KU-543-657

MARK BEVIR

University of Liverpool

Withdrawn from stock

Key Concepts in
Governance

Los Angeles • London • New Delhi • Singapore • Washington DC

© Mark Bevir 2009

First published 2009

Apart from any fair dealing for the purposes of research or
private study, or criticism or review, as permitted under the
Copyright, Designs and Patents Act, 1988, this publication
may be reproduced, stored or transmitted in any form, or by
any means, only with the prior permission in writing of the
publishers, or in the case of reprographic reproduction, in
accordance with the terms of licences issued by the Copyright
Licensing Agency. Enquiries concerning reproduction outside
those terms should be sent to the publishers.

SAGE Publications Ltd
1 Oliver's Yard
55 City Road
London EC1Y 1SP

SAGE Publications Inc.
2455 Teller Road
Thousand Oaks, California 91320

SAGE Publications India Pvt Ltd
B 1/I 1 Mohan Cooperative Industrial Area
Mathura Road, New Delhi 110 044

SAGE Publications Asia-Pacific Pte Ltd
33 Pekin Street #02-01
Far East Square
Singapore 048763

Library of Congress Control Number Available

British Library Cataloguing in Publication data

A catalogue record for this book is available from the
British Library

ISBN 978-1-4129-3569-2
ISBN 978-1-4129-3570-8 (pbk)

Typeset by C&M Digitals (P) Ltd, Chennai, India
Printed in India by Replika Press Pvt. Ltd.
Printed on paper from sustainable resources

contents

key concepts in governance

preface

The language of governance is increasingly prominent in discussions of changes in the nature and role of the state. Governance has become a topic of concern to political and non-profit actors; it even has a place among the lending criteria of institutions such as the World Bank. In addition, the language of governance includes new ways of thinking about social coordination and patterns of rule as they appear in civil society, political institutions, and the international arena. Corporate governance, for example, has become a staple ingredient of company reports and the business pages of financial newspapers.

Despite its prominence, the language of governance remains bewildering. One problem is that the key concepts of governance derive from diverse disciplines – public administration, political science, economics, business, sociology – and these disciplines rely tacitly on different assumptions. This book addresses this problem: it illuminates the key concepts in terms of their respective contexts. Yet the language of governance is also bewildering because it covers both specific narratives about changes in the state and new theories of social coordination in general. This book addresses this problem: it provides an opportunity to step back from particular narratives and contexts in order to consider theoretical and conceptual debates.

I hope that this book will make it easier for students to learn about new ways of thinking about governance as well as the changing nature of the state. Students should find it a useful companion to broader literatures. I hope they will use it to learn about the concepts that inform governance today, and to reflect on these concepts in ways that will lead them to try to reform and improve governance.

Readers will realize that no book of this size could possibly cover all the concepts of relevance to governance. I have necessarily selected some concepts for inclusion at the expense of others. The process of selection was a rather incremental one, conducted in the context of discussions with colleagues and students. Yet I was loosely guided in my selections by principles that reflect the general account of governance provided in the introductory essay, 'What is Governance?' I have tried to balance theoretical concepts that refer to social coordination and how to study it with empirical ones that refer to the changes in the nature and role of the state. I have also tried to balance concepts that seek to describe the world as it is with concepts that appear within more normative accounts about how we ought to conduct public policy and promote democracy. Part of me would have liked to include more concepts that refer to technical innovations in public policy. However, I was also eager to capture the theoretical breadth that we surely associate with the term 'governance' when we remember that it did not originate in debates about public administration and that it remains as prominent in international relations, rational choice theory, comparative politics, and other areas of scholarly and practical concern as it does within public administration. Besides, I remain convinced that students in professional schools of public policy benefit greatly from learning about the broader theoretical issues by which alone we can decide the appropriateness and desirability of any given policy technique. Hence the selected concepts cover not only changing policy instruments but also theoretical debates about patterns of rule and how they are changing.

acknowledgements

It is a pleasure to record my debt to a recent cohort of my students. This book was conceived, written, and tested with them in mind and with their input. Thanks to Bethany Gerdemann, Orion Haas, Minna Howell, Justin Norval, Prashant Reddy, Brittany Sachs, Ana Schwartz, Andre Tutundjian, Tony Zhao, and Lechuan Zhou. I am also grateful to the contributors to Sage's *Encyclopedia of Governance*. They taught me much about topics on which I otherwise would have known too little. Perhaps I am biased, but I believe the *Encyclopedia* is the perfect resource for readers who would explore further the key concepts of governance.

Part I: What is Governance?

What is Governance?

INTRODUCTION

Governance can be used as a specific term to describe changes in the nature and role of the state following the public sector reforms of the 1980s and 1990s. Typically, these reforms are said to have led to a shift from a hierarchical bureaucracy towards a greater use of markets, quasi-markets, and networks, especially in the delivery of public services. The effects of the reforms were intensified by global changes, including an increase in transnational economic activity and the rise of regional institutions such as the European Union. So understood, governance expresses a widespread belief that the state increasingly depends on other organizations to secure its intentions and deliver its policies.

By analogy, governance also can be used to describe any pattern of rule that arises either when the state is dependent upon others or when the state plays little or no role. For example, the term 'global governance' refers to the pattern of rule at the international level where the United Nations is too weak to resemble the kind of state that can impose its will upon its territory. Likewise, the term 'corporate governance' refers to patterns of rule within businesses – that is, to the systems, institutions, and norms by which corporations are directed and controlled. In this context, governance expresses a growing awareness of the ways in which forms of power and authority can secure order even in the absence of state activity.

More generally still, governance can be used to refer to all patterns of rule, including the kind of hierarchical state that is often thought to have existed prior to the public sector reforms of the 1980s and 1990s. This general use of governance enables theorists to explore abstract analyses of the construction of social orders, social coordination, or social practices irrespective of their specific content. Theorists can divorce such abstract analyses from specific questions about, say, the state, the international system, or the corporation. However, if we are to use governance in this general way, perhaps we need to describe the changes in the state since the 1980s using an alternative phrase, such as 'the new governance'.

Whether we focus on the new governance, weak states, or patterns of rule in general, the concept of governance raises issues about public policy and democracy. The increased role of non-state actors in the delivery of public services has led to a concern to improve the ability of the state to oversee these other actors. The state has become more interested in various strategies for creating and managing networks and partnerships. It has set up all kinds of arrangements for auditing and regulating other organizations. In the eyes of many observers, there has been an audit explosion. In addition, the increased role of unelected actors in policy-making suggests that we need to think about the extent to which we want to hold them democratically accountable and about the mechanisms by which we might do so. Similarly, accounts of growing transnational and international constraints upon states suggest that we need to rethink the nature of social inclusion and social justice. Political institutions from the World Bank to the European Union now use terms such as 'good governance' to convey their aspirations for a better world.

A CONCEPTUAL HISTORY OF GOVERNANCE

The general concept of governance as a pattern of rule or as the activity of ruling has a long lineage in the English language. The medieval poet Geoffrey Chaucer wrote, for example, of 'the gouernance of hous and lond' (the governance of house and land). Nonetheless, much of the current interest in governance derives from its specific use in relation to changes in the state since the late twentieth century. These changes date from neoliberal reforms of the public sector in the 1980s.

Neoliberalism

Neoliberals argue that the state is inherently inefficient when compared with markets. Often they also suggest that the post-war Keynesian welfare state is in crisis; it has become too large to be manageable, it is collapsing under the burden of excessive taxation, and it is generating ever higher rates of cyclical inflation. Neoliberals believe that the post-war state cannot be sustained any longer, especially in a world that is now characterized by highly mobile capital and by vigorous economic competition between states. Hence they attempt to roll back the state. They often suggest, in particular, that the state should concentrate on making policy decisions rather than on delivering services. They want the state to withdraw from direct delivery of services. They want to replace state provision of public services with an entrepreneurial system based on competition and markets. In *Reinventing Government*, David Osborne and Ted Gaebler distinguish between the activity of making policy decisions, which they describe as steering, and that of delivering public services, which they describe as rowing. They argue that bureaucracy is bankrupt as a tool for rowing. And they propose replacing bureaucracy with an 'entrepreneurial government', based on competition, markets, customers, and measurement of outcomes.

Because neoliberals deride government, many of them look for another term to describe the kind of entrepreneurial pattern of rule they favor. Governance offers them such a concept. It enables them to distinguish between 'bad' government (or rowing) and necessary governance (or steering). The early association of governance with a minimal state and the spread of markets thus arose from neoliberal politicians and the policy-wonks, journalists, economists, and management gurus who advised them.

The advisers to neoliberals often draw on rational choice theory. Rational choice theory extends a type of social explanation found in micro-economics. Typically, rational choice theorists attempt to explain social outcomes by reference to micro-level analyses of individual behavior, and they model individual behavior on the assumption that people choose the course of action that is most in accordance with their preferences. Rational choice theorists influence neoliberal attitudes to governance in large part through a critique of the concept of public interest. They insist that individuals, including politicians and civil servants, act in their own interest, which undermines the idea that policy-makers act benevolently to promote a public interest. Indeed, their reduction of social facts to the actions of individuals casts doubt on the very idea of a public interest over and above the aggregate interests of individuals. More specifically, rational choice theorists provide neoliberals with a critique of bureaucratic government. Often they combine the claim that individuals act in accordance with their preferences with an assumption that these preferences are typically to maximize one's wealth or power. Hence they argue that bureaucrats act to optimize their power and career prospects by increasing the size of their fiefdoms even when doing so is unnecessary. This argument implies that bureaucracies have an inherent tendency to grow even when there is no good reason for them so to do.

Because rational choice theory privileges micro-level analyses, it might appear to have peculiar difficulties explaining the rise of institutions and their persistent stability. Micro-economic analysis has long faced this issue in the guise of the existence of firms. Once rational choice theorists extend such micro-analysis to government and social life generally, they face the same issue with respect to all kinds of institutions, including political parties, voting coalitions, and the market economy itself. The question is: if individuals act in accordance with their preferences, why don't they break agreements when these agreements no longer suit them? The obvious answer is that some authority would punish them if they broke the agreement, and they have a preference for not being punished. But this answer assumes the presence of a higher authority that can enforce the agreement. Some rational choice theorists thus began to explore how they might explain the rise and stability of norms, agreements, or institutions in the absence of any higher authority. They adopted the concept of governance to refer to norms and patterns of rule that arise and persist even in the absence of an enforcing agent.

Social Science

The neoliberal concept of governance as a minimal state conveys a preference for less government. Arguably, it often does little else, being an example of empty political rhetoric. Indeed, when social scientists study neoliberal reforms of the public sector, they often conclude that these reforms have scarcely rolled back the state at all. They draw attention instead to the unintended consequences of the reforms. According to many social scientists, the neoliberal reforms fragmented service delivery and weakened central control without establishing markets. In their view, the reforms have led to a proliferation of policy networks in both the formulation of public policy and the delivery of public services.

The 1990s saw a massive outpouring of work that conceived governance as a proliferation of networks. Much of this literature explores the ways in which neoliberal reforms created new patterns of service delivery based on complex sets of organizations drawn from all of the public, private, and voluntary sectors. It suggests that a range of processes – including the functional differentiation of the state, the rise of regional blocs, globalization, and the neoliberal reforms themselves – have left the state increasingly dependent on other organizations for the delivery and success of its policies. Although social scientists adopt various theories of policy networks, they generally agree that the state can no longer command others. In their view, the new governance is characterized by networks in which the state and other organizations depend on each other. Even when the state still remains the dominant orga-nization, it and the other members of the network are now interdepen-dent in that they have to exchange resources if they are to achieve their goals. Many social scientists argue that this interdependence means that the state now has to steer other organizations instead of issuing com-mands to them. They also imply that steering involves a much greater use by the state of diplomacy and related techniques of management. Some social scientists also suggest that the proliferating networks often have a considerable degree of autonomy from the state. In this view, the key problem posed by the new governance is that it reduces the ability of the state to command and even to steer effectively.

Social scientists have developed a concept of governance as a complex and fragmented pattern of rule composed of multiplying networks. They have done so in part because of studies of the impact of neoliberal reforms on the public sector. But two other strands of social science also gave rise to this concept of governance. First, a concept of governance as networks arose among social scientists searching for a way to think about the role of transnational linkages within the European Union. Second, a concept of governance as networks appeals to some social scientists interested in general issues about social coordination and inter-organizational links. These latter social scientists argue that networks are a distinct governing structure through which to coordinate activities and allocate resources. They develop typologies of such governing structures – most commonly hierarchies, markets, and networks – and they identify the characteristics associated with each such structure. Their typologies often imply that networks are preferable, at least in some circumstances, to the hierarchic structures of the post-war state and also to the markets favored by neolib-erals. As we will see, this positive valuation of networks sometimes led to what we might call a second wave of public sector reform.

Resistance and Civil Society

Radicals, socialists, and anarchists have long advocated patterns of rule that do not require the capitalist state. Many of them look towards civil society as a site of free and spontaneous associations of citizens. Civil society offers them a non-statist site at which to reconcile the demands of community and individual freedom – a site they hope might be free of force and compulsion. The spread of the new governance has prompted such radicals to distance their visions from that of the neolib-eral rolling back of the state. Hence we find two main uses of the word 'governance' among radicals: they use it to describe new systems of force and compulsion associated with neoliberalism, and they use it to refer to alternative conceptions of a non-statist democratic order.

There is disagreement among radicals about whether the new governance has led to a decline in the power of the state. Some argue that the state has just altered the way in which it rules its citizens; it makes more use of bribes and incentive, moral exhortation and threats to withdraw benefits. Others believe that the state has indeed lost power. Either way, radicals distinguish the new governance sharply from their visions of an expansion of democracy. In their view, if the power of the state has declined, the beneficiaries have been corporations; they associate the hollowing out of the state with the growing power of financial and industrial capital. Radical analyses of the new governance explore how globalization – or perhaps the myth of globalization – finds states and international organizations acting to promote the interests of capital.

Radicals typically associate their alternative visions of democratic governance with civil society, social movements, and active citizenship. Those who relate the new governance to globalization and a decline in state power often appeal to parallel shifts within civil society. They appeal to global civil society as a site of popular, democratic resistance to capital. Global civil society typically refers to non-governmental groups such as Amnesty International, Greenpeace, and the International Labor Organization as well as less formal networks of activists and citizens. Questions can arise, of course, as to whether these groups adequately represent their members, let alone a broader community. However, radicals often respond by emphasizing the democratic potential of civil society and the public sphere. They argue that public debate constitutes one of the main avenues by which citizens can participate in collective decision-making. At times they also place great importance on the potential of public deliberation to generate a rational consensus. No matter what doubts radicals have about contemporary civil society, their visions of democracy emphasize the desirability of transferring power from the state to citizens who would not just elect a government and then act as passive spectators but rather participate continuously in the processes of governance. The association of democratic governance with participatory and deliberative processes in civil society thus arises from radicals seeking to resist state and corporate power.

These radical ideas are not just responses to the new governance; they also help to construct aspects of it. They inspire new organizations, and new activities, by existing social movements. At times, they influence political agreements – perhaps most notably the international regimes and norms covering human rights and the environment. Hence social scientists interested in social movements sometimes relate them to new national and transnational forms of resistance to state and corporate power. To some extent these social scientists again emphasize the rise of networks. However, when social scientists study the impact of neoliberal reforms on the public sector, they focus on the cooperative relations between the state and other institutionalized organizations involved in policy-making and the delivery of public services. In contrast, when social scientists study social movements, they focus on the informal links among activists concerned to contest the policies and actions of corporations, states, and international organizations.

THE NEW GOVERNANCE

The current interest in governance derives primarily from reforms of the public sector since the 1980s. The new governance refers to the apparent spread of markets and networks following these reforms. It points to the varied ways in which the informal authority of markets and networks constitutes, supplements, and supplants the formal authority of government. It has led many people to adopt a more diverse view of state authority and its relationship to civil society.

Recent public sector reform has occurred in two principal waves. The first wave consisted of the New Public Management (NPM) as advocated by neoliberals. These reforms were attempts to increase the role of markets and of corporate management techniques in the public sector. The second wave of reforms consisted of attempts to develop and manage a joined-up series of networks informed by a revived public sector ethos. They were in part responses to the perceived consequences of the earlier reforms.

Some advocates of NPM imply it is the single best way for all states at all times. The same can be said of some advocates of partnerships and networks. Studies of both waves of reform can imply, moreover, that change has been ubiquitous. It is thus worth emphasizing at the outset both the variety and the limits of public sector reform. Reforms have varied from state to state. NPM is associated primarily with neoliberal regimes in the United Kingdom and United States, as well as a few other states, notably Australia and New Zealand. Although many other developed states introduced similar reforms, they did so only selectively, and when they did so, they often altered the content and the implementation of the reforms in accordance with their institutions and traditions. Typically, developing and transitional states adopted similar reforms only under more or less overt pressure from corporations, other states, and international organizations. Public sector reform has also varied across policy sectors within any given state. For example, even in the United Kingdom and the United States, there have been few attempts to introduce performance-related pay or outsourcing to the higher levels of the public service, which are responsible for providing policy advice. The varied extent of public sector reform should itself make us wary of overstating the degree to which governance has been transformed. Of course there have been extensive and significant reforms. But bureaucratic hierarchies still perform most government functions in most states.

The New Public Management

The first wave of public sector reform was NPM. It is inspired by ideas associated with neoliberalism and public choice theory. At first NPM spread in developed, Anglo-Saxon states. Later it spread through much of Europe – though France, Germany, and Spain are often seen as remaining largely untouched by it – and to developing and transitional states. In developed countries, the impetus for NPM came from fiscal crises. Talk of the overloaded state grew as oil crises cut state revenues, and the expansion of welfare services saw state expenditure increase as a proportion of gross national product. The result was a quest to cut costs. NPM was one proposed solution. In developing and transitional states, the impetus for NPM lay more in external pressures, notably those associated with structural adjustment programs.

NPM has two main strands: marketization and corporate management. The most extreme form of marketization is privatization, which is the transfer of assets from the state to the private sector. Some states sold various nationalized industries by floating them on the stock exchange. Other state-owned enterprises were sold to their employees through, say, management buyouts. Yet others were sold to public shareholders, including telecommunications, railways, electricity, water, and waste services. Smaller privatizations have involved hotels, parking facilities, and convention centers, all of which are as likely to have been sold by local governments as by central states.

Other forms of marketization remain far more common than privatization. These other measures typically introduce incentive structures into public service provision by means of contracting-out, quasi-markets, and consumer choice. Marketization aims to make public services not only more efficient but also more accountable to consumers, who are given greater choice of service provider. Prominent examples of marketization include contracting-out, internal markets, management contracts, and market testing. Contracting-out (also known as outsourcing) involves the state contracting with a private organization, and on a competitive basis, to provide a service. The private organization can be for-profit or non-profit; it is sometimes a company hastily formed by those who have previously provided the service as public sector employees. Internal markets arise when departments are able to purchase support services from several in-house providers or outside suppliers who in turn operate as independent business units in competition with one another. Management contracts involve the operation of a facility – such as an airport or convention center – being handed over to a private company in accordance with specific contractual arrangements. Market testing (also known as managed competition) occurs when the arrangements governing the provision of a service are decided by means of bidding in comparison with private sector competitors.

Typically, marketization transfers the delivery of services to autonomous or semi-autonomous agencies. Proponents of NPM offer various arguments in favor of such agencies. They argue that service providers are then able to concentrate on the efficient delivery of quality services without having to evaluate alternative policies. They argue that policy-makers can be more focused and adventurous if they do not have to worry about the existing service providers. And they argue that when the state has a hands-off relationship with a service provider, it has more opportunities to introduce performance incentives.

Corporate management reform involves introducing just such performance incentives. In general, it means applying to the public sector ideas and techniques from private sector management. The main ideas and techniques involved are management by results, performance measures, value for money, and closeness to the customer, all of which are tied to various budgetary reforms. Although these ideas and techniques are all attempts to promote effective management in the public sector, there is no real agreement on what would constitute effective management. To the contrary, the innocent observer discovers a bewildering number of concepts, each with its own acronym. For example, Management by Objectives (MBO) emphasizes clearly defined objectives for individual managers, whereas Management by Results (MBR) emphasizes the use of past results as indicators of future ones, and Total Quality Management (TQM) emphasizes awareness of quality in all organizational processes. Performance measures are concrete attempts to assure effective management by auditing inputs and outputs and relating them to financial budgets. Such measures also vary widely because there is disagreement about the goals of performance as well as how to measure results properly. Nonetheless, value for money is promoted mainly through the use of performance measures to influence budgetary decisions.

The success of NPM has been unclear, and remains the source of considerable debate. Few people believe it proved the panacea it was supposed to be. Studies suggest that it generates at best about a three per cent annual saving on running costs, which is pretty modest, especially when one remembers that running costs are typically a relatively small component of total program costs. Even neoliberals often acknowledge that most savings have come from privatization, not reforms in public sector organizations. The success of NPM also appears to vary considerably with contextual factors. For example, the reforms are often counterproductive in developing and transitional states because these states lack the stable framework associated with elder public disciplines such as credible policy, predictable resources, and a public service ethic. It is interesting to reflect that, in this respect, NPM appears to require the existence of aspects of just that kind of public service bureaucracy that it is meant to supplant.

Networks, Partnerships, and Inclusion

Although discussions of the new governance often highlight NPM, public sector reform is a continuous process. Typically, managerial reforms have given way to a second wave of reform focusing on institutional arrangements – networks and partnerships – and administrative values – public service and social inclusion. The second wave of reforms includes a number of overlapping trends, which are often brought together under labels such as 'joined-up governance', 'one-stop government', 'service integration', 'whole-of-government', or *'Aktivierender Staat'* (activating state). Some commentators even describe this second wave as a 'governance approach' or 'new governance' defined in contrast to NPM.

Several connected reasons can be given for the altered nature of public sector reform. One is the shifting tide of intellectual and political fortunes. To an extent, the fortunes of public choice theory and neoliberalism have ebbed, while those of reformist social democrats and network theorists have risen. The rise of New Labor within the United Kingdom is perhaps the most obvious example of this tide. A second reason is a growing sensitivity to a new set of external problems, including terrorism, the environment, asylum-seekers, aging populations, and the digital divide. Many of these problems have led people to turn to the state, rather than markets, and to do so with concerns about equity, rather than efficiency. Yet another reason for the changing content of public sector reform resides in the unintended consequences of the earlier managerial reforms. Observers emphasize that NPM has led to a fragmentation of the public sector: because public services are delivered by networks composed of a number of different organizations, there is a new need to coordinate and manage networks. Observers also emphasize that NPM has raised dilemmas of accountability: even if the autonomous and semi-autonomous organizations now involved in delivering services are more efficient, they are not always easy to hold accountable on matters of equity. These worries about accountability have been exasperated by recent exposures of corruption in the private sector and by studies emphasizing the public's lack of trust in government.

The main thrust of the second wave of reforms is to improve coordination across agencies. This ambition to join up networks reflects concerns that the earlier reforms have led to the fragmentation of public service delivery. Joined-up governance promotes horizontal and vertical coordination between the organizations involved in an aspect of public policy. Although the boundary between policy-making and policy implementation is blurred, joined-up approaches look rather different in each case. Joined-up policy-making brings together all the agencies involved in dealing with intractable problems such as juvenile crime or rural poverty. Joined-up policy implementation coordinates the actions of agencies involved in delivering services so as to simplify them for citizens: an example is one-stop shops at which the unemployed can access benefits, training, and job information.

Joined-up governance often draws on the idea that networks can coordinate the actions of a range of actors and organizations. Indeed, its proponents often suggest that there are many circumstances in which networks offer a superior mode of coordination to both hierarchies and markets. For example, they tie an enabling or facilitative leadership within a network to greater flexibility, creativity, inclusiveness, and commitment. Hence joined-up governance is as much about fostering networks as it is about managing them. Indeed, the second wave of reforms characteristically attempts to promote networks or partnerships rather than markets. These partnerships can be ones between public, private, and voluntary bodies, as well as between different levels of government or different state agencies. In many countries, the emphasis has shifted from competitive tendering to the public sector building long-term relationships based on trust with suppliers, users, and other stakeholders. Public–private partnerships are said to have a number of advantages based on their ability to combine the strengths of each sector. For example, they can ease the burden of capital investment on the public sector while reducing risks of development for the private sector.

Partnerships and joined-up governance are often advocated as ways of promoting social inclusion as well as increasing efficiency. Ideally, they increase citizen involvement in the policy process. Citizen groups participate as partners in aspects of policy-making and policy implementation. The second wave of public sector reforms seeks to activate civil society. Partnerships and joined-up governance are supposed to provide settings in which public sector bodies can engage stakeholders – citizens, voluntary organizations, and private companies – thereby involving them in democratic processes. It is also hoped that involving stakeholders in the policy process will build public trust in government.

GOVERNANCE BEYOND THE STATE

The literature on the new governance highlights the role of markets, networks, and non-state actors. It thereby weakens the distinction between states and other domains of social order. All social and political regimes appear to depend on a pattern of rule, or form of governance, no matter how informal. Hence the term 'governance' has come to refer to social and political orders other than the state.

Some patterns of rule appear in civil society. The most discussed of these is corporate governance, which refers to the means of directing and controlling business corporations. Current interest in corporate governance owes something to theoretical questions within a microeconomic framework about how to account for the stability of firms: most responses to these questions parallel those that rational choice theorists give to questions about the origins of social norms, laws, and institutions. Yet, the main source of interest in corporate governance is probably public, shareholder, and governmental concerns about corporate scandals, corruption, the abuse of monopoly power, and the high salaries paid to top executives. Three broad themes dominate the resulting literature on corporate ethics: openness through disclosure of information, integrity through straightforward dealing, and accountability through a clear division of responsibilities.

Although much has been written on corporate governance, it need not detain us longer. Our concern is with political orders. Hence the main forms of governance beyond the state that interest us are regional and global governance.

Regional Governance

The rise of new regional regimes and institutions, such as the European Union (EU), plays two roles in discussions of the new governance. Many commentators suggest that the rise of these regional regimes has eroded the autonomy of nation states, which contributes to the rise of new governance. They also suggest that the new regional regimes are often taken to be examples of a networked polity and therefore of the new governance, rather than an older government.

The most prominent case of the new regional governance remains the EU. Studies of the EU gave rise to an extensive literature on multi level governance: the EU is a level of governance above the nation state, which, in turn, often contains various levels of local and federal government. The literature on multilevel governance in the EU posits links in the Commission, national ministries, and local and regional authorities. It emphasizes the rise of transnational policy networks, especially where policy-making is depoliticized and routinized, supranational agencies depend on other agencies to deliver services, and there is a need to aggregate interests.

Transnational policy networks are arguably the defining feature of a new pattern of regional and global governance. We should recognize, though, that these transnational networks do not always lead to the deep linkages associated with the EU. Regional projects can consist of little more than loose preferential trading agreements. We should also recognize that transnational agreements do not always correspond to actual geographic regions. Much north–south regionalism consists, for example, of agreements between one or more developed state and one or more less developed state – agreements that secure access to one another's markets while also diffusing particular regulatory and legal standards.

Global Governance

The concept of global governance has much the same relation to the new governance as does that of regional governance. On the one hand, some commentators suggest that international processes are eroding the importance of the state; the relevant processes include the internationalization of production and of financial transactions, the rise of new international organizations, and the growth of international law. On the other hand, the international sphere is itself portrayed as being a case of governance in the total or near total absence of the state.

Regional governance is, moreover, a prominent part of the pattern of rule that currently operates at the global level. Of course there are global organizations, such as the United Nations or the World Bank, which help to create and sustain the laws, rules, and norms that govern international politics. Nonetheless, even when we allow for these organizations, many of the interactions and agreements between states and other global actors are situated in the context of the transnational policy networks associated with the new regionalism. If the Cold War was a bipolar era based on the predominance of the USA and the Soviet Union, global governance now consists of a multipolar regionalism, albeit in the context of US hegemony.

The new regional and transnational organizations appear to share certain broad characteristics. They are typically fairly open to countries from outside the region: they are perhaps less a series of protectionist pacts and more a series of interconnected webs within an increasing global economy. Their policy objectives extend beyond the economy to areas such as security, the environment, human rights, and 'good' governance. Lastly, they often incorporate a variety of non-state actors as well as states themselves. This new type of regional governance has combined with increased economic flows and older international organizations to transform the world order – that is, to create a new form of global governance.

THEORIES OF GOVERNANCE

Although recent interest in governance owes much to public sector reforms of the late twentieth century, these reforms and the interest they inspired cannot easily be separated from theories such as rational choice and the new institutionalism. It is important to recognize that the meaning of governance varies not only according to the level of generality at which it is pitched, but also the theoretical contexts in which it is used.

Rational Choice

The neoliberal narrative of governance overlaps somewhat with rational choice theory. Both of them draw on micro-economic analysis with its attempt to unpack social life in terms of individual actions, and its attempt to explain individual actions in terms of rationality conceived as utility-maximizing actions. Yet, while neoliberals deployed such analysis to promote marketization and the New Public Management, rational choice theorists were often more interested in exploring cases where institutions or norms were honored even in the absence of a higher authority to enforce them.

Rational choice theory attempts to explain all social phenomena by reference to the micro-level of rational individual activity. It unpacks social facts, institutions, and patterns of rule entirely by analyses of individuals acting. It models individuals acting on the assumption that they adopt the course of action most in accordance with their preferences. Sometimes rational choice theorists require preferences to be rational: preferences are assumed to be complete and transitive. Sometimes they also make other assumptions, most notably that actors have complete information about what will occur following their choosing any course of action. At other times, however, rational choice theorists try to relax these unrealistic assumptions by developing concepts of bounded rationality. They then attempt to model human behavior in circumstances where people lack relevant information.

The dominance of the micro-level in rational choice theory raises issues about the origins, persistence, and effects of the social norms, laws, and institutions by which we are governed. One issue is the abstract one of how to explain the rise and stability of a pattern of rule in the absence of any higher authority. Rational choice theorists generally conclude that the absence of any effective higher authority means that such institutions must be conceived as self-enforcing. Another issue is a more specific interest in the effects of norms, laws, and institutions on individuals' actions. Rational choice theorists argue that institutions structure people's strategic interactions with one another: stable institutions influence individuals' actions by giving them reasonable expectations about the outcome of the varied courses of action that they might chose. Another more specific issue is to model weakly institutionalized environments in which the absence of a higher authority leads people to break agreements and so create instability. Examples of such weak institutions include the international system and also nation states in which the rule of law is weak. Rational choice theorists explore self-enforcing agreements, the costs associated with them, and the circumstances in which they break down.

The New Institutionalism

An institutional approach dominated the study of public administration and politics up until sometime around the 1940s. Scholars focused on formal rules, procedures, and organizations, including constitutions, electoral systems, and political parties. Although they sometimes emphasized the formal rules that governed such institutions, they also paid attention to the behavior of actors within them. This institutional approach was challenged in the latter half of the twentieth century by a series of attempts to craft universal theories: behavioralists, rational choice theorists, and others attempted to explain social action with relatively little reference to specific institutional settings. The new institutionalism is often seen as a restatement of the older institutional approach in response to these universal theories. The new institutionalists retain a focus on rules, procedures, and organizations: institutions are composed of two or more people; they serve some kind of social purpose; and they exist over time in a way that transcends the intentions and actions of specific individuals. Yet the new institutionalists adopt a broader concept of institution that includes norms, habits, and cultural customs alongside formal rules, procedures, and organizations.

It has become common to distinguish various species of new institutionalism. Rational choice institutionalists examine how institutions shape the behavior of rational actors by creating expectations about the likely consequences of given courses of action. Because it remains firmly rooted in the type of micro-analysis just discussed, we will focus here on new institutionalists who eschew deductive models based on assumptions about utility-maximization. These other institutionalists typically explain outcomes by comparing and contrasting institutional patterns. They offer two main accounts of how institutions shape behavior. Historical institutionalists tend to use metaphors such as 'path dependency' and to emphasize the importance of macro-level studies of institutions over time. Sociological institutionalists tend to argue that cognitive and symbolic schemes give people identities and roles.

Historical institutionalists focus on the way past institutional arrangements shape responses to political pressures. They argue that past outcomes have become embedded in national institutions which prompt social groups to organize along particular lines and thereby lock states into paths of development. Hence they concentrate on comparative studies of welfare and administrative reform across states in which the variety of such reforms is explicable in terms of path dependency.

Sociological institutionalists focus on values, identities, and the ways in which they shape actors' perceptions of their interests. They argue that informal sets of ideas and values constitute policy paradigms that shape the ways in which organizations think about issues and conceive political pressures. Hence they adopt a more constructivist approach to governance – an approach that resembles the social constructivism we will consider later on. They concentrate on studies of the ways in which norms and values shape what are often competing policy agendas of welfare and administrative reform.

Systems Theory

Although sociological institutionalism can resemble social constructivism, it often exhibits a distinctive debt to organizational theory. At times its exponents perceive cognitive and symbolic schemes not as intersubjective understandings, but as properties of organizations. Instead of reducing such schemes to the relevant actors, they see them as a kind of system based on its own logic. In doing so, they echo themes that are developed more fully in systems theory.

A system is the pattern of order that arises from the regular interactions of a series of interdependent elements. Systems theorists suggest that such patterns of order arise from the functional relations and interactions of the elements. These relations and interactions involve a transfer of information. This transfer of information leads to the self-production and self-organization of the system even in the absence of any center of control.

The concept of governance as a socio-cybernetic system highlights the limits to governing by the state. It implies that there is no single sovereign authority. Instead, there is a self-organizing system composed of interdependent actors and institutions. Systems theorists often distinguish here between governing, which is goal-directed interventions, and governance, which is the total effect of governing interventions and interactions. In this view, governance is a self-organizing system that emerges from the activities and exchanges of actors and institutions. Again, the new governance has arisen because we live in a centerless society, or at least a society with multiple centers. Order arises from the interactions of multiple centers or organizations. The role of the state is not to create order but to facilitate socio-political interactions, to encourage varied arrangements for coping with problems, and to distribute services among numerous organizations.

Regulation Theory

Just as sociological institutionalism sometimes draws on systems theory, so historical institutionalism sometimes draws on Marxist state theory.

The main approach to governance derived from Marxism is, however, regulation theory. Marx argued that capitalism was unstable because it led to the over-accumulation of capital and to class struggle. Regulation theorists examine the ways in which different varieties of capitalism attempt to manage these instabilities. They study forms of governance in relation to changes in the way these instabilities are masked.

Typically, regulation theorists locate the new governance in relation to a broader socio-economic shift from Fordism to post-Fordism. Fordism refers to a combination of 'intensive accumulation' and 'monopolistic regulation' – a combination associated with the mass production pioneered by Henry Ford in the 1920s. Intensive accumulation relied on processes of mass production such as mechanization, the intensification of work, the detailed division of tasks, and the use of semi-skilled labor. Monopolistic regulation involved monopoly pricing, the recognition of trade unions, the indexing of wages to productivity, corporatist tendencies in government, and monetary policies to manage the demand for commodities. According to regulation theorists, intensive accumulation and monopolistic regulation temporarily created a virtuous circle: mass production created economies of scale thereby leading to a rise in productivity; increased productivity led to increased wages and so greater consumer demand; the growth in demand raised profits due to the full utilization of capacity; and the rising profits were used to improve the technology of mass production, creating further economies of scale, and so starting the whole circle going again.

Regulation theorists ascribe the end of Fordism to various causes. Productivity gains decreased because of the social and technical limits to Fordism. Globalization made the management of national economies increasingly difficult. Increased state expenditure produced inflation and state overload. Competition among capitalists shifted the norms of consumption away from the standardized commodities associated with mass production. All of these causes contributed to the end not only of Fordism but also the bureaucratic, Keynesian, welfare state associated with it. Although regulation theorists can be reluctant to engage in speculations about the future, they generally associate the new post-Fordist era with the globalization of capital, neoliberal politics, contracting-out, public–private partnerships, and the regulatory state.

Social Constructivism

Constructivist and interpretive approaches to governance often emphasize contingency. They reject the idea that patterns of rule can be properly understood in terms of a historical or social logic attached to capitalist development, functional differentiation, or even institutional settings. Instead, they emphasize the meaningful character of human actions and practices. In this view, because people act on beliefs, ideas, or meanings – whether conscious or not – we can explain their actions properly only if we grasp the relevant meanings. Some of the older constructivist approaches suggest that beliefs, ideas, or meanings are more or less uniform across a culture or society. Hence they inspire studies of the distinctive patterns of governance associated with various cultures. Other constructivist and interpretive approaches place a greater emphasis on contests and struggles over meaning. Hence they inspire studies of the different traditions or discourses of governance that are found within any given society.

Although social constructivists analyze governance in terms of meanings, there is little agreement among them about the nature of such meanings. The meanings of interest to them are variously described, for example, as intentions and beliefs, conscious or tacit knowledge, subconscious or unconscious assumptions, systems of signs and languages, and discourses and ideologies. Social constructivists often explore many of these varied types of meanings both synchronically and diachronically. Synchronic studies analyze the relationships between a set of meanings abstracted from the flux of history. They reveal the internal coherence or pattern of a web of meanings: they make sense of a particular belief, concept, or sign by showing how it fits in such a web. Diachronic studies analyze the development of webs of meanings over time. They show how situated agents modify and even transform webs of meanings as they use them in particular settings.

The diverse constructivist studies of the synchronic and diachronic dimensions of meanings all have in common a reluctance to reduce meanings to allegedly objective facts about institutions, systems, or capitalism. In this view, patterns of rule arise because of the contingent triumph of a web of meanings. The new governance arose, for example, alongside neoliberalism, which inspired much of the New Public Management, and also discourses in the social sciences, which inspired the turn to networks and public–private partnerships. Sometimes social constructivists relate the rise of neoliberalism and network theory to new relations of power, changes in the global economy, or problems confronted by states. Even when they do, however, they usually suggest that these social facts are also constructed in the context of webs of meanings.

PUBLIC POLICY

Public policy refers very generally to the actions – plans, laws, and behaviors – of government. Concern with the new governance draws attention to the extent to which these actions are often performed now by agents of the state rather than directly by the state. There are a vast number of studies of specific policy areas, and even specific policy problems and governmental responses to them. These studies offer detailed accounts of the impact of the New Public Management and the rise of the new governance within particular policy sectors, such as health care, social welfare, policing, and public security. However, policy analysis often includes a prescriptive dimension as well as a descriptive one. Students of public policy attempt to devise solutions to policy problems as well as to study governmental responses to them. Of course their solutions are sometimes specific proposals aimed at a particular policy problem. At other times, however, they concern themselves with the general question of how the state should seek to implement its policies.

The rise of the new governance raises the question: how should the state try to implement its policies given the proliferation of markets and networks within the public sector? Answers to this question typically seek to balance concerns over efficiency with ones over ethics. To some extent, the leading answers reflect the leading theories of governance. Rational choice theory tends to promote market solutions; its exponents typically want to reduce the role of the state in implementing policies. Institutionalists tend to concentrate on strategies by which the state can manage and promote particular types of organization; its exponents typically offer advice about how the state can realize its policy agenda within a largely given institutional setting. Social constructivism tends to promote dialogic and deliberative approaches to public policy; its exponents typically want to facilitate the flow of meanings, and perhaps thereby the emergence of a consensus.

Planning and Regulating

The stereotype of 'old governance' is of a bureaucratic state trying to impose its plan on society. Formal strategic planning did indeed play a prominent role in much state activity in the latter half of the twentieth century. However, there remains widespread recognition that strategic planning is an integral feature of government. Plans help to establish the goals and visions of the state and its agencies, and they facilitate the concentration of resources in areas where they are thought to be most likely to improve an organization's efficiency in relation to its dominant goals. Of course plans are not set in stone. Rather, they are made on the basis of assumptions that might prove inaccurate and visions that might change in ways that require the plan to be modified.

Although planning remains an integral feature of government, there has been much debate over how the state should implement its plans and policies. Earlier we saw how neoliberals wanted the state to concentrate on steering not rowing. Sometimes they argue that a focus on steering would actually enable the state to plan more effectively: when state actors step back from the delivery of policies, they have more time to consider the big picture. Neoliberalism represented less a repudiation of planning than an attempt to contract out or otherwise devolve the delivery of policies to non-state actors. Typically, its advocates suggested that devolving service delivery would do much to foster a more entrepreneurial ethos within public services – they said that the New Public Management would free managers to manage. Nonetheless, if some neoliberals appear to think that market mechanisms can ensure non-state actors will do as the state (or citizens) wish (or should wish), others recognize that the state still has to structure and oversee the policy process. The state still has to set the goals for other actors; and it has to audit and regulate these actors in relation to these goals. Even as the state forsook direct intervention, so it expanded arm's length attempts to control, coordinate, and regulate other organizations. The new governance includes expanded regimes of regulation. A growing number of agencies, commissions, and special courts enforce rules to protect economic competition and social welfare.

Managing Networks

Social scientists often conclude that the withdrawal of the state from service delivery has led to a proliferation of networks as well as regulatory institutions. The spread of networks appears to further undermine the ability of the state to control and coordinate the implementation of its policies. Social scientists, notably institutionalists, thus argue that effective public policy now depends on mechanisms for controlling and coordinating networks. There are a number of different approaches to the management of policy networks. Some approaches attempt to improve the ability of the state to direct the actions of networks by means of law, administrative rules, or regulation. Others focus on the ability of the state to improve the cooperative interactions between the organizations within networks; typically, they suggest that the state can promote cooperation by altering the relevant incentive structures. Yet other approaches concentrate on negotiating techniques by which the state might promote incremental shifts in the dominant norms and cultures within networks.

The different strategies of network management can be seen as complementing one another. In this view, the state should deploy different policy styles as appropriate in different settings. This perspective returns us to the idea that public policy is an incremental process of muddling through. Public sector managers respond to citizen references and specific problems in concrete settings. Generally, they have to bear in mind multiple objectives, including meeting quality standards, promoting efficiency, remaining democratically accountable, and maintaining public trust and legitimacy. Their responses to problems are typically pragmatic ones that aim to satisfy all of these objectives rather than to maximize performance in relation to any one of them.

Many of the current approaches to network management reject the command-and-control strategies associated with hierarchic bureaucracies. In this view, because the state now depends on other organizations, it has to rely on negotiation and trust. Some social scientists thus suggest that the new governance requires a new ethic of public service. The state should neither row nor merely steer. It should act as a facilitator or enabler. It should help foster partnerships with and between public, voluntary, and private sector groups. It should encounter citizens not merely as voters or as consumers of public services, but as active participants within such groups and policy networks. Instead of defining the goals of public policy in advance, it might even allow the public interest to emerge from dialogues within networks.

Dialogue and Deliberation

Sociological institutionalism and social constructivism theory highlight the ways in which meanings, beliefs, cognitive symbols, and conceptual schemes impact upon the policy process. Some of their advocates suggest that the state might try to manage public policy by means of negotiation and other techniques designed to produce incremental shifts in the culture of networks. Others are less focused on the state; they advocate dialogue and deliberation as the means to give greater control of the policy process to citizens. These later advocate giving greater control to citizens partly for democratic reasons and partly on the grounds that doing so can improve policy-making and policy implementation. Some of them argue that the direct involvement of citizens has become both more important and more plausible as a result of the rise of the new governance and the emergence of new information technologies.

Advocates of dialogue and deliberation argue that they facilitate social learning. In their view, public problems are not technical issues to be resolved by experts. Rather, they are questions about how a community wants to act or govern itself. Dialogue and deliberation better enable citizens and administrators to resolve these questions as they appear in concrete issues of policy. They enable a community to name and frame an issue and so to set an agenda. They inform those involved about their respective concerns, preferences, and ideas for solutions. They help to establish trust and so cooperative norms within a community. And, perhaps most importantly, they are said to help reveal common ground, even to generate a consensus about the public good. Hence they appear to pave the way for common action.

Critics point to various problems with dialogic and deliberative policy-making. They argue that it is unrealistic given the size of modern states, it ignores the role of expertise in making policy decisions, it inevitably excludes groups or viewpoints, it is slow, and it cannot respond to crises. Critics also suggest that some policy areas, such as national security, are particularly inappropriate for direct citizen involvement. Despite such criticisms, citizen involvement, even if only through voting, is surely a necessary requisite of good, democratic governance.

DEMOCRATIC GOVERNANCE

Questions about public policy are partly normative. We want the policy process to reflect our values. Today these values are generally democratic ones. However, the new governance raises specific problems for our democratic practices. Democracy is usually associated with elected officials making policies, which public servants then implement. The public servants answer to the elected politicians who, in turn, are accountable to the voting public. However, the rise of markets and networks has disrupted these lines of accountability. In the new governance, policies are being implemented and even made by private sector and voluntary sector actors. There are often few lines of accountability tying these actors back to elected officials, and those few are too long to be effective. Besides, the complex webs of actors involved can make it almost impossible for the principle to hold any one agent responsible for a particular policy. Similar problems arise for democracy at the global level. States have created regulatory institutions to oversee areas of domestic policy, and the officials from these institutions increasingly meet to set up global norms, agreements, and policies governing domains such as the economy and the environment.

There is no agreement about how to promote democracy in the new governance. To some extent the different proposals again reflect different theories of governance in general. Rational choice theorists sometimes suggest markets are at least as effective as democratic institutions at ensuring popular control over outcomes. Institutionalists are more likely to concern themselves with formal and informal lines of the accountability needed to sustain representative and responsible government. These institutional issues merge gradually into a concern to promote diverse forums for dialogue – a concern that is common among constructivist and interpretive theorists.

'Good' Governance

Concerns about democratic governance first arose in discussions of economic development. Economists came to believe that the effectiveness of market reforms was dependent upon the existence of appropriate political institutions. In some ways, then, the quality of governance initially became a hot topic not because of normative, democratic concerns, but because it impinged on economic efficiency, notably the effectiveness of aid to developing countries. International agencies such as the International Monetary Fund and the World Bank increasingly made 'good governance' one of the criteria on which they based aid and loans. Other donors followed suit.

The concept of 'good governance' was thus defined by institutional barriers to corruption and by the requirements of a functioning market economy. It was defined as a legitimate state with a democratic mandate, an efficient and open administration, and the use of competition and markets in the public and private sectors. Various international agencies sought to specify the characteristics of good governance so conceived. They wanted checks on executive power, such as an effective legislature with territorial (and perhaps ethno-cultural) representation. Likewise, they stressed the rule of law, with an independent judiciary, laws based on impartiality and equity, and an honest police force. They included a competent public service characterized by clear lines of accountability and by transparent and responsive decision-making. They wanted political systems to effectively promote a consensus, mediating the various interests in societies. And they emphasized the importance of a strong civil society characterized by freedom of association, freedom of speech, and the respect of civil and political rights. Some international agencies, such as the World Bank, also associated good governance with the New Public Management; they encouraged developing states to reform their public sectors by privatizing public enterprises, promoting competitive markets, reducing staffing, strengthening budgetary discipline, and making use of non-governmental organizations. Other organizations, such as the United Nations, place greater emphasis on social goals, including inclusiveness, justice, and environmental protection.

Non-Majoritarian Institutions

It was perhaps ironic that international agencies and western donors began to emphasize 'good governance' just as the proliferation of markets and networks posed questions about their own democratic credentials. The new governance sits oddly beside the ideal of representative and responsible government in accordance with the will of the majority. It involves private and voluntary sector actors in policy processes even though these actors are rarely democratically accountable in as straightforward a way as are public sector actors.

There are many responses to the tension between governance and democracy. These responses vary from the suggestion that we might benefit from less democracy, through proposals to make networks and markets more accountable to elected officials, and on to calls for a radical transformation of our democratic practices. The suggestion that we might benefit from less democracy generally comes from people indebted to rational choice theory. Their argument contrasts democracy, which allows citizens to express their preference by voting only once every few years and only by a simple 'yes' or 'no' for a whole slate of policies, with the market, which allows consumers to express their preferences continuously, across a range of intensities, and for individual items. In addition, they worry that democracy entails certain political transaction costs that make it liable to lead to incessant increases in public expenditure: one problem is that the costs of any item of expenditure are thinly distributed across a large population, which thus has little reason to oppose them, whereas the benefits are often concentrated in a small population, which thus clamours for them. Hence they advocate non-majoritarian institutions as ways of protecting crucial policy areas, such as banking and budgeting, from democracy.

Democratic Visions

Many people are uncomfortable with the growing role of non-majoritarian (or undemocratic) organizations in government. Often they associate the growing role of such organizations with growing public disinterest in or distrust of government. There has been much discussion about the democratic legitimacy of new forms of governance. Parts of this discussion aim to reconcile the new governance with democracy by rethinking the concept of democratic legitimacy. Historically, this concept has privileged electoral accountability together with a bureaucratic accountability in which the actions of unelected agents are controlled, evaluated, sanctioned, and answered for by elected officials. Perhaps we should expand this concept of democratic legitimacy to incorporate efficacy, legal accountability, or social inclusion.

So, perhaps the legitimacy of organizations and their decisions might rest on their effectiveness in providing public goods – a possibility that clearly resonates with the arguments for the efficiency of markets and non-majoritarian institutions. Alternatively, we might ascribe legitimacy to organizations that are created and regulated by democratic states no matter how long and obscure the lines of delegation. In this view, democratic legitimacy is maintained whenever elected assemblies set up independent organizations in accordance with rules that are monitored by independent bodies such as courts. Legitimacy is maintained here because the independent organizations are legally accountable, and a democratic government passed the relevant laws. Alternatively again, the legitimacy of institutions and decisions might rest on their being fair and inclusive. Proponents of this view often especially emphasize the importance of a strong civil society in securing a form of accountability based on public scrutiny. Voluntary groups, the media, and active citizens monitor institutions and decisions to ensure that these are fair and inclusive. They thereby give or deny organizations the credibility required to participate effectively in the debates, negotiations, and networks that generate policy.

Discomfort with the democratic credentials of the new governance can also lead people to search for new avenues of citizen participation, or at least to try to enhance established avenues of participation. Here we might divide the democratic policy process into stages such as those of deliberation, decision, implementation, evaluation, and review.

Typically, citizens already have avenues of participation at several stages. Citizens often can participate, for instance, by writing to newspapers, voting on ballot measures, and serving on advisory boards. Nonetheless, because many stages of the policy process are increasingly outside the direct control of elected officials, there is a case for enhancing opportunities for participation even if one does not believe in participatory democracy as a political ideal. Proposals for enhancing participation include: public hearings, town hall forums, referenda, deliberative polls, citizen representatives on committees, various types of self-steering, and citizens juries. Advocates of more participatory democracy are often acutely aware that different citizens possess different resources for participating. Hence they often attend carefully to process issues about who participates in what ways and under what circumstances. So, for example, they might advocate state support for under-represented groups. Typically, their goal here is to increase equality and social inclusion in relation to participation.

CONCLUSION

We have seen how the term 'governance' can be used at various levels of generality and within various theoretical contexts. The diversity of uses exceeds any attempt to offer a comprehensive account of governance by reference to a list of its properties. There does not appear to be a single feature shared by all those cases to which we might apply the term. Perhaps we would do well to look instead for a series of family resemblances between its various uses.

The concept of the new governance refers, most prominently, to an institutional shift at all levels of government – from the local to the global – from bureaucracy to markets and networks. Of course, it is important to remember that this shift is neither universal nor uniform, and that bureaucracy probably remains the prevalent institutional form. Nonetheless, the shift from bureaucracy to markets to networks means that the central state often adopts a less hands-on role. Its actors are less commonly found within various local and sectoral bodies, and more commonly found in quangos concerned to steer, coordinate, and regulate such bodies.

The concept of governance conveys, most importantly, a more diverse view of authority and its exercise. In the new governance, the neoliberal quest for a minimal state and the more recent attempts to promote networks are attempts to increase the role of civil society in practices of rule.

Likewise, theories of governance generally suggest that patterns of rule arise as contingent products of diverse actions and political struggles informed by the varied beliefs of situated agents. Some of these theories even suggest that the notion of a monolithic state in control of itself and civil society was always a myth. The myth obscured the reality of diverse state practices that escaped the control of the center because they arose from the contingent beliefs and actions of diverse actors at the boundary of state and civil society. In this view, the state always has to negotiate with others, policy always arises from interactions within networks, the boundaries between the state and civil society are always blurred, and transnational links and flows always disrupt national borders.

Part II: The Concepts

Accountability

DEFINITION

The word 'accountability' derives from the Latin word *computare*, which literally meant 'to count', and which denoted book-keeping and forms of financial record-keeping. Today, however, the word 'accountability' conveys a more general sense of 'giving a report of oneself'. As such, it overlaps with concepts like 'responsibility' and 'liability'.

So, accountability can be defined in the following manner: when people are meant to pursue the will and/or interests of others, they give an account of their actions to those others who are then able to decide whether to reward or censure them for the actions. Accountability thus conveys the idea that an agent (such as an elected politician or a civil servant) is responsible for acting on behalf of a principal (such as a citizen or government minister, respectively) to whom they should respond and report. The principal is thereby able to hold the agent accountable for his or her actions.

CONTEXT

'Accountability' rarely appeared in dictionaries prior to the twentieth century. The emphasis fell instead on representative and responsible government. Social scientists thought of representative democracy as a historical achievement, and, in their opinion, the civil society (or stage of civilization) that sustained representative democracy also would support the moral ideals and behavior that made for responsible government. Responsibility referred here to the character of politicians and officials at least as much as to their relationship to the public. Politicians and officials had a duty to respond to the demands, wishes, and needs of the people. To act responsibly was to act so as to promote the common good rather than to seek personal advantage. To act responsibly was to overcome petty factionalism in order to pursue the national interest.

The concept of accountability rose to prominence in the early twentieth century. The First World War precipitated a loss of faith in the old belief in the progress of nations towards statehood, liberty, representative democracy, and responsible government. Social scientists began to describe the nation as fragmented. They viewed democracy less as a means of expressing a common good and more as a contest among factions or classes. At the same time, social scientists themselves appeared to provide a neutral expertise that might guide policy-making: social science could show us what policies would best produce whatever results or values our democratic representatives decided upon. Hence a neutral bureaucracy appeared to be a possible check on political factionalism.

In the bureaucratic narrative, politics and administration were separate activities. The political process generated values and political decisions. Public officials provided a politically neutral expertise to formulate and implement policies that were in accordance with these values and decisions. The bureaucratic narrative thereby made responsibility seem less important than political and administrative accountability.

Political accountability involves politicians being held to account through the institutions of representative democracy. Legislators are accountable to the voters who periodically decide whether or not to return them to office. The executive – especially Presidents in political systems with a strong separation of powers – can also be directly accountable to the electorate. Alternatively, the executive – especially Prime Ministers in Westminster systems – can be held accountable by a legislature that is capable of revoking its authority. In practice, these forms of political accountability are fairly weak, for while politicians and governments can be voted out of office, they typically control knowledge, agendas, and resources in ways that make them more powerful than those who might seek to hold them to account.

Administrative accountability is an ideal within bureaucratic hierarchies. Bureaucratic hierarchies are meant to clearly define a specialized, functional division of labor. They are meant to specify clear roles to individuals within the decision-making process, thereby making it possible to identify who is responsible for what. Typically, individual officials are thus directly answerable to their superiors (and ultimately their political masters) for their actions. Administrative accountability also occurs through ombudsmen and other judicial means for investigating maladministration and corruption.

If administrative accountability appears stronger than political accountability, it is nonetheless a blunt instrument. Administrative accountability provides a theoretical account of how to apportion blame and seek redress in cases of maladministration. Critics of the bureaucratic narrative complain, however, that it does not provide an adequate way of assessing different levels of performance. Moreover, the new governance has made the ideal of administrative accountability appear increasingly implausible as an account of reality. The involvement of diverse actors in the formulation and delivery of services makes it increasingly difficult to say who should be held responsible for what. Hence the new governance has inspired a shift of emphasis from the procedural accountability that we have just discussed to new concepts of performance accountability.

DEBATE

Performance accountability identifies legitimacy primarily with satisfaction with outputs. In doing so, it sidesteps the problems associated with procedural accountability. For example, if the state is judged by its outputs, then there is less need to cling to the illusion of a distinction between the administrative and political domains. Similarly, if we focus on performance, we can be less concerned that the actions of the agent are overseen and judged by the principal.

Although the shift from procedural to performance accountability solves some problems, it remains extremely controversial. Prominent debates concern how we should understand performance accountability and whether or not performance accountability adequately reflects our democratic values.

Let us look at the question of how to understand performance accountability. Sometimes performance accountability is understood in quasi-market terms: citizens act as customers, and they express their satisfaction by buying or selecting services delivered by one agency rather than another. In practice, however, public agencies often lack the kind of pricing mechanisms, profit levels, and hard budgets that are believed to make the market an indicator of customer satisfaction. Hence an alternative way of conceiving performance accountability is in terms of measurements of outputs. Targets, benchmarks, and other standards and indicators provide a basis for monitoring and even auditing the performance of public agencies. Finally, performance accountability can be embedded in horizontal exchanges among a system of actors. Whereas procedural accountability privileged vertical relationships such as that of public officials to their political masters, performance accountability is equally at home within horizontal relationships within which various actors provide checks and balances on one another.

Consider, finally, the fit between performance accountability and our democratic values. For many people, democracy is not just a matter of people being happy with the performance of their government. Democracy requires that citizens participate in making decisions and oversee their implementation. If we take these democratic values seriously, then surely proper accountability requires clear-cut arrangements such that particular officials and politicians should be answerable respectively to elected politicians and to citizens for their actions and decisions.

Perhaps we need to be able to specify: Who is accountable? To whom are they accountable? For what are they accountable? In the new governance, where actions and decisions are shared among multiple actors, the answers to these questions are becoming less and less clear. Who is accountable? As decisions are made by many actors – with various degrees of public visibility, terms of office, and sources of funding – it becomes extremely difficult to attribute causation to one specific actor or decision. To whom are they accountable? To say that they ought to be accountable to the public is perhaps to assume that the public has a more homogeneous voice than it actually does. For what are they accountable? If elected politicians promote a policy, should they be accountable for its implementation by other actors over whom they have little control? Conversely, if a government agency implements a law correctly, but the law undermines performance, then should the agency be accountable for that?

CROSS REFERENCES

Bureaucracy, Representative democracy

FURTHER READING

Behn, R.D. (2001) *Rethinking Democratic Accountability*. Washington, DC: Brookings Institution Press.

Dunsire, A. (1978) *Control in a Bureaucracy*. New York: St Martin's Press.

Przeworski, A., Stokes, S.C. and Manin, B. (eds) (1999) *Democracy, Accountability, and Representation*. Cambridge: Cambridge University Press.

Radin, B. (2006) *Challenging the Performance Movement: Accountability, Complexity, and Democratic Values*. Washington, DC: Georgetown University Press.

Bureaucracy

DEFINITION

A bureaucracy is an organization characterized by hierarchy, fixed rules, impersonal relationships, strict adherence to impartial procedures, and specialization based on function. Bureaucratic organizations can be found in the private sector as well as the public sector.

This definition of bureaucracy as a type of organization overlaps with other ways in which the word is used. Bureaucracy can be used as a synonym for a hierarchical mode of social coordination – a usage based on the hierarchical nature of such organizations. It can be used as a synonym for the public administration – a usage that suggests the public sector is the archetype of a hierarchical organization. It can be used to refer to the people who work in the public sector or other large, hierarchical organizations; these people are bureaucrats. And it can be used to describe conduct that rigidly applies general rules to particular cases – a type of conduct associated with officials in hierarchical organizations.

Government bureaucracies expanded for much of the twentieth century. To some, bureaucracy appeared to be the ideal organizational type for the performance of complex yet repetitive tasks: it allowed separate parts of the state to specialize in particular tasks, while providing the center with effective control over each of the parts. Yet, by the late twentieth century, a growing number of critics argued that government bureaucracies had become too big and complex, leading to a lack of responsiveness and inefficiency. Some of these critics argued that bureaucracies were inherently unresponsive and inefficient in that they were shielded from the disciplines of the market. Popular culture abounded with jokes and complaints about lazy, self-serving bureaucrats and their love of red tape: the British sitcom *Yes Minister* is a classic of this genre. The backlash against bureaucracy led to attempts to reform government. It led, in particular, to attempts to replace hierarchy with markets and networks – to move from government to governance.

CONTEXT

Etymologically, 'bureaucracy' combines 'bureau', which referred to a place of work for officials, with 'cracy', which was the Greek term for a pattern of rule. Vincent de Gournay, an eighteenth-century economist, introduced the word 'bureaucracy' as an addition to the classic typology of government systems: it was a form of government in which officials dominated.

Although the word 'bureaucracy' only arose in the eighteenth century, social scientists have been quick to apply it to earlier times. They have argued that the Egyptian monarchy created a bureaucratic system to build waterworks projects throughout its empire, that the Romans used bureaucratic systems to govern their vast territories, or that the monarchs of medieval and early modern Europe used bureaucrats for tax collection, trade regulation, and early forms of policing. Generally, however, bureaucracy retains a clear association with the rise of modern industrial and political systems. Social scientists often argue that industrialization led – and historians now emphasize just how slow and uneven the process was – to a shift away from small-scale craft production to a system of mass production, and the greater concentration of capital and the rise of factories then led to the rise of the modern, bureaucratic corporation. Social scientists also often argue that industrialization created a myriad of new and increasingly complex social problems, and that from the nineteenth century onwards the state began to establish departments and bureaux to govern and mitigate these problems. Hence, the argument goes, large-scale hierarchical organizations came to dominate both the private and public sectors.

Democrats often had mixed feelings about the rise of government bureaucracy. They worried about the legitimacy of handing aspects of government over to unelected officials, although many of them accepted that democracy could still operate provided there were clear lines of accountability to ensure the officials were answerable to elected politicians and so ultimately to the people. Equally, they often thought that bureaucracy was necessary because of the range of specialized tasks that governments had to perform. It is difficult to imagine elected politicians dealing with the complexities of patent law, or even economic policy, without the help of expert advisers.

DEBATE

Max Weber, the German sociologist, has been by far and away the most influential theorist of bureaucracy. Weber believed that societies evolved from the primitive and mystical to the complex and rational. He paid particular attention to changing forms of political authority in this process of evolution. In his view, political authorities secured obedience by acquiring various kinds of legitimacy. He identified three types of authority, each of which had a different source of legitimacy: traditional, charismatic, and rational. Tribal societies, and also absolute monarchs, rely on traditional authority legitimized by the sanctity of tradition. Military, religious, and other leaders often rely on charismatic authority legitimized by the personal standing of the leader. Finally, rational-legal societies rely on legal authority legitimized by reason. Law defines the obligations and rights of rulers and ruled. Reason leads the ruled to obey the rulers. Weber claimed that there was a general pattern of social evolution towards the kind of rational-legal authority found in modern states.

Weber described bureaucracy as the institutional form of rational-legal authority. Bureaucracy does not involve public officials dominating government. It means only that full-time, professional officials are responsible for the everyday affairs of government. Elected politicians might formulate policy, but officials implement it. Many of the themes in our earlier definition of bureaucracy derive, in Weber's analysis, from its rational-legal setting. The dominance of legal authority entails an impersonal rule in which abstract rules are applied to particular cases. The dominance of rationality appears in the division of an organization into specialized functions carried out by experts.

Most social scientists endorse something akin to Weber's characterization of bureaucracy. Although Weber thought modern rationality was a mixed blessing, he is often read as claiming bureaucracy as the ideal and most efficient type of organization, and many critics disagree strongly with such claims.

Critics of bureaucracy often argue that the features of Weber's ideal type have self-defeating consequences. Rational choice theorists argue that hierarchical organizations encourage bureaucrats to respond to their superiors at the expense of citizens. Neoliberals argue that the emphasis on general rules and stability leads to inertia and to an inability to respond to a rapidly changing environment. Institutionalists argue that the specialization of functions leads to fragmentation; it results in a plethora of sub-units, each of which goes its own way, leaving the center facing problems of coordination and control. Yet other critics argue that bureaucracy threatens democracy: whereas Weber suggested that bureaucracy offered a neutral and technical structure for implementing policies formed by elected politicians, these critics emphasize the impossibility of distinguishing policy implementation from policy formation and so bureaucratic administration from democratic decision-making.

Today Weber's concept of bureaucracy might seem an outdated relic. Certainly, the rational choice, neoliberal, and institutionalist criticisms of bureaucracy helped to inspire various attempts to replace hierarchies with markets or networks. Still, we should not over-emphasize the extent to which the reforms genuinely succeeded in supplanting older bureaucratic structures. For a start, large parts of the public sector remain heavily bureaucratic. In addition, even when we do find a proliferation of markets and networks, these new organizations still operate within a realm constituted in part by the lingering presence of the bureaucratic state. Finally, bureaucracy appears to be as relevant as ever for organizations that must have impartially to process vast numbers of similar, routine cases. We would not want immigration issues, welfare payments, airport security, and the like to depend on the whim of the particular official someone encountered. Hence, even if the state contracts out some of these tasks, the organizations that take them over are likely to appear rather bureaucratic. And there are tasks that we would rather the state did not contract out.

Bureaucracy remains with us. It is likely to do so for a considerable time. Critics might say that its persistence reflects institutional inertia and the ability of bureaucrats to defend their fiefdoms. Others might say that bureaucracy persists because of its utility and desirability.

CROSS REFERENCES

Accountability, Coordination, Hierarchy

FURTHER READING

Beetham, D. (1996) *Bureaucracy*. Buckingham: Open University Press.
Gerth, H. and Mills, C.W. (eds) (1973) *From Max Weber: Essays in Sociology*. Oxford: Oxford University Press.
Im, S. (2001) *Bureaucratic Power, Democracy and Administrative Democracy*. Burlington, VI: Ashgate.
Page, E. (1985) *Political Authority and Bureaucratic Power*. Brighton: Wheatsheaf Books.
Smith, B.C. (1988) *Bureaucracy and Politial Power*. New York: St Martin's Press.

key concepts in governance

Capacity

DEFINITION

Capacity is the state's ability to overcome opposition in order to accomplish its policy aims. This general concept of capacity is, however, often too vague to be of much use. The state's diverse domestic and international activities defy a monolithic approach to capacity. State strategies to improve domestic capacity can create weaknesses on the international front, and state strategies to develop international capacity can create weaknesses on the domestic front. What is more, state capacity can vary within either the domestic or international sphere. State capacity can vary, in particular, across policy sectors. A state might have a strong capacity to provide foreign aid but be weak at projecting its military power. Or a state might have a strong capacity to enforce taxation but be weak at providing basic welfare services.

CONTEXT

State capacity may be determined by analyzing policy capacity and administrative capacity. Policy capacity is the state's ability to make intelligent choices and set strategic agendas that optimally use its resources. Administrative capacity is the state's ability to manage and implement its policy choices. Consider the example of central banking. The policy capacity of central banks lies in their ability to gather and assess information critical to economic decision-making. They employ extensive systems of data collection and tested analytical principles to create interest rate policies that will ensure economic stability. The administrative capacity of central banks lies in states' recognition of their independence and their monopoly status in money markets.

In the context of governance, capacity is mainly used to express worries about the prospects for good governance in developing states. Some states are unable to perform basic functions, including raising fiscal resources, enforcing law, implementing policies, maintaining internal coherence, and responding to citizens and interest groups. They lack the capacity to create a stable environment conducive to economic, social, and political growth.

These worries about failing states have directed attention to ways of increasing the capacity of a state. State capacity builds up as individuals and groups (which might be either state actors or social actors) develop the ability to take part in various processes of governance. Their participation increases their skills, attitudes, and knowledge. Over time they thus can become the cornerstones of governing institutions.

Global institutions such as the World Bank have attempted to devise remedies for problems of state capacity, typically by providing logistical support and financial loans. It is worth recognizing, however, that the approach of the World Bank to building capacity has met with considerable criticism. Critics argue that the conditional loans offered by the Bank damage capacity; first, by requiring the rapid dismantling of overarching state structures in the economy, and, second, by providing direct resources and services in a way which circumvents stable, indigenous institutions.

DEBATE

Analyses of state capacity can vary considerably with one's view of states' aims, let alone one's views of how these aims are best realized. Broadly speaking, however, we might identify three dominant approaches to state capacity – the corporatist approach, the strong-state approach, and the policy instruments approach.

The corporatist approach to state capacity emphasizes the importance of creating a strong network of domestic social partnerships. The state officially recognizes substantial interests groups. It includes them in negotiations over major policy issues, thereby lending them legitimacy. The corporatist approach typically promotes a tripartite bargaining system between the state, labor, and business. In return for the state so lending legitimacy to business and labor organizations, it relies on them to endorse and even implement the policy outcomes. The endorsement of policies by these organizations also enhances the legitimacy of the state among the population. Contemporary approaches to corporatist bargaining typically emphasize that wage bargaining can lead to a stable labor market, which, in turn, contributes to other goals such as low inflation and low unemployment. Critics of the corporatist approach argue that it is poorly suited to issues related to a state's international capacity.

Whereas corporatism focuses on the necessity of providing a stable environment for state–society interactions, the strong-state approach focuses on the state's ability to assert control over state–society relations. The strong-state approach derives from a statist model in which society is subordinate. In this view, the state uses coercion to control and mold societal interests. Strong states rely on the bureaucracy to implement policies and even to restructure social and economic relations. Indeed, the capacity of strong states to implement pervasive domestic restructuring is what enables them to overcome organized domestic opposition. Strong states can directly enforce regulations upon industries and factional interests. The most common examples of the strong-state approach to capacity are arguably the Asian developmental states of the 1970s.

Finally, the policy instruments approach is associated with states that are trying to preserve institutions and policies that are now threatened by globalization. Advocates of this approach argue that the capacity of a state derives from the policy instruments that it is empowered to employ. States that use these policy instruments effectively retain their capacity. States that do not do so lose their capacity. Many social scientists identify a state's financial system as its core policy instrument. The extent to which the state can allocate capital appears to distinguish states with high and low capacities to intervene in social and economic relations. If the state is the key provider of credit and plays an intelligent role in administering prices, it develops a high capacity to manage the economy. If credit and prices are predominantly left to private corporations and international capital flows, the state's capacity to intervene decreases; it loses any established foothold in the economy.

CROSS REFERENCES

Corporatism, Implementation, Managing networks, Metagovernance

FURTHER READING

Cheema, S. and Rondinelli, D. (eds) (2003) *Reinventing Government for the Twenty-first Century*. Bloomfield, CT: Kumarian Press.

Painter, M. and Pierre, J. (eds) (2005) *Challenges to State Policy Capacity*. Basingstoke: Palgrave Macmillan.

Weiss, L. (1998) *The Myth of the Powerless State: Governing the Economy in a Global Era*. Cambridge, NY: Polity Press.

capacity

Center–Local
Relations

DEFINITION

Center–local relations refer to the political and administrative relationships that exist between a central state and the local governments within its territorial borders. Some analyses of center–local relations focus on the spectrum that runs from centralization to decentralization. A state favoring centralization will amass power at the center: the center develops a top-down chain of command through which to play a prominent role in formulating and implementing policies throughout its territory. Conversely, a state favoring decentralization will distribute power to local governments: sub-national bodies play a more active role in the policy process.

Other analyses of center–local relations consider the institutional relationships and control mechanisms that exist between a state and its local parts. A common distinction here is the one between unitary and federal states. Generally, sub-national governments in federal states have entrenched constitutional protections in a way sub-national governments in unitary states do not. Constitutions in federal systems give sub-national governments rights and powers that the federal government cannot infringe upon. Local governments within unitary systems are usually seen as lacking such constitutional protection. Their rights and duties are more susceptible to alteration by the central state.

CONTEXT

Center–local relations vary widely across the globe. It is difficult to generalize without oversimplifying. Yet, the rise of new worlds of governance in the 1980s seems to have led to widespread changes in center–local relations not only in Britain and the USA but also in many other states, including much of Latin America and the post-Communist world. We might highlight two such changes. First, there has been a rising trend of devolving certain powers of discretion to local bodies. Second, this devolution has been accompanied, ironically, with the rise of new instruments of central control.

Many states have witnessed considerable decentralization since the 1980s. The Reagan Presidency in the USA, for example, marked a shift to a 'new federalism' in which the states were given increased discretion over how they chose to spend the federal funds allocated to various welfare programs: the states acquired far greater autonomy over decisions about eligibility requirements and aid amounts. Not all neoliberal governments pursued decentralization. The Thatcher governments in Britain gave barely any new powers to local governments, and they showed little compunction in abolishing tiers of local government that opposed them politically, most notably the Greater London Council. In general, neoliberal governments obsessed over rolling back the state. If decentralization appeared to offer a means to do so, they devolved some powers. If it did not, they were equally happy to increase the center's powers over local bodies.

Irrespective of whether neoliberal governments did or did not devolve some decision-making powers, they almost always introduced new forms of central control. The Thatcher governments in Britain were particularly centralist, imposing a vast number of new laws and regulations on local governments in an attempt to force them to reduce taxes and public expenditure and to promote marketization. Likewise, when neoliberal regimes devolved powers, they almost always simultaneously introduced new patterns of regulation. So, for example, while the center often gave local governments greater freedom to develop policy initiatives, they also adopted increasingly tight regulation of the fiscal aspects of such initiatives.

DEBATE

The new theories of governance have altered the ways in which scholars think about center–local relations. Historically, the study of center–local relations concentrated on formal institutions and rules. Now it is often studied in terms more indebted to organizational theory. As a result, there has been much debate about the rival claims of formal institutions of government and policy networks as units of analysis in understanding sub-central politics. The newer policy network approach pays more attention to the fragmentation of government activities at both the central and local level. It suggests that sometimes we would be better advised to think in terms of policy sectors than in terms of territorial divisions. It highlights the close relationships between civil servants, local government officers, and technocratic experts within particular policy domains.

This policy network perspective, together with the experience of neoliberal regimes, has inspired a growing skepticism about the distinction between unitary and federal states and the distinction between centralization and decentralization. Consider the distinction between unitary and federal states. It now seems clear that all states have political struggles between central and local governments in the context of written or unwritten constitutional norms. All states have a central government that negotiates its relationship to sub-central parts. Hence the distinction between federal and unitary systems becomes, at most, one of degree rather than one of kind. Consider also the spectrum between centralized systems and decentralized ones. We have already seen how neoliberal reforms often appeared to devolve powers to local bodies while actually adding new modes of central control. In addition, scholars have noted how the uneven bargaining power of central and local bodies can mean that apparently decentralizing measures actually return power back to the center. Devolution can create 'institutional voids' within which central state actors are able to gain greater power and control. Central state actors can use decentralizing measures as an opportunity to promise or withhold central resources from local actors, thereby building up a system of patronage that consolidates or maintains their popularity among local constituencies. From this perspective, decentralization looks like a political tool with which actors at the center might seek to increase their own power.

CROSS REFERENCES

Decentralization, Local governance, Multilevel governance, Pluralism

FURTHER READING

Agranoff, R.J. (1986) *Intergovernmental Management*. Albany, NY: State University of New York Press.

Bogason, P. (2000) *Public Policy and Local Governance: Institutions in Postmodern Society*. Cheltenham: Edward Elgar.

Page, E. (1991) *Localism and Centralism in Europe: The Political and Legal Basis of Local Self-government*. Oxford: Oxford University Press.

Rhodes, R.A.W. (1988) *Beyond Westminster and Whitehall: The Sub-central Governments of Britain*. London: Routledge.

Collaborative Governance

DEFINITION

Collaborative governance refers to attempts to create and conduct policy that involve the participation of non-governmental and non-traditional political actors. At times it refers specifically to attempts to bring all the relevant stakeholders together for face-to-face discussions during which policies are developed. The actors from civil society who are interested in a policy play an active role in the policy process from initial discussions over the agenda to completion. Examples of relevant non-governmental organizations include not only businesses and unions but also citizens' groups such as local residents and activist groups. Collaborative governance is an interactive process in which myriad actors with various interests, perspectives, and knowledge are brought together. The hope is that the resulting policies will be better conceived, more suitable to the local context, more workable, and also more legitimate than would policies formed through more closed policy-making processes.

CONTEXT

Collaborative governance parallels a broader trend away from top-down hierarchical approaches to public policy – a trend that also includes marketization and joined-up government. Yet collaborative governance differs from other moves away from hierarchy in its emphases on discussion and ultimately agreement and cooperation among stakeholders. Unlike marketization, collaborative governance relies on negotiation, not competition, to define acceptable outcomes. Unlike joined-up governance, collaborative governance focuses on the involvement of citizens' groups in the policy process, not the bringing together of the diverse government agencies involved in a given policy area.

There is a sense, of course, in which the policy process has always included non-state actors whose interests are affected by the relevant policy. However, the main actors involved in the formation of policy have been large institutionalized interests, with the involvement of citizens' groups being limited to responding to policy proposals in settings such as public hearings and formal complaints. Policy formation is, indeed, still usually dominated by state-level actors, including legislators and technocrats, and insider interest groups, such as businesses and unions. Collaborative governance remains radical in its insistence on the importance of citizen participation.

Advocates of collaborative governance argue that it has several advantages. First, it accelerates the policy-making process. Because more actors are involved in the earlier stages, there is more support for the policy once it is proposed and implemented. Second, the involvement of diverse actors leads to a more thorough exploration of any proposed policy: there is less chance that an aspect or consequence of a policy will be overlooked or ignored. Third, collaborative governance brings new skills, expertise, and perspectives into the policy-making process: it expands the range of people involved, and it might thus lead to more innovative policies. Fourth, collaborative governance can increase the legitimacy of public policies. It opens up the policy-making process, thereby increasing transparency, accountability, and trust. Besides, when non-state actors are involved in the policy-making process, they have a greater sense of ownership of the policies. Finally, collaborative governance that widens public participation in the policy-making process has spin-off benefits for society. Participation makes citizens feel empowered and promotes civic pride. Citizens come to view the state not as an external imposition watching over them, monitoring them, and regulating them, but as an active partner in making a better society.

DEBATE

By no means does everyone agree that collaborative governance has the advantages its advocates suggest it does. To the contrary, critics vociferously debate its desirability. One debate is about whether or not collaborative governance is more efficient than other, more top-down styles of decision-making. Critics suggest that involvement of more actors seriously increases the transaction costs involved in deciding on a policy. Many more interests have to be reconciled or at least placated, and managing the diverse interests often proves excessively costly if not outright impossible.

Critics of collaborative governance also debate the claim that it increases legitimacy. They argue that the policies that arise from collaborative governance represent only the interests of the few selected groups that participated in the policy process. They point out that some interests are often too diffuse to be readily organized and voiced. They also suggest that collaborative processes typically favor groups that have better finances and knowledge. In so far as relatively weak social actors are excluded from collaborative processes, or marginalized within them, collaborative governance is in danger of expressing special interests rather than fostering a sense of common good.

A final set of debates concern the practicalities of collaborative governance. Both advocates and critics of collaborative governance sometimes argue that the current infrastructures for policy-making are poorly suited to it. In this view, collaborative governance requires a change in the culture and the organization of the civil service. Public officials need to rethink their role as one that facilitates dialogue rather than advising politicians, managing departments, and implementing decisions. Some critics of collaborative governance argue more dramatically that the infrastructure it requires is impossible or at least highly undesirable. They argue, in particular, that the mere fact of actors having collaborated in the formation of a policy is not enough to ensure that these actors later keep their commitments. For example, if an actor realizes that he can achieve his interests in other contexts, such as the legal system or elections, it is likely he will not be as committed to the collaborative process. Hence the critics conclude that collaborative governance requires powerful enforcement mechanisms that would undermine much of what it is meant to achieve.

CROSS REFERENCES

Dialogic policy-making, Participatory democracy, Social inclusion

FURTHER READING

Hajer, M. and Wagenaar, H. (eds) (2003) *Deliberative Policy Analysis: Understanding Governance in the Network Society*. Cambridge: Cambridge University Press.

Healey, P. (1997) *Collaborative Planning: Shaping Places in Fragmented Societies*. London: Macmillan.

Meadowcroft, J. (1999) 'Cooperative Management Regimes: Collaborative Problem Solving to Implement Sustainable Development', *International Negotiation*, 4: 225–254.

Wondolleck, J. and Yaffee, S. (2000) *Making Collaboration Work: Lessons from Innovation in Natural Resource Management*. Washington, DC: Island Press.

Collective Action Problem

DEFINITION

The collective action problem suggests that even when members of a group have a common good they might fail to act to attain it. The relevant common goods are those that, once attained, are made available to everyone irrespective of whether or not they acted to attain it. An example of such a common good is clean air: clean air benefits everyone regardless of the extent to which they cause air pollution. Collective action problems occur because the fact that everyone benefits from these common goods means that the rational strategy for each individual is to try to reap the benefits without having to put any work into attaining them. Rational individuals aim to freeride: they aim to have others pay the costs of providing the good from which they then benefit. The result is that nobody works to provide the good, so it is not attained. Again, individuals do not have to incur the cost of cooperation to benefit from the common good, so if they are rational, they will try to leave the costs to others, with the result that if they all act rationally, nobody pays the costs, and the good is not attained. Individual rational behavior thereby leads to a collectively irrational result.

The failure to attain common goods because of collective action problems is commonly referred to as the 'tragedy of the commons'. The 'tragedy of the commons' refers primarily to the case of cattle grazing on common lands. Suppose there is a large area of land for common grazing. Several cattle-owners use the land. All the owners benefit from the common grazing ground. They thus have a collective interest in preserving its fertility by limiting the number of cattle that graze on it. Yet, the benefits of the land and its fertility go to all the owners irrespective of the extent to which each of them contributes to maintaining it, so an individual owner benefits most if she puts many cattle on the land while the others restrict the numbers they put on it. Hence if each owner pursues her individual interests, the number of cattle on the land will increase quickly and the grazing lands will be depleted in a way that harms every owner. If each owner acts rationally, the result will be collectively irrational – a 'tragedy of the commons'.

CONTEXT

The analysis of collective action problems draws on rational choice theory. It is, in other words, less a set of empirical observations than a model based on the assumption that people act rationally in pursuit of their individual interests. Moreover, rational choice theory and so the serious analysis of collective action problems really only arose in the twentieth century. For much of the nineteenth century, social theorists typically assumed that if a group of people shared common interests, then they would act in consort to pursue those interests. Social theorists wanted to protect the wider public from the consorted action of powerful groups. In politics, they worried about oligarchy. In economics, they worried about cartels. They feared that groups of powerful businesses would act collectively so as to regulate output and prices in ways that would increase their profits at the expense of the consumer. Rational choice theory and neoclassical economics challenge these older accounts of collective action because they analyze action in terms of individuals seeking to maximize their particular gains. On the one hand, neoclassical economics and rational choice theory erode fears about oligarchy and cartels. Economists began to argue that cartels formed solely to boost profits were inherently unstable since efficient businesses would profit more from breaking any agreement. On the other hand, as we have seen, neoclassical economics and rational choice theory inspire new fears about the difficulties of ensuring social cooperation, and particularly about the ways in which individually rational actions lead to collectively irrational results.

Collective action problems are found in a variety of settings. One important setting is environmental policy. Consider the example of recycling. Most people recognize that recycling is good for the environment, and that a better environment benefits all of us. Nonetheless, each individual reaps the benefits of other people recycling irrespective of whether or not they themselves do so; hence they can gain the rewards without paying any costs. What is more, the contribution of any individual to the overall benefits of everyone recycling is statistically rather low; hence the amount of benefits each individual reaps are almost wholly unaffected by whether or not they recycle. In both these respects, recycling is a clear case where the rational strategy for each individual is to do nothing and try to reap the rewards of others doing something. Yet if everyone acted rationally, the result would be that nobody would recycle and the quality of the environment would decline. Clearly, the same type of collective action problem occurs with many kinds of environmental goods from the local level to the global level.

Social scientists have tried to explore a range of issues as analogous to collective action problems. One example is the widespread decline in levels of voting. The supporters of a party have a collective interest in the victory of their candidate. But each of them benefits from their candidate winning irrespective of whether or not they vote: they can gain the rewards without paying any costs, such as the time taken up by casting a vote. What is more, their single vote is unlikely to make any significant difference to the outcome of the election: their actions are unlikely to have any impact on whether or not they attain the reward. Hence the rational strategy is not to vote.

DEBATE

Many debates about collective action problems concern the validity of the rational choice perspective upon which it draws. Critics argue that rational choice theory makes a number of unrealistic assumptions about the selfish and rational nature of humans. Many of them argue that human action owes more to social norms or conventions. Such arguments imply that we need not worry quite so much about collective action problems. These arguments imply that people might cooperate even when it is not strictly in their interests to do so. They imply that social norms might lead people to contribute to collective goods even though they could benefit from the goods even if they did not so contribute to them.

The more credence one gives to the analysis of collective action problems, however, the more one is likely to debate possible solutions to them. One proposed solution is to limit the size of groups. The idea here is partly that small groups tend to be more homogeneous, which increases the likelihood of cooperation, and partly that individuals in a small group are more likely to contribute because they can more easily perceive the effects of their contribution. Another proposed solution is to introduce some kind of membership cost that individuals have to pay if they are to benefit from a collective good. Alas, however, the proposed solutions to collective actions are widely seen as flawed. A small group might encourage cooperation, but small groups typically have fewer resources and are unable to deal with many of the large-scale collective action problems that bedevil us today. Similarly, membership costs are likely to reduce membership levels, leading to smaller groups that lack the resources to deal with large-scale collective action problems.

CROSS REFERENCES

Coordination, Environmental governance, Rational choice theory

FURTHER READING

Hardin, G. (1968) 'The Tragedy of the Commons', *Science*, 162: 1243–1248.
Hardin, R. (1982) *Collective Action*. Baltimore, MD: Johns Hopkins University Press.
Olson, M. (1965) *The Logic of Collective Action: Public Goods and the Theory of Groups*. Cambridge, MA: Harvard University Press.
Sandler, T. (1992) *Collective Action: Theory and Applications*. Ann Arbor, MI: University of Michigan Press.

Communitarianism

DEFINITION

Communitarianism refers to various social and political theories that exhibit a broad emphasis on the social nature of individual human existence, as well as the advantages of a society based on strong, shared moral values. Many communitarians also emphasize the role of religion, work, and family in sustaining shared moral values and so society.

There are two main varieties of communitarianism – the philosophical and the sociological. Philosophical communitarians oppose meta-ethical ideas that are prominent in contemporary liberalism (notably, the thin concept of self and the priority of the right over the good). They argue that we are embedded in communities, traditions, and ways of life, which give us our values, identities, and loyalties. And they argue that we can justify moral principles, at least initially, only from within particular communities and traditions. The meta-ethical arguments of philosophical communitarians do not entail any particular approach to governance. Some philosophical communitarians insist, for example, that their meta-ethic is quite compatible with a liberal politics. Philosophical communitarians can be quite hostile to sociological communitarianism.

Sociological communitarianism itself consists primarily of an emphasis on the importance of strong, shared values as a prerequisite of a well-functioning society. Unlike philosophical communitarianism, socio-logical communitarianism has had a clear impact on the new governance, notably as an inspiration for various welfare reforms. The leading expo-nent of sociological communitarianism is Amitai Etzioni, a professor of sociology who spent a year in the White House as a senior adviser on domestic affairs, and who later founded the Communitarian Network.

CONTEXT

Sociological communitarianism arose to prominence in the 1980s. It was a reaction to the neoliberal governments of Ronald Reagan in the USA and Margaret Thatcher in the UK. The neoliberals were widely seen as promoting individualism and, according to some of their critics, thereby condoning materialism and selfishness.

Sociological communitarians employ a chronological narrative to explicate their ideas in opposition to neoliberalism. According to Etzioni, the 1950s were, at least in the USA, a time of stable values and so a viable community. A widely shared set of values, based to some degree on the dominance of Christianity, gave people a strong sense of duty to family, community, and society. Although the society based on these values involved coercive breaks on autonomy, especially for groups such as women and ethnic minorities, it had an admirable moral vitality. For Etzioni, moral vitality is the foundation of social order and so of primary importance even though it involves a loss of autonomy. He argues for a balance between community and autonomy, between indi-vidual rights and social responsibilities. In his view, the 1960s and 1970s brought an excess of autonomy that destroyed the healthy community of the 1950s. The excess of autonomy appeared in a growing sense of entitlement, a neglect of responsibilities, a decline in respect for author-ity, and in consequent social problems, including welfare dependency among the underclass. Communitarians typically locate the source of this excessive autonomy in the counter-cultural movements of the 1960s: these movements undermined the values of hard work and thrift, and they encouraged new socio-economic patterns, such as the entry of women into the labor market, which limited the amount of time that people could give to family and voluntary action in the community. According to the communitarians, the excess of autonomy appears in both the welfare liberalism of the 1960s and 1970s, with its emphasis on rights, and the neoliberalism of the 1980s, with its individualism, materialism, and selfishness.

DEBATE

Sociological communitarians call for a reassertion of strong values to stop the moral drift that they believe has occurred since the early 1960s. They associate strong values with religion, work, and family. In their view, work and family teach people responsibility and self-reliance, while integrating them into society. Work and family bolster self-esteem, purpose, and the sense of contributing to a community. Work and family encourage people to relate their individual choices to their responsibilities. Hence sociological communitarians often advocate welfare-to-work programs and measures to support families. Some argue, for example, that the state should promote marriage actively and make divorce more difficult for couples with children. Many sociological communitarians also suggest that an emphasis on work and family is the best way to attack poverty: they think that stable intact families offer the best solution to poverty for children, and they think that paid employment offers the best solution to the adult poverty of the underclass. More generally still, communitarians advocate policies to promote family and work as ways of ensuring a general shift from a culture of autonomy towards one of community. They want to re-establish a link between rights and responsibilities, tying the rights we enjoy to our fulfilment of corresponding duties. In their view, much of the value of work and family derives from the fact that they are where we learn to be responsible. The state is, in contrast, the paradigmatic institution from which we demand rights.

In the UK and USA, governments drew on communitarian ideas in their programs of welfare reform. The communitarian emphasis on work as a tutor of responsibility has inspired welfare-to-work schemes. In these schemes, the state attempts to tackle social exclusion by bouncing people into work where, it is hoped, they will learn responsibility and gain self-esteem as well as becoming financially self-supporting. Governments have established 'New Deals', under which the state accepts a responsibility to provide work and training, while in return the unemployed accept the reciprocal responsibility to seek and accept such opportunities. These New Deals sometimes require the unemployed to undertake full-time education or voluntary work, or else they have their benefits cut.

We might divide up the innumerable criticisms of sociological communitarianism according to their focus on its narrative, theory, or policy. As a counter-narrative, we might describe sociological communitarianism itself as nostalgia for a mythical golden age of social order conveniently projected onto the 1950s. In theoretical terms, we might point to a clear tension between the invocation of strong values and the commitment to an inclusive community. At times, sociological communitarians elide inclusion with those activities by which people fulfil their duties: the unemployed are socially excluded but to bring them into the workforce is to include them by enabling them to participate in the economy. At other times, they suggest that the inclusive community consists of umbrella institutions that bind people together within civil society. Yet neither of these visions of inclusion appears particularly appealing or convincing. Finally, in policy terms, critics have argued that welfare-to-work schemes do relatively little to solve the structural causes of unemployment.

CROSS REFERENCES

Social capital, Social inclusion

FURTHER READING

Bevir, M. (2005) *New Labor: A Critique*. London: Routledge.

Etzioni, A. (1993) *The Spirit of Community: Rights, Responsibilities, and the Communitarian Agenda*. New York: Crown.

Etzioni, A. (ed.) (1998) *The Essential Communitarian Reader*. Lanham, MD: Rowman & Littlefield.

Henderson, P. and Salmon, H. (1998) *Signposts to Local Democracy: Local Governance, Communitarianism, and Community*. London: Community Development Fund.

Mulhall, S. and Swift, A. (1996) *Liberals and Communitarians*. Oxford: Blackwell.

Coordination

DEFINITION

Coordination is both a driving force of governance and one of its goals. Policy actors are unable to change or implement policies by themselves and must work with each other at all stages of the policy process. Coordination occurs whenever two or more policy actors pursue a common outcome and work together to produce it. We can say that coordination is a driving force of governance in that policies can often only be introduced effectively if actors coordinate their actions. Equally, we can say that coordination is a goal of governance in so far as policy actors aim to establish it so that the policy process and public services operate smoothly.

Governmental coordination occurs at a variety of political levels as well as between the different levels. On the national level, legislators often coordinate their interests and actions to introduce legislation. In some states the legislature also has to coordinate with the head of the executive branch of government to approve the legislation. Within the executive branch, public officials coordinate with one another, often in the context of hierarchical chains of command that assign specialized functions to each of them. Increasingly, public officials also coordinate their actions with various private and voluntary agencies. Similarly complex processes of coordination occur at the local level, between central and local governments within a given state, and also in transnational and international contexts. Certainly, international organizations generally rely on the coordination of diverse states and sometimes also non-governmental bodies. For example, military alliances such as the North Atlantic Treaty Organization (NATO) bring member states together in a common defence agreement that requires coordination to ensure inter-operability of military hardware and unified military action.

CONTEXT

The discussion of coordination in governance is often framed around three ideal types: hierarchy, market, and network. A dominant account of the new governance portrays it as a shift from hierarchical coordination to markets and especially networks.

Coordination by hierarchy occurs in a structure in which functions are organized in and executed through a well-defined, multi-tiered system. The medium of coordination is power or authority. The actors in the higher tiers have the power to command those below them, thereby establishing coordination. The authority of the actors at the top of a hierarchy can derive from several sources, including law, reason, and charisma. The most common examples are public actors – local and central agencies. Yet hierarchy can also define coordination for non-state actors. Many private corporations remain profoundly hierarchical: employers can command the employees, and higher-level managers can command those beneath them. Similarly, families are often hierarchical, at least in so far as the adults coordinate the contributions of the children to the unit as a whole.

In markets, the medium of coordination is price. In a market, a resource is allocated among diverse actors according to how much they are willing to pay for a quantity of that resource. Much economic theory suggests that markets produce an optimal outcome. Early social theorists emphasized the way in which markets could turn private vices into public virtues. In their view, even if individuals made their decisions based on selfish motives, the market was such that their decisions would lead to an efficient distribution of resources that would further stimulate the production of those resources. Modern economists often adopt the similar, albeit more static, idea of a Pareto optimum. In their view, properly functioning markets typically lead to a competitive equilibrium in which consumers maximize utility and producers maximize profit. The most common examples are indeed the relationships of consumers and producers in a free market economy. However, markets also play a role within particular organizations: private corporations often make one subdivision purchase a service or good from another in a somewhat competitive market context. Similarly, markets play an increasingly prominent role in the public sector, especially when the state contracts out the delivery of public services to private sector actors.

Finally, coordination can arise in networks. Much recent work on governance has been preoccupied with the question of how coordination can work in the absence of both a central authority and a functioning market. One way of approaching network coordination is to list the factors that appear to be most conducive to its success. Network coordination is most likely to arise when the relevant actors:

- have a common goal
- are unable to realize that goal on their own
- have different resources that can contribute to the collective realization of the goal
- communicate and exchange information with one another
- have trust or confidence in one another.

Such networks can be between friends arranging a holiday, between companies researching a new technology, or between state and non-state actors. Sometimes they can be established for a particular purpose. But the importance of trust means that they are more likely to arise out of repeated interactions. The medium of coordination appears indeed to be something like trust in the context of interdependence.

DEBATE

There are theoretical and practical debates about what types of coordination operate best under what circumstances. To some degree, however, these debates reflect rival theories of social practices: neoclassical economics and rational choice theory typically privilege markets while institutionalists and constructivists often look more favorably on hierarchies and networks.

Hierarchies remain dominant in many systems of governance. They initially appeared to offer some fairly clear advantages. Their clear structures facilitate accountability: it is clear who is responsible to whom for what. They could institutionalize a permanent and neutral form of expertise as a counter to party bias. Yet critics have increasingly pointed to characteristic flaws or limitations of hierarchical bureaucracies. Hierarchies are said to be inefficient, inflexible, and unresponsive. They are inefficient because they lack the structure of incentives that characterize markets. They are inflexible because they have many layers, each of which must be kept in the loop and perhaps even agree to decisions made at lower tiers: they put a premium on abiding by organizational rules and norms, rather than innovation and entrepreneurial activity. They are unresponsive because they encourage officials to concentrate on following rules and fulfilling the intentions of their superiors, rather than on trying to satisfy citizens or consumers.

These criticisms of hierarchy did much to inspire those neoliberals who attempted to reform the public sector by means of marketization. In accordance with the formal analyses of neoclassical economics, properly functioning markets were thought to provide an efficient distribution of resources, and also to be responsive to individual demands. Yet even if we grant the formal analysis of markets, there remain a larger number of goods for which markets cannot properly function due to the absence of competition or information, the presence of a monopoly, or transaction costs. Indeed, public goods are characteristically ones for which it is difficult to construct properly functioning markets. Think, for example, of law and order, transportation infrastructure, education, public housing, or environmental standards. Even if we could get competition between different producers all supplying these goods, we still might want the outcomes to depend less on market forces than on regulation and control in accordance with certain social values.

The problem of markets in public goods helps to explain why the new governance has often come to rely more on networks. Yet networks too have failings. They often make central steering difficult, thereby reducing control and accountability. Network actors can protect their autonomy and have little ownership of system-wide policies. All too often, moreover, the central state, having facilitated the rise of networks, then balks at its inability to command and control them. In these circumstance the hands-off management and diplomacy of network actors is soon challenged by the center trying yet again to impose a command operating code.

CROSS REFERENCES

Hierarchy, Institutionalism, Market, Network, Rational choice theory

FURTHER READING

Chisholm, D. (1989) *Coordination without Hierarchy: Informal Structures in Multiorganizational Systems*. Berkeley, CA: University of California Press.

Jordan, A. and Schout, A. (2007) *The Coordination of the European Union: Exploring the Capacities of Networked Governance*. New York: Oxford University Press.

Olson, M. (1965) *The Logic of Collective Action: Public Goods and the Theory of Groups*. Cambridge, MA: Harvard University Press.

Scharpf, F. (1997) *Games Real Actors Play: Actor-centered Institutionalism in Policy Research*. Boulder, CO: Westview Press.

Corporatism

DEFINITION

Today corporatism generally refers to a pattern of rule in which the state has strong ties with business and labor organizations. Business and labor organizations are treated as having a legitimate right to represent their group's interests in policy networks formed with the central state. In exchange for this privileged position, these organizations take on considerable responsibility for the implementation of the collective agreements that arise out of such policy networks. The state thereby gains some control over the demands, and perhaps even the leadership, of business and labor organizations. Although corporatist bargaining typically acts to limit competition within individual industrial sectors, it is generally compatible with a high level of competition between various sectors, such as that between agrarian and manufacturing interests.

CONTEXT

Corporatism has a long and diverse history. Before the rise of modern states, corporate organizations, such as guilds and churches, had considerable autonomy in pronouncing and enforcing rules for their membership. The guilds regulated entry to particular trades and also cooperation and competition among those who practised the relevant trades. Yet over time these corporate bodies lost much of their autonomous rights to self-governance, for the modern state increasingly claimed the sole right to make laws while free market ideas led to a liberalization of many professions.

The Catholic Church was the first major institution to attempt to integrate corporatist governance into a modern state and a free market economy. Pope Leo XIII took note of the surge of trade unions that swept through Europe in the late nineteenth century. He disagreed with the economists who argued for the inevitability of class conflict or the superiority of market-based competition. In 1891, he published *Rerum Novarum*, advocating associations to link employers and workers so that they would understand one another better. The Catholic Church began to promote, in particular, the idea that social conflict could be managed through representative institutions based on occupations and professions. Later, in the twentieth century, Fascist regimes in southern Europe adopted representation along professional lines as an alternative to parliamentary democracy. Spain under Franco, Portugal under Salazar, and Italy under Mussolini tried to control the population using occupational groupings derived from civil society.

Other modern forms of corporatism have been far less coercive than those found in Fascist Europe. In particular, neo-corporatism refers to increasing attempts by the state to intervene in the industrial relations so as to foster economic growth and social justice. This neo-corporatism arose in Europe in the aftermath of the Second World War as an alternative to both Soviet Marxism and liberal capitalism. At the end of the war, many states guaranteed jobs to returning soldiers, thereby producing a sudden rise in employment rates, but also raising the spectre of inflation. Some states used corporatist relationships with business and labor organizations to build a consensus on effective anti-inflationary economic policies and then to implement them.

Neo-corporatism relies heavily on collective bargaining agreements to economic issues and especially to incomes policy. These agreements involve multiple actors in contexts where no one actor is able to ensure implementation of the agreement on their own. Explanations of neo-corporatism often imply that, of the three principal actors, the state prefers an authoritative solution, and labor prefers a redistribution of wealth, while business prefers a market solution. In contexts where none of these actors can secure their own preference, they can agree on a system that combines state authority, the organized representation of labor and business, and the commitment of labor and business to the implementation of state policies.

Many political scientists argue that neo-corporatism declined after the economic crises of the 1970s, and even that it was virtually abandoned as a macro-economic strategy during the 1980s. The most popular explanation for the decline of neo-corporatism is the rising interdependence of national economies. In this view, globalization has undermined the ability of states to manage their own economies whether or not they try to do so with the cooperation of organized labor and business: attempts to manage wage levels and rates of employment are now doomed to fail. Hence, the argument continues, neo-corporatism has yielded to a more competitive approach to global markets. States, as well as labor and business, now have to adopt strategies that will prove competitively viable within the global market.

Some political scientists argue, however, that the changes in some states since the 1970s are best understood as a shift from macro-level forms of corporatism to alternative forms of meso-corporatism and micro-corporatism. Here meso-corporatism involves state agencies interacting more with smaller, specialized interest associations, and less with the big organized expressions of capital and labor. Likewise, micro-corporatism involves state agencies developing bilateral arrangements with particular private firms and labor groups.

DEBATE

Among the main debates sparked by the literature on neo-corporatism are those about its viability and its relationship to other forms of interest intermediation. The debate about the relationship of neo-corporatism to other forms of interest intermediation, especially neo-pluralists, highlighted both similarities and differences. The neo-pluralists portrayed US politics as a political market analogous to a market economy. In this view, there are limited amounts of power, influence, money, and cooperation in politics, and groups compete to accrue as much influence as possible in order to gain access to policy-makers and affect outcomes. Some pluralist theorists added that the state, far from being on an equal footing with other groups, was an adjudicator that weighed competing interests, actively chose the final policy and then implemented it.

Neo-corporatism is clearly a type of interest mediation between capital, labor, and the state, and, as such, it resembles neo-pluralism. Yet there are significant differences between neo-corporatism and neo-pluralism:

- Whereas pluralism focuses on interest groups competing for scarce resources, corporatism emphasizes their limited cooperation. Indeed, corporatist divisions are based on, and brought together through, effective hierarchical management.
- Corporatism privileges producer interests. It gives producers (labor and business) an institutionalized voice in policy-making in a way it does not give consumers.
- A corporatist state thus often reinforces status quo power relationships and discourages the creation of new groups.
- Whereas pluralism places the state in charge of policy administration, corporatism has capital and labor themselves involved in the implementation of collective agreements.

Let us turn, finally, to discussions of the viability of neo-corporatism. Many social scientists argue that corporatism is most successful in smaller nations and most likely to arise in states that have comparatively little autonomy. Small nations are more likely to be able to sustain collective agreements among actors from civil society, such as labor and business. And states that are unable to impose policies are likely to seek the cooperation of actors from civil society. However, a significant number of states deliberately cultivate neo-corporatism because of the close connections that it creates between the state, labor, and capital. In their view, the integration of state, labor, and capital promotes economic flexibility and so competitiveness in the global market. Neo-corporatism has thus become as much a competitive strategy for states as a means of promoting social justice and harmony.

Pluralism, Policy network, Regulation theory

FURTHER READING

Cawson, A. (1986) *Corporatism and Political Theory*. New York: Basil Blackwell.
Cox, A. and O'Sullivan, N. (1988) *The Corporatist State*. Cheltenham: Edward Elgar.
Grant, W. (1985) *The Political Economy of Corporatism*. London: Macmillan.
Schmitter, P. and Lehmbruch, G. (1982) *Patterns of Corporatist Policy Making*. London: Sage.

Decentralization

DEFINITION

Decentralization is a process that reallocates resources from a higher, more central authority to a lower one. Administrative decentralization redistributes tasks and duties in a bureaucracy to lower levels, special agencies, or local bodies. Political decentralization delegates powers and responsibilities to lower, local tiers of government. It might involve either devolution – the delegation of responsibilities to subordinates – or regionalization – the division of areas of government into smaller regions. Decentralization generally tries to bring power and authority closer to the citizens it affects in order to promote more efficient and democratic politics.

There has also been some recent talk of economic decentralization. Economic decentralization disperses economic responsibilities across regions or private businesses. It may refer to a political process in which local governments supplant the central state in some of the activities associated with economic development, planning, and regulation. Yet it also can refer to little more than attempts to spread markets through society. The idea here is that markets locate choices about consumption closer to citizen-consumers which promotes a more efficient system of distribution. Nonetheless, there is something very misleading about equating marketization with decentralization. Unless we are willing to equate democratic participation with a choice of goods and services, we should recognize that marketization does not relate to our democratic values in the same way as do administrative and political decentralization.

Empirical studies highlight just such distinctions between political and economic decentralization. Consider three different approaches to decentralization. The first seeks both political and economic decentralization. Examples include Bolivia and Indonesia in the 1970s and South Africa in the 1990s. States that pursue such dual decentralization are generally democracies with heavily centralized political systems. The second approach concentrates on dispersing political power with little or no economic power going to local governments, let alone non-state actors. Examples include Brazil and India. The final approach to decentralization, in contrast, concentrates on economic reform with little or no political powers being transferred. Examples of states that have adopted this approach include China, Pakistan, and Uganda.

CONTEXT

Although people from the left and right wings of political debate often advocate decentralization, they do so for rather different reasons. On the left, the 1960s witnessed a resurgence of various liberationist critiques of the centralized governments and extensive bureaucracies. These critiques depicted an increasingly centralized and interfering state extending its reach into continually wider ranges of civil society and private life. At times they even went so far as to present the welfare state as an attempt to control and discipline people in the interests of market capitalism. In sharp contrast, neoliberal economists from the right argued that state action and bureaucratic hierarchies were less efficient and less responsive to individual choices than were markets. Hence, those on the left generally advocate decentralization to smaller political units or to voluntary groups in civil society, while those on the right characteristically try to associate decentralization with marketization.

If advocates of decentralization have different visions of it as well as different reasons for advocating it, they nonetheless agree that it is important for democratization and good governance. Social scientists often argue that levels of decentralization are one key difference between democratic and authoritarian states. Authoritarian regimes rely on centralized power to direct and dominate civil society: the elite retain tight control over decision-making while the rest of the population has little political, economic, or social freedom. Hence attempts to spread democracy are often entwined with decentralization. Democratization depends on a successful reallocation of power away from the elite and towards citizens.

Historically, some states resisted decentralization, and so perhaps democratization, on the grounds that it hampered development. In contrast, some scholars and international institutions have begun to argue that decentralization is itself a key feature of the 'good governance' needed to sustain successful development. The World Bank recommends, for example, that developing states strengthen local and regional governments, increasing their independence from the central state. It suggests that weak local bureaucracies and an inadequate distribution of resources and power to lower tiers of the government can lead to corruption and failed development.

DEBATE

Not everyone agrees that decentralization leads to more efficient governance. On one hand, many people argue that decentralization typically creates a government that is more responsive to citizens' needs. They believe that decentralization locates power with local politicians and local officials who are more familiar with local situations and more directly answerable to local people. So, for example, a city council can promote education, health, and infrastructure projects that reflect the particular nature of that city in a way a central state cannot. On the other hand, people are sceptical of the evidence that decentralization is so conducive to efficiency and responsiveness. Some empirical studies suggest that decentralization often creates inefficient bureaucracies that lack the capacity (human and financial) to adequately implement policies.

Of course the views for and against decentralization are not strictly incompatible with one another. Perhaps decentralization is likely to fail and lead to weak government if the local bodies do not have sufficient resources, whereas if decentralization is done with proper resources, then it can lead to greater responsiveness and democratic participation.

The idea that the effectiveness of decentralization depends on certain resources inspires another debate: what conditions are necessary for the empowerment of local governance to be effective? Three conditions are particularly prominent in this debate. The first is the existence of a functioning local democracy or at least the capability for such a democracy. The idea is that democracy itself is vital even for efficient local economic governance. It challenges the viability of economic decentralization without corresponding political decentralization – the approach associated, as we saw above, with states such as China and Pakistan. The argument is that democracy fosters responsiveness and accountability, without which decentralization is likely to merely exasperate problems of corruption at local levels. The second condition is that local governments must have fiscal autonomy. The ability of local governments to raise revenue gives them legitimacy and independence. Without this ability, decentralization is likely to result either in local governments that merely enact the wishes of the center or in disputes between the tiers of government. The final condition is that local officials must be competent and adroit. If local officials are incompetent, then decentralization will lead to inefficient government, which might undermine the legitimacy of the whole political system.

CROSS REFERENCES

Good governance, Local governance, Marketization, State

FURTHER READING

Bardhan, P. and Mookherjee, D. (2006) *Decentralization and Local Governance in Developing Countries: A Comparative Perspective.* Cambridge, MA: MIT Press.

Cheema, G. and Rondinelli, D. (eds) (2007) *Decentralizing Governance: Emerging Concepts and Practices.* Washington, DC: Brookings Institution Press.

Keating, M. (ed.) (2004) *The New Regionalism in Western Europe: Territorial Restructuring and Political Change.* Cheltenham: Edward Elgar.

Oxhorn, P., Tulchin, J. and Selee, A. (2004) *Decentralization, Democratic Governance, and Civil Society in Comparative Perspective: Africa, Asia, and Latin America.* Washington, DC: Woodrow Wilson Center Press.

Dialogic Policy-Making

DEFINITION

Dialogic policy-making is a process in which citizens actively participate in the creation of public policies. It encourages and values collective deliberation. To be more specific, dialogic and deliberative approaches to policy give citizens an opportunity to exchange relevant viewpoints and arguments prior to the adoption of a policy. The dialogic process might be overseen or facilitated by public officials. Alternatively, public officials might provide one voice among the many in the dialogue. The dialogic process might be a way of reaching a decision or an exercise in consultation.

Advocates of dialogic approaches argue that they encourage joint learning and collective agreements. Typically, dialogic policy-making is an iterative process. The repeated negotiation of conflicting interests and beliefs discourages participants from remaining stubbornly uncompromising. Hence, even if there is no consensus at the outset, dialogue is likely to move participants towards substantial compromises and agreements at the end. Similarly, as participants move towards agreement during the dialogues, so satisfaction with the outcome is likely to increase. Besides, participants are likely to develop some kind of investment in a policy that they played an active role in formulating.

The prospects for dialogic public policy vary widely. Many observers highlight several preconditions for its success. First, the state, perhaps with the help of citizens, should set the stage for a dialogue; in particular, it should make sure that the participants all have clear roles. Second, the participants should enter the dialogue with openness; they should not hold hidden agendas since these undermine the trust that is crucial for meaningful deliberation and negotiation. Third, the state should express its sincerity and its confidence in the process, for by doing so it encourages citizens to treat their own participation as relevant and important. Finally, the dialogue should concern appropriate types of policy, where appropriate issues are generally understood to be concrete matters of direct concern to the participants. For example, finding strategies for reducing crime in a neighbourhood is perhaps a more appropriate topic for dialogue than strategies for solving world poverty.

CONTEXT

Contemporary discussions of dialogic and deliberative approaches to public policy have arisen out of several overlapping theories. One theoretical basis for dialogue is the literature on participatory democracy. In the 1960s and 1970s radical political theorists began to argue that our democratic ideals, notably that of self-rule, required that citizens play a far more extensive role in processes of government. They proposed that citizens should not only elect representatives to legislative assemblies, but also actively participate in the formation and even implementation of particular policies. Dialogic approaches to public policy are often attempts to institutionalize the idea of citizens actively making the decisions that determine how they are governed. So conceived, the dialogic ideal might encourage us to promote the direct participation of citizens not only in government but also in intermediary associations such as businesses, unions, places of worship, and consumer groups.

An alternative theoretical basis for dialogue or deliberation is the literature on communicative action. Jürgen Habermas, the German philosopher, located rationality firmly in interpersonal communication, as opposed to private mental habits or a cosmic teleology. In his view, we can decide what is rational, right, and good only by appeal to the nature of communicative action, and, more particularly, the universal pragmatics of speech acts. The key idea here is that we reach rational outcomes through a free exchange of beliefs in the absence of domination. Deliberative democrats, many of whom take their inspiration from Habermas, thus argue that legitimate public decisions depend less on practices of voting than on public dialogue or deliberation among citizens. So conceived, the deliberative ideal implies that public decisions should reflect a fair exchange of information and arguments among citizens.

When dialogic and deliberative ideals first arose among political theorists, they appeared far removed from actual democratic practice. More recently, however, the gap between ideals and practices has shrunk. On one hand, some political theorists have begun to run deliberative (and less frequently dialogic) experiments, at times with the support and funding of social movements or television channels. On the other hand, a few states have begun to toy with small-scale uses of deliberative (and again less frequently dialogic) measures.

The appeal of deliberation and dialogue to states appears to lie primarily in their potential as a source of legitimacy. The last two decades have seen considerable falls in the electoral turnout in many states. This decline in the percentage of eligible voters who actually vote is often perceived as a threat to states' legitimacy. States appear to lack the support or interest of their citizens. Politicians are becoming concerned, in other words, that the falling rates of voter participation reflect a growing discontent with government and even a growing distrust of politicians. Some of them believe that deliberative democracy and dialogic policy-making might provide a means of renewing civic life and generating a greater legitimacy for the state.

DEBATE

The main debate around both deliberative democracy and dialogic policy-making is about their desirability. Yet this debate almost inevitably spills over into discussions of the impact they would have on the quality of public decisions.

Proponents of dialogic policy-making ascribe to it multiple virtues. Dialogue can be conceived, as we have seen, as a way of promoting democratic ideals such as self-rule. It can also be seen as a way of generating legitimacy for political institutions, thereby promoting a more harmonious community. Certainly advocates of dialogic policy-making often suggest that it counters the balkanizing effects of the rise of individualism and the concomitant disintegration of community life. Many suggest that when citizens engage one another in deliberative settings, they are likely to reach a tolerant understanding of differences if not a reasoned consensus. At the very least, dialogue might serve, then, to push extreme interests and hostility to the periphery of the policy-making process. These claims on behalf of dialogue and deliberation often rely on the hope that citizens will not only bargain and negotiate among their interests, but also forge new social bonds, concepts, and practices. In a sense, therefore, deliberative and dialogic approaches are transformative – their aim is not simply to solve practical policy problems but also, and arguably more importantly, to transform the lived context in which those problems arise.

Criticisms of dialogic and deliberative approaches can be either practical or theoretical. The practical criticisms typically point to the difficulties or costs of making such approaches work. Dialogue and deliberations require time and resources. Besides, dialogue and deliberation are unlikely to be as free and equal as their advocates would wish since some individuals and groups have greater resources of time, money, and knowledge than others, and so are likely to be able to dominate. The theoretical criticisms of dialogic approaches often challenge the idea that they will promote rational, just solutions. One such criticism points to the role of self-interest and negotiated bargains in the policy process, arguing either that the distinction between such negotiations and deliberation is untenable in practice or even that such negotiations are themselves a way of arriving at collectively rational solutions. Another theoretical criticism suggests that dialogue and deliberation are as likely to lead to adversarial relationships as to greater understanding and solidarity.

CROSS REFERENCES

Collaborative governance, Participatory democracy, Social inclusion

FURTHER READING

Bohman, J. (1996) *Public Deliberation: Pluralism, Complexity, and Democracy.* Cambridge, MA: MIT Press.
Fischer, F. and Forester, J. (eds) (1993) *The Argumentative Turn in Policy Analysis and Planning.* Durham, NC: Duke University Press.
Habermans, J. (1985) *The Theory of Communicative Action,* 2 vols, trans. T. McCarthy. Boston: Beacon Press.
Hajer, M. and Wagenaar, H. (eds) (2003) *Deliberative Policy Analysis: Understanding Governance in the Network Society.* Cambridge: Cambridge University Press.
Roberts, N. (ed.) (2002) *The Transformative Power of Dialogue.* Oxford: Elsevier.

Differentiated Polity

DEFINITION

A differentiated polity consists of a number of interdependent organizations such as governments, departments, and agencies. The political integration of the organizations is limited, as is the degree of administrative standardization across them. A differentiated polity is fragmented between organizations that cover different territories, deliver varied functions, or both. Hence governance occurs through a maze of institutions that give rise to a complex pattern of decentralized functions. Governance occurs, in other words, in and through networks composed of the relevant governments, departments, agencies, and other social and political actors. The organizations in the networks are interdependent: each organization relies on cooperative exchanges with the others to secure parts of its agenda. The networks themselves are often self-organizing, and they have at least some autonomy from the center.

One of the best ways to make sense of the concept of a differentiated polity is to see it as representing a sharp contrast with the concept of a unitary state. A unitary state is generally defined as an identifiable polity with clear boundaries and a sovereign center that formulates law for, and rules over, the territory within those boundaries. In contrast, a differentiated polity is characterized by fuzzy boundaries and by the flow of power and authority downwards, upwards, and outwards. It is often suggested that these flows of power have increased recently as a result of devolution, contracting-out, and globalization.

CONTEXT

The Anglo-governance school is the main source of the phrase 'differentiated polity'. They introduced it to correct what they believed to be the misleading or outdated image provided by the Westminster model of government in the United Kingdom. The Westminster model privileges themes such as parliamentary sovereignty, cabinet government, executive authority, and a neutral civil service. The Anglo-governance school uses the phrase 'differentiated polity' to offer an alternative image of a hollow state, a core executive, and multiple networks. This image of the UK as a differentiated polity drew on accounts of governance that had arisen in discussions of policy networks, the European Union, and the New Public Management. The Anglo-governance school argues that power is diffuse, and that central government is just one of several public, voluntary, and private bodies involved in the policy process. They argue that although the core executive might have a pre-eminent place within networks, it can rarely dictate or control policy. Rather, the center attempts to steer and regulate networks by means of financial controls, audits, and negotiation. This image of a differentiated polity draws attention to gaps between the Westminster model and the actual practice of governance in the UK. For example, it highlights the importance of links between the European Union and sub-national authorities in the administration of structural funds.

Although the phrase 'differentiated polity' remains closely associated with the Anglo-governance school, similar phrases are increasingly common in discussions of the new governance more generally. Concepts such as 'networked polity' or 'disaggregated state' closely resemble that of a differentiated polity. These other concepts are often used to describe emerging patterns of European and global governance. As such, they refer to territories that, unlike the UK, social scientists never really thought were governed by a unitary state. The European Union resembles a networked polity in that it relies on a complex web of committees and societal associations to advise, manage, and regulate varied aspects of governance. Similarly, global governance resembles a disaggregated state in that it relies on diverse transgovernmental networks. States collaborate with non-state actors within diverse networks in order to address shared concerns. Although some global networks are composed solely of states and are constituted by legal treaties, others are informal networks composed of organizations such as national regulators and the main private organizations that they regulate. Transnational groups and corporations often generate private governance regimes of rules, norms, and principles that then guide their actions. Global governance consists in part of attempts to regulate and coordinate such private governance regimes.

DEBATE

It is often unclear whether the differentiated polity represents a fundamental change in patterns of rule, a gradual process of change, or an abstract concept that seeks to rectify simplistic concepts of the state.

We might distinguish here between two accounts of the differentiated polity that embody rather different analyses of differentiation. On the one hand, differentiation can refer to a process based on functional differences. This concept of differentiation inspires accounts of governance as a complex set of institutions defined by their social roles. It leads to a concept of the differentiated polity as a fairly recent outcome of the process of specialization within government: institutions and the links between them have multiplied in order to serve increasingly specialized purposes. In this view, the differentiated polity is primarily a temporal phenomenon – part of the new governance.

On the other hand, differentiation can refer to the different interpretations, beliefs, or meanings that are often within an institution or practice. This concept of differentiation inspires decenterd accounts of governance. Patterns of governance arise out of contingent and competing actions inspired by distinct webs of belief. In this view, the differentiated polity is not just a description of recent changes in the world. It is an abstract account of how we should think about all states, perhaps even all patterns of rule. It is a new theory of governance.

It is possible, of course, that both versions of the differentiated polity are correct. Perhaps we should combine a new decenterd theory of governance with recognition of the rise of new patterns of governance. The new governance at the national, the regional, and the global level is often portrayed as differentiated, networked, and disaggregated. These portraits combine to offer a vivid alternative to the older one of sovereign and unitary states located in a largely anarchical international society. They evoke, instead, a world that is composed of networks of networks. Individuals and groups organize themselves into multiple, overlapping, and interdependent networks to address common problems. States and international organizations are just groups within these diverse networks.

CROSS REFERENCES

Interdependence, Policy network

FURTHER READING

Ansell, C. (2000) 'The Networked Polity: Regional Development in Western Europe', *Governance*, 13: 303–333.

Bevir, M. and Rhodes, R. (2003) *Interpreting British Governance*. London: Routledge.

Marinetto, M. (2003) 'Governing Beyond the Center: A Critique of the Anglo-governance School', *Political Studies*, 51: 592–608.

Rhodes, R., Carmichael, P., McMillan, J. and Massey, A. (2003) *Decentralizing the Civil Service: From Unitary State to Differentiated Polity in the United Kingdom*. Buckingham: Open University Press.

Slaughter, A. (2004) *A New World Order*. Princeton, NJ: Princeton University Press.

Enabling State

DEFINITION

The enabling state suggests a view of the state's relationship to the public sector and to its citizens. This view of the state is typically juxtaposed to the historic role of the welfare state. Historically, the welfare state provided social services to its citizens in order to ensure they had a minimum standard of welfare. In contrast, the enabling state is meant to form partnerships with other groups so as to provide the context in which citizens can improve themselves.

Discussions of the enabling state yoke together two different ideas. First, the enabling state points to a change in the relation of the state to service provision. In this sense, the enabling state 'enables' because it brings together networks of private and voluntary sector bodies to provide services. It differs from the welfare state in that it manages these networks rather than directly providing the services. Advocates of the enabling state argue that it increases efficiency and promotes choice.

Second, the enabling state points to a change in the relation of the state to its citizens. In this sense, the enabling state 'enables' because it provides the opportunities for individuals to escape poverty and make better lives for themselves. It differs from the welfare state in that it provides opportunities rather than substantive material benefits. Advocates of the enabling state describe this change as one from paternalism to partnership.

While the enabling state refers to changes in the state's relationship to both public services and its citizens, these two changes do not have to go together. We could imagine a state that tried directly to provide services and opportunities that would foster responsibility. We could also imagine a state that promoted networks of voluntary and private sector actors to provide material goods to its citizens.

CONTEXT

The enabling state is a reaction to the perceived failings of the welfare state. In general, critics of the welfare state characterize it as excessively bureaucratic, unresponsive to citizens and their different preferences, and increasingly antiquated in a brave new world of global markets. Some critics believe that the welfare state was always flawed because it required too much taxation and public expenditure, or because it relied on hierarchical institutional structures. Other critics of the welfare state argue that it once served us well, but that it is incompatible with contemporary developments such as the rise of a global economy and individualized patterns of consumption.

The enabling state's new relationship to public services is in large part a response to steadily mounting economic pressures on the welfare state. The financial capacity of welfare states to provide social services has been severely strained by demographic, economic, and political developments. Demographically, many developed states have witnessed a rise in life expectancy and a fall in the birth rate. They face the prospect of a higher percentage of the population claiming social benefits such as pensions while a lower percentage work to fund these benefits through taxes. Economically, globalization is often believed to have led to intense competition between states for finance capital, where if states are to compete successfully, they cannot raise taxes and increase public expenditure. Besides, politically, citizens are increasingly reluctant to vote for political parties that openly advocate the higher taxes needed to extend welfare provision. Much of the middle-class appears to have concluded either that the welfare state wastes the high level of taxation that is imposed on them or that they simply do not want to contribute towards collective services.

So, the enabling state is an attempt to reduce the costs of state-provided welfare. Its advocates argue that it reduces the costs of welfare services by tapping sources of finance and expertise located in the private and voluntary sectors. Sometimes they also suggest that the involvement of the private sector brings entrepreneurialism, competition, and so greater efficiency to the public sector. One example of the involvement of the private and voluntary sectors is the use of tax incentives to promote private pensions or private health schemes. Another example is the use of vouchers for housing and education, where the vouchers can be cashed in with private providers instead of the state.

If we turn now to the enabling state's new relationship to its citizens, we might portray the change as a response to claims about an underclass and about bureaucratic inflexibility. The welfare state seemed to some to be failing the population, including those most in need. Some observers suggested that the welfare state had created an underclass that lacked the means and incentives necessary to break free from their dependence on state-provided welfare. Welfare dependency can be explained in several different ways. Some social scientists argue that the balance of benefits and taxation is such that some people would be no better off if they got a job. Others argue that the provision of welfare benefits without any corresponding duties undermines individual responsibility, thereby creating a psychology of dependence. Of course, we might also conclude that there is no such thing as welfare dependency; perhaps it is just convenient political rhetoric or a form of moral panic.

The enabling state is an attempt to promote choice and especially individual responsibility among welfare recipients. Advocates of the enabling state argue that it replaces a paternalistic approach to welfare with one based on the idea of partnership. In this view, the state forges a partnership with welfare recipients: the state has a duty to provide them with the opportunities to improve themselves, and they in turn have a duty to take up these opportunities. Advocates of the enabling state also argue that the shift from paternalism to partnership replaces a culture of dependency and victimhood with one of individual responsibility and hard work. One example of the attempt to foster individual responsibility is the rise of various New Deals for welfare recipients. These New Deals typically require citizens to take up opportunities offered by the state or have their welfare benefits cut.

DEBATE

As with any significant change in the role of government, there are many controversies about the enabling state. To illustrate these controversies, let us consider one that surrounds the enabling state's relationship to public services and one that surrounds its relationship to individual citizens.

With respect to public services, there is an important debate about accountability. When the state shifts the burdens of delivering social services, let alone financing them, to the private sector, it appears to increase the risk of conflicts of interest at the very same time as it weakens the capacity of the legislature to oversee such services and to hold accountable those responsible for them.

The enabling state's emphasis on individual responsibility has also created a debate about the moral principles that inform the welfare state. Advocates of the enabling state sometimes claim that they are merely relying on new means to realize the historic ideal of social justice. But surely the change in means entails a change in the nature of the ethic institutionalized by the state? For a start, citizens now appear to be as much bearers of duties as holders of rights. Whereas the discourse of the welfare state evoked the idea of duty primarily to convey the obligation of the well-to-do to improve the lot of the less privileged among their fellows, the discourse of the enabling state refers to the duties welfare recipients owe to society. Similarly, the enabling state effectively replaces the ideal of a substantive minimal level of welfare with one of minimal access to certain opportunities. In the welfare state, citizens owed one another a certain standard of living simply by virtue of being members of the same political community. Now, the enabling state seeks only to enhance the ability of citizens to compete with one another and thereby advance themselves in their own ways and by their own merits.

To conclude, we might explicitly mention a debate over how to explain the rise of the enabling state. Advocates of the enabling state portray it as a sensible response to failings of the welfare state. For many critics, however, the enabling state is little more than a smoke screen obscuring the reality of steadily declining benefits. In this view, 'the enabling state' is a cost-cutting exercise: the enabling state is a neoliberal state in which the disadvantaged must fend for themselves.

CROSS REFERENCES

Communitarianism, Managing networks, Public–private partnerships, Social inclusion

FURTHER READING

Gilbert, N. and Gilbert, B. (1989) *The Enabling State: Modern Welfare Capitalism in America*. New York: Oxford University Press.

Latham, M. and Botsman, P. (eds) (2001) *The Enabling State: People before Bureaucracy*. Sydney: Pluto Press.

Page, E. (ed.) (2007) *From the Active to the Enabling State: The Changing Role of Top Officials in European Nations*. Basingstoke: Palgrave Macmillan.

Environmental Governance

DEFINITION

Environmental governance refers to all the processes by which political, economic, and social actors regulate interactions between humans and nature. These processes include the legislation, administration arrangements, and judicial enforcement by which local, regional, and national governments attempt to manage natural resources. Yet, just as the term 'governance' is broader than 'government', so environmental governance also refers to the actions of non-governmental and supranational organizations in so far as these concern ecological issues. Many prominent environmental concerns are transnational collective action problems that are unlikely to be resolved by action at the level of the nation state.

CONTEXT

Developments in environmental governance exhibit many of the trends associated with the rise of the new governance. These trends include the increasing prominence of marketization, networks based in part on civil society, and transnationalism.

Markets provide a mechanism by which all kinds of people seek to influence the ways in which others affect the environment. Increasing numbers of citizens are trying to affect the environment through their choices about what to consume. Citizens boycott some products, pay more for others, invest only in some companies, and so on. In doing so they often hope to influence the decisions of corporations. Markets also play a more indirect role in the measures by which political actors attempt to impact upon the actions of organizations and individuals alike. Environmental policies often rely on costs and benefits, along with market forces, to encourage or to discourage activities. Relevant costs include taxes and fines. Relevant benefits include partnerships and subsidies. For example, China, Colombia, the Philippines, and several other states have introduced pollution taxes to influence the decisions of industrial organizations. Market mechanisms also appear in some transnational and supranational schemes to address environmental issues. So, for example, the Montreal Protocol defines a set of rules for the exchange of pollution rights among states: these rules establish a market in pollution rights so that the total amount of pollution is limited, but states have more choice about the amount they are willing to pay in order to persist in creating more pollution than is the norm.

Contemporary environmental governance owes much not only to marketization but also to networks based in part on organizations from civil society. Non-governmental organizations, such as Greenpeace and the World Wildlife Fund, are among the best-known actors in environmental governance. These non-governmental organizations typically play a dual role in environmental governance. On the one hand, they are campaigning organizations that mobilize popular activism, and often hostility, to the decisions made by states and corporations. On the other, they are often part of the policy networks upon which political actors rely for expertise and advice when they formulate, implement, or monitor public policies.

We might add, finally, that environmental issues are often transnational or supranational. The most obvious transnational issues concern worldwide changes in the environment, such as global climate change and the depletion of species. Other such issues are raised by the adverse impact that all kinds of transnational actors, from multinational corporations to criminal networks, can have on the environment: their transnational character often makes it difficult for states to effectively track and regulate their actions. Yet other transnational issues concern natural resources that spill over state borders. Water is a prominent example. Pollution, or overuse, in one state can lead to problems like drought downstream in an entirely different state.

Transnational, global environmental issues are surely among the most pressing issues of the twenty-first century. Various international agreements seek to coordinate the activity of states in addressing these problems. Prominent global agreements here include the Montreal Protocol, which seeks to limit pollution, and the Kyoto Protocol, which seeks more specifically to reduce the levels of greenhouse gas emissions. Alas, however, although these international agreements are a step forward, they also illustrate the difficulties of securing effective cooperation in the face of common action problems. The United States has refused to sign the Kyoto Protocol, for example, in a way that may look suspiciously like an attempt to avoid contributing to the costs of a collective good.

DEBATE

One way to approach debates about environmental governance is to divide them into discussions of means and of ends. Discussions of means often revolve around just the kind of collective action problems exemplified in getting every state to sign the Kyoto Protocol. No doubt some environmental problems can be dealt with through legislation, state administration, and judicial enforcement. Yet, when the state is too weak to enforce its will in this way, other forms of coordinated action are needed. Global environmental issues are perhaps paradigmatic here: the absence of anything resembling a strong world government means that many global environmental problems can be dealt with only through negotiation, diplomacy, and agreement among different states, and often non-state actors. Optimists might believe that good will, moral persuasion, and reason will suffice to ensure a suitable response to issues such as global climate change. Others are likely to disagree. Rational choice theorists might emphasize that the rational strategy for each individual or state is to free-ride: individuals will typically try to let others pay the costs of improving the environment since they reap the benefits irrespective of whether or not they contribute towards these costs. Similarly, neo-realist theories of international politics often imply that states pursue their own interests and remain wary of one another in ways that make it difficult to achieve coordinated action to address environmental issues. The arguments of rational choice theorists and neo-realists have inspired attempts to find more market-based means of preserving the environment.

Debates about the ends of environmental governance are at least as lively as those over the means. Green political theory contains a number of ethical debates about why exactly we should care about nature. Should we care about it for its own sake or because of its role in human life? Green political theory also contains a number of debates about the more specific goals of environmental policy-making. In what circumstances should we try to preserve things as they are, encourage restorative projects, or manage facets of change? A common way of describing the overall goal of environmental governance is to evoke sustainability. Typically, sustainability refers to the long-term viability of our interactions with the environment. Yet sustainability remains a difficult concept to pin down. As a concept, sustainability might refer to one or more of a society, a pattern of development, or a yield. In all these cases, moreover, there is room for considerable disagreement about what exactly is or is not sustainable. If we are very optimistic about the prospects for technological advances, we might even believe that our current activities are sustainable. But more radical environmentalists argue that we need to return to small-scale communities that use local resources and relatively few of those.

There is, of course, something artificial about an attempt to distinguish between debates on means and those on ends. Political disputes about environmental governance typically merge practical concerns with matters of justice. Consider, for example, the distribution of the costs of environmental regulations between developed and underdeveloped states. Individuals in developed states use far more natural resources and energy to sustain their lifestyles than do those in underdeveloped states. Similarly, developed states used up vast amounts of resources and caused vast amounts of pollution as they industrialized. Hence some people argue that developed states should contribute more towards the costs of environmental regulations, or that the regulations should be stricter for developed states. Some even suggest that developing countries, including China and India, with their high rates of population and industrial growth, should have the same opportunity for industrialization and urbanization as did Europe and the United States.

CROSS REFERENCES

Collective action problem, Good governance

FURTHER READING

Dodson, A. (2000) *Green Political Thought*. London: Routledge.
Levy, D. and Newell, P. (eds) (2004) *The Business of Global Environmental Governance*. Cambridge, MA: MIT Press.
World Commission on Environment and Development (1987) *Our Common Future*. Oxford: Oxford University Press.
Young, O. (1998) *Global Governance: Learning Lessons from the Environmental Experience*. Cambridge, MA: MIT Press.

Evidence-Based Policy

DEFINITION

Evidence-based policy-making is the analysis of many forms of empirical data as a guide to the creation, modification, or retention of effective public policies. Evidence-based policy-making appears to have originated in health policy in the UK. Policy-makers began to worry that the selection and use of medicines was not based on evidence derived from appropriate tests, such as randomized controlled trials. This worry gave rise to calls for 'evidence-based medicine', such that drugs would be used only if there was appropriate laboratory evidence of their effectiveness. From UK health policy, evidence-based policy-making spread to states such as Australia and the USA, as well as to diverse policy sectors, including criminal justice, education, the environment, housing, and social welfare. Back in the UK, the New Labor governments have increasingly appealed to evidence-based policy-making as an important part of their attempt to reform the public sector. Yet, as we will see, the concept of evidence can remain dangerously empty.

CONTEXT

Evidence has always been relevant to policy-making. What, we might thus ask, is new about evidence-based policy? The rise of explicit appeals to evidence seems to point to a more deliberate use of scientific research and analysis to evaluate and amend existing policies. Indeed, the main reason for the excitement about evidence-based policy is its aura of scientific authority. The appeal to evidence contrasts with alternative views of policy-making that either try to extend democratic participation (such as dialogic policy-making) or advocate a kind of muddling through (such as incrementalism). Yet, beneath the aura of scientific authority, the concept of 'evidence' is often far too vague. All kinds of empirical evidence might enter into the policy process in all kinds of ways. There are diverse ways of getting information on policies, and there are diverse ways of assessing such information. Even if we restrict our attention to the treatment of proposed policies, there are diverse ways of conducting both randomized control trials and other pilot projects.

In general, there is no clear definition of 'evidence', no clear guidelines on how evidence should be assessed, and no clear principles on the use of evidence in different policy sectors. When the concept of 'evidence-based policy-making' has more specific content, it is usually because a particular institution, such as the United States Office of Management and Budget, has established a unified set of organizational standards and language for its own purposes.

To be fair, advocates of evidence-based policy-making sometimes contrast their approach with earlier forms of evaluation research. For a start, they criticize earlier forms of evaluation research on the practical grounds that they analyzed the effects of a policy immediately after its implementation and for a short period of time: a proper long-term evaluation was stymied by deadlines and by demands for results. In addition, they argue that previous evaluation research assessed the effectiveness of policies once they were in place, whereas a properly scientific approach requires that the evidence comes before the policy. In doing so, they associate evidence-based policy-making particularly closely with experimental evidence based on randomized control trials and other pilot projects.

DEBATE

It is obvious that policy-makers should try to make informed assessments of the impact of policies. It is also obvious that in many policy sectors an informed assessment requires a grasp of the relevant scientific knowledge. Yet, many academics and policy-makers feel that there are problems associated with labelling particular policies as backed by scientific evidence. The main problem is that evidence implies a kind of neutrality that social science rarely provides. Given that there is no agreement about what constitutes relevant evidence, let alone how to assess such evidence, claims about the scientific basis of particular policies appear to be mere attempts to justify contestable preferences and even thereby to foreclose democratic procedures.

Problems of defining and assessing evidence reappear in several more specific debates about evidence-based policy-making. A prominent example is the debate over the evaluation of pilot programs. Evidence-based policy-making often relies on models and small-scale pilot programs to assess a potential policy. However, critics argue that the architects of pilot policies often construct them so as to make them fit peculiarly well in the controlled setting in which they operate; the architects thereby create an artificial impression of success. It seems, in other words, that although pilot programs are well-respected in scientific fields such as pharmacology, they are easily manipulated into a form of prototyping when they are used in other areas of public policy. What is more, if pilot programs can be manipulated, it is difficult to see how evidence-based policy-making differs from earlier attempts to assess the impact of existing policies and respond accordingly. There is nothing new in the idea that policy-makers have contestable stories about the way a given policy works or is likely to work, and they make a decision based on their assessment of the plausibility and meaning of those stories.

Debates about the neutrality of allegedly scientific evidence have influenced people's assessments of cases in which evidence-based approaches have been used. Broadly speaking, however, evidence-based policy-making appears to have worked best in policy sectors with a clear basis in natural science, such as drug prescriptions in health care. It also seems to have worked fairly well in policy sectors with established measures of outputs, such as child poverty in social welfare. But it appears to have been far less successful in other policy sectors, such as education.

Perhaps evidence-based policy-making will spread further. For now, however, it is both too ambiguous in its conceptualization and too uncertain in its implementation. Its advocates and its critics alike might agree that a sound framework of evaluation standards must be established.

CROSS REFERENCES

Dialogic policy-making, Incrementalism, Managing networks, New Public Management

FURTHER READING

Nutley, S.M., Smith, P.C. and Davies, H.T.O. (2000) *What Works?: Evidence-based Policy and Practice in Public Services*. Bristol: The Policy Press.

Pawson, R. (2006) *Evidence-based Policy: A Realist Perspective*. London: Sage.

Sanderson, I. (2002) 'Evaluation, Policy Learning and Evidence-based Policy Making', *Public Administration*, 80: 1–22.

Wholey, J.S., Hatry, H.P. and Newcomer, K.E. (eds) (1994) *Handbook of Practical Programme Evaluation*. San Fransisco: Jossey-Bass.

Global Governance

DEFINITION

Global governance refers to the ways in which a variety of actors come together to address global problems. The varied actors produce a global pattern of rule even in the absence of an overarching world state. Historically, states have been regarded as the principal actors in producing global governance. States engaged in overlapping and interlocking processes, often within international organizations, which produced a world order. States create and enforce a range of international rules, norms, and standards, often in the setting of international organizations such as the United Nations (UN). Recently, however, social scientists have drawn attention to the increasing prominence of multinational corporations and non-governmental organizations within global governance. Non-state actors play an important role by influencing the actions of states as well as acting globally in their own right.

CONTEXT

Although some theorists have developed blueprints for a world government, attempts to create one have had limited success. The League of Nations was established in 1919 after the First World War, but it proved unable to prevent the growing aggression of Fascist states in the 1930s and later the Second World War. Many of the most visible aspects of contemporary global governance arose at the end of the

Second World War. The UN was formed in 1945 by a Charter signed by fifty countries. The UN inherited several of the agencies established by the League. Its aims are to promote international law, international security, economic development, and to some extent global justice. The UN has a formally established, but highly circumscribed, capacity to use force in pursuit of these aims. The end of the Second World War also witnessed the creation of the International Court of Justice (ICJ), which had been preceded by *ad hoc* regional tribunals in Nuremburg and Tokyo for trying war criminals. International courts and tribunals have since played a large part in the creation and enforcement of international law, and perhaps most notably human rights. Finally, the end of the Second World War saw the creation of a number of institutions to oversee the international economy. The United Nations Monetary and Financial Conference, held at Bretton Woods in 1944, led, after several years, to the creation of the World Bank, the International Monetary Fund, and the General Agreement on Tariffs and Trade, which has since become the World Trade Organization. The international organizations created at the end of the Second World War soon became one focus for the vast number of global policy networks, regional associations, and intergovernmental organizations, covering an equally vast range of issues, which make up the increasingly complex pattern of contemporary global governance.

Analytically, we might identify four major trends in contemporary global governance. First, states have sought to coordinate their activities on an increasing number of issues and concerns. Many environmental issues, including global warming, offer clear examples of problems that transcend state boundaries and so appear to require cooperation and coordination among states if they are to be dealt with satisfactorily. The degradation of the environment in one state often has costs for people in other states. Hence the monitoring and enforcement of all kinds of environmental norms appears to depend on transnational or international arrangements. Other examples of global issues that require transnational responses include terrorism, drug trafficking, and world health concerns such as HIV/AIDS.

A second trend in contemporary global governance is the growing concern to promote international standards that are seen to transcend national boundaries. Certain standards are no longer left to the discretion of sovereign states. Human rights is the prime example. International laws have been created to restrict states' treatment of their own citizens within their own borders. Domestic courts, international courts, and tribunals have been established to try individuals who are accused of genocide, war crimes, and crimes against humanity. The rise of these international legal institutions has inspired various non-governmental organizations to try to monitor compliance with international standards around the world. Today the international community has acquired a legitimate role in condemning violations of human rights, and even intervening forcibly to curtail such violations.

The third trend in global governance is the multiplication of actors in international affairs. Individuals, multinational corporations, international organizations, and domestic groups all play an increasing role in international governance. They promote policies, standards, and action both with and without the cooperation of states. They often contribute to the design of multilateral treaties between states. They monitor and publicize particular issues.

A final trend in global governance is the growing economic interconnectedness that many social scientists identify with globalization. The reconstruction of the world economy after the Second World War has led to greater and greater transnational economic exchanges across state borders. The resulting economic interdependence of states has led some observers to argue for all kinds of new governance arrangements. In this view, we need new rules, standards, and regulatory agencies to foster and maintain accountability and responsibility among economic actors, especially multinational companies.

DEBATE

The main debates about global governance revolve around the question of whether or not states are in decline. Most observers agree that the role of the state has changed following the rise of global networks that include international and transnational agencies, multinational corporations, and voluntary sector organizations. Yet observers are far from agreed about the character, impact, and desirability of the changing role of the state.

Some scholars argue that states are perhaps no longer the dominant actors in global governance. In this view, the spread of markets and networks has hollowed out the state from below, while the growth of transnational, regional, and international organizations has hollowed it out from above. An increasing number of rules and regulations are created and enforced by transnational and international groups, and these rules and regulations restrict the options that are available to states. Most states certainly appear to have lost some of their ability to issue tariffs and subsidies by signing up to international trade agreements and regional blocs. The rise of international standards appears to restrict the ability of states to acquire nuclear weapons, for example. The most hotly discussed restrictions on states are those linked to globalization. It seems to many policy-makers that globalization means that states can no longer pursue certain economic and social policies since the consequences of their doing so depend on non-state actors, including, in particular, global finance capital.

Other scholars argue that states, far from declining in importance, have reaffirmed their dominance. These scholars emphasize the ways in which states can simply ignore the limitations set by transnational and other non-state actors. While they acknowledge the newly enhanced role of non-governmental organizations, they maintain that the policies that these organizations promote are typically ones that have to be carried out by states. In this view, the influence of non-state actors is constrained by the international system, and the international system is still dominated by states and the organizations within which they interact, negotiate, and coordinate their activities so as to establish international norms, agreements, and policies.

Other debates about global governance concern the question of who governs and how they might be accountable to those they govern. Whether or not the prominence of supranational actors and institutions suggests that the role of the state is diminishing, concerns remain over the difficulty of making the international order democratically accountable to citizens or even their governments. The rise of new global networks often exasperates this problem of accountability. Networks of bureaucrats, judges, and other unelected officials are increasingly formulating a range of international norms and policies. Some social scientists want to stretch our concept of democracy to cover such networks. They suggest, for example, that these networks are legitimate because of the outcomes they produce. Other social scientists, in contrast, want to devise new ways of promoting democracy within contemporary global governance. While there is no clear agreement about what democracy means on the global level, many of these social scientists want those whose interests are affected by decisions made by international institutions to be able to participate directly or indirectly in the decision-making process.

CROSS REFERENCES

Globalization, Regionalism, Transnationalism

FURTHER READING

Barnett, M.N. and Finnemore, M. (2004) *Rules for the World: International Organizations in Global Politics*. Ithaca, NY: Cornell University Press.

Hewson, M. and Sinclair, T. (eds) (1999) *Approaches to Global Governance Theory*. Albany, NY: State University of New York Press.

Nye, J. (2001) 'Globalization's Democratic Deficit: How to Make International Institutions More Accountable', *Foreign Affairs*, 80: 2–6.

Slaughter, A. (2004) *A New World Order*. Princeton, NJ: Princeton University Press.

Wilkinson, R. (ed.) (2005) *The Global Governance Reader*. London: Routledge.

Globalization

DEFINITION

Globalization refers to the changing nature of the world economy. The changes are associated with the growth in economic interactions across state borders. The main changes are generally thought to be increasing trade flows, greater mobility of finance capital, and the internationalization of production chains. Many observers associate these changes with the rapid development of information technology.

Although globalization carries an aura of energy and excitement, critics argue that it has negative consequences. From a sociological standpoint, globalization might imply greater cultural conformity, perhaps even a type of cultural imperialism by the major western economies. From a political standpoint, globalization is often seen as part of a neoliberal program that forces governments to adopt a severely restricted and arguably unjust set of public policies. Such criticisms illustrate how debates about globalization often relate economic and technological issues to changing patterns of international and national governance.

The new governance is, indeed, often portrayed as a response to globalization. In this view, globalization has eroded the importance of national barriers and even the state itself; it has increased the economic interdependence of states, thereby undermining the ability of each state to govern its own economy. However, despite the ubiquity of talk of globalization, notably in the rhetoric of policy-makers, there remains a

globalization

89

lack of general consensus on its extent and its implications for governance. Globalization can refer, in narrow terms, to increased volumes of transnational trade. Or it can refer to a broader pattern of global economic integration. Or it can refer to the activities of those firms that have scattered their production activities across a number of states, and those states that have promoted a liberal world order.

CONTEXT

The transnational flows associated with globalization appear to have risen in the 1970s. It was, after all, in the 1970s, notably in the wake of the oil crisis, that some states, including the UK and the USA, sought to liberalize their economies. A few social scientists even began to discuss globalization at that time. Nonetheless, we can date the massive explosion of talk of globalization, among both social scientists and policy actors, to the 1990s. This explosion appears to have owed much to the end of the Cold War. Talk of globalization represented a way of characterizing a new global order. It reflected the perception of a shift from superpowers and their political conflicts to a broader range of actors concerned with economic exchanges.

Once we locate globalization in the wake of the Cold War, we are likely to become more sensitive to the intellectual currents and political forces that have made it possible. Neoliberal ideas became extremely prominent in the late 1970s, and they emphasized the supposed benefits of rolling back the state and spreading free markets and free trade. The USA, unchecked by a rival superpower, occupied an increasingly hegemonic role, which it used to promote and guarantee globalizing initiatives. International economic institutions, such as the International Monetary Fund, World Bank, and World Trade Organization, also promoted norms and agreements that facilitated marketization and free trade.

Just as globalization arose in part because of changes in global politics, so it has inspired new accounts of global governance. Globalization is said to have undermined the state-based system established in 1648 by the Treaty of Westphalia. We no longer have the old image of largely autonomous states possessing territorial sovereignty, and interacting in terms set by law, diplomacy, and even war. Instead we have a new picture of diverse actors, including firms and non-profits as well as states, engaged in all kinds of transnational activities. We have a new world order consisting of networks based on the negotiations and exchanges of interdependent actors. Coordination and order arise less from states and more from markets and networks.

DEBATE

Globalization is one of the most disputed terms in contemporary social science. Many of the disputes concern whether or not the term captures any actual process, and if it does, then how far this process extends, and what implications it has for governance.

Some social scientists believe that globalization is a myth. On the one hand, they might argue that there have always been transnational flows, and that these flows are not necessarily of more importance today than they were earlier. Or, on the other hand, they might highlight the persistence of state borders and other impediments to transnational economic flows, and they thereby might argue that states are nothing like as constrained as the literature on globalization suggests. There is, for example, an extensive literature on varieties of capitalism that suggests different historical legacies have led capitalist states to respond differently to the economic changes associated with globalization.

Other social scientists debate the scale and scope of globalization. They might point out that the costs and benefits of globalization are not distributed evenly throughout the world. In this view, developed states have reaped most of the supposed economic benefits from the increasing levels of trade, while some developing countries have seen little of the much-vaunted new technologies. Even if there are ever increasing exchanges between London, New York, and Tokyo, little might have changed for the impoverished villagers of large parts of Africa and Asia.

It is perhaps worth adding that some critics think of globalization primarily as the spread of international institutions and norms that facilitate the exploitation of poor states by rich capitalist ones, and believe that, in particular, the spread of a liberal trading order exacerbates economic problems while restricting the available strategies for economic development.

A final debate about globalization concerns its implications for governance, especially at the level of the nation state. As we have seen, discussions of globalization often suggest that it restricts the range of policies that states might adopt. Neoliberals often suggest, for instance, that globalization requires states to introduce liberalization and marketization if they are to compete successfully. Many social democrats similarly worry that the increased freedom of financial capital means that if they introduce radical policies, finance capital will flow out of their borders, leading to a currency collapse. In sharp contrast, when social scientists argue that globalization is a myth, they often hope thereby to suggest that social democratic policies remain viable.

CROSS REFERENCES

Global governance, Regionalism, Transnationalism

FURTHER READING

Cameron, A. and Palan, R. (2004) *The Imagined Economies of Globalization*. London: Sage.

Hay, C. and Marsh, D. (eds) (2001) *Demystifying Globalization*. Basingstoke: Palgrave Macmillan.

Scholte, J. (2005) *Globalization: A Critical Introduction*. Basingstoke: Palgrave Macmillan.

Strange, S. (1996) *The Retreat of the State: The Diffusion of Power in the World Economy*. Cambridge: Cambridge University Press.

Good Governance

DEFINITION

There is no agreed definition of good governance. Definitions usually consist of a wish-list of reforms, practices, and outcomes, usually with a particular eye on developing states. Yet each organization that is concerned with good governance appears to construct its own wish-list. Some definitions of good governance emphasize political and legal institutions – participation, accountability, rule of law, and human rights. Others emphasize neoliberal economic reforms and better management of resources. Yet others emphasize social structures and practices. If we had to specify something that the items on these wish-lists have in common, we might do worse than point to a concern with the interactions of state and society. Most wish-lists concern the rules, processes, and behavior that define the nature and limits of political authority. They try to ensure that political actors, at all levels, are responsive and accountable to stakeholders. They also seek to ensure that states act impartially and fairly, and restrict themselves to particular domains.

Although good governance concentrates on the interactions of state and society, its origins lie in economic concerns. Aid donors came to believe that development depended on issues of governance. Even today, most wish-lists of good governance echo this early concern with economic growth. The purpose of good governance is commonly seen as being to promote development. 'Bad' governance is identified with corruption, wastefulness, incompetence, and unresponsiveness, all of which impede economic development and perpetuate poverty.

Consider two particular views of good governance. The first is that of the World Bank. Here good governance is primarily a strategy for development, or at least a principle to guide donors and investors when they make decisions. The Bank's economic liberalism ensures that its wish-list includes the promotion not only of liberal democratic political institutions, but also of a market economy, free trade, and reduced public sectors. The second example is the definition of good governance offered by the United Nations Development Program (UNDP). Because the UNDP is less dominated by economic liberalism, its definition of good governance focuses on socio-political conditions. Its wish-list contains eight items:

- equality of participation in decision-making
- responsiveness to stakeholders
- attempts to secure a broad consensus
- accountability to stakeholders
- transparency in decision-making
- the rule of law
- the productive use of resources
- guaranteed rights.

CONTEXT

The term 'good governance' became prominent in the early 1990s when it was used in relation to economic and social development. The World Bank introduced the concept in 1992 as part of its lending requirements. Good governance referred here to changes in the public sector – changes broadly associated with neoliberalism (the New Public Management, marketization, and privatization). Other international organizations, notably the International Monetary Fund (IMF) and the United Nations, followed suit. They required good governance of developing countries that wanted to receive financial assistance. As we have seen, however, they defined 'good' in different ways according to their own beliefs and purposes.

Although 'good governance' arose in a neoliberal context, it represented a retreat from a development policy constructed almost wholly on the basis of market economics. The neoliberal and monetarist agendas of the 1980s led the World Bank and IMF to shift from aiding projects that might stimulate growth to a policy of financing structural readjustment programs. The idea was that growth was best served by a stable macro-economic environment and the spread of the free market. Before long, however, the Bank concluded that the effectiveness of aid depended in part on social and political factors: its landmark report of 1989 on Sub-Saharan Africa referred explicitly to a 'crisis of governance' as a key barrier to economic development. Thereafter the Bank turned to good governance in an attempt to specify and promote the social and political factors that influence economic development. (It did so even though its Articles of Agreement technically forbade it from considering non-economic issues when making lending decisions.)

It is possible that we should recognize changes in the concept of good governance promoted by the World Bank, if not the IMF. The original neoliberal agenda of the Bank and IMF arose in the context of a 'Washington Consensus' that consisted of a particularly stark neoliberal agenda of rolling back the state to enable markets to flourish. Recently there has been much talk of a post-Washington Consensus. It is said that the post-Washington Consensus gives greater emphasis to topics such as institutions, information, public goods, and policy execution. Good governance might be redefined, therefore, to put more emphasis on state capacity and social capital.

The spread of the language of governance means, more generally, that it is increasingly difficult to restrict the concept of 'good governance' to issues of aid and development. Good governance is obviously an issue for public management in general, and, indeed, for corporations and voluntary sector organizations.

DEBATE

We might distinguish four loosely related debates about good governance. The first is about the development strategies pursued by the World Bank and the IMF. Critics reject the neoliberal assumptions that underpin these strategies. Often they argue that the actual effects of these strategies have been damaging. Some suggest that international organizations restricted the economic freedom of recipient countries in a way that stopped them from adopting more viable strategies for growth, including perhaps strategies based on state action and public investment. Often the critics draw on alternative socio-economic theories to promote different development strategies. Some argue that developing states, instead of constantly responding to agendas set by donors and their international organizations, should develop their own programs and then ask donors for support.

A second debate concerns the appropriateness of public sector reform for developing states. It has become obvious that fads such as the New Public Management were often particularly unsuited to developing states. The initial impetus for public sector reform came from a belief that the state was too strong and too active. But developing states often have the opposite problem – the state is too weak and inept. It is important to distinguish between state scope and state strength. Scope refers to the range of activities pursued by the state. Strength refers to how effective the state is in pursuing its activities. Public sector reforms attempted to restrict the scope of state activity, but the main obstacle to modernization in developing states is a lack of state strength. As a result, the reforms often proved to be tragically inappropriate to developing states. The pressing need in many developing states is to establish bureaucratic institutions with clear lines of accountability, impartial officials, and abstract rules to guide them.

Yet another debate concerns the very association of good governance with the issue of economic development. Some critics complain that this association perpetuates the ethnocentric idea that bad governance is a particular problem for Africa, Asia, and Latin America. Perhaps they cavil at the suggestion that the developed western world is free of ills such as political corruption. Or perhaps they oppose the imposition of a western concept of political corruption upon other parts of the world. This second criticism pushes us to recognize that, irrespective of the economic theories we hold, we have to be aware that good governance is an issue at home as well as abroad.

The final debate about good governance thus concerns the patterns of rule that we think desirable at home as well as – or instead of – abroad. To some extent this debate takes us back to the classical topics of political theory, including liberty, equality, order, and democracy. Equally, however, this debate might also involve considering the relative importance we would ascribe to an efficient public sector or a transparent and accountable one, or it might involve considering trade-offs between, say, economic growth and social inclusion.

CROSS REFERENCES

Accountability, Rule of law, Social inclusion

FURTHER READING

Demmers, J. Fernández Jilberto, A.E. and Hogenboom, B. (eds) (2004) *Good Governance in the Era of Global Neoliberalism: Conflict and Depolitisation in Latin America, Eastern Europe, Asia and Africa*. New York: Routledge.

Doornbos, M. (2001) '"Good Governance": The Rise and Decline of a Policy Metaphor?', *Journal of Development Studies*, 93: 93–108.

Munishi, S. and Abraham, B. (eds) (2004) *Good Governance, Democratic Societies and Globalization*. New Delhi: Sage.

Siddiqui, T. (2001) *Towards Good Governance*. New Delhi: Oxford University Press.

Williams, D. and Young, T. (1994) 'Governance, the World Bank, and Liberal Theory', *Political Studies*, 42: 84–100.

Governance Indicators

DEFINITION

Governance indicators are measurements that describe and evaluate a state's ability to govern. Governance itself is usually understood here as the arrangements and qualities of a set of institutions and rules by which decisions are made and authority exercised. There are indicators of both the processes and outcomes of governance so conceived. Indicators of the outcomes of governance measure the ability of policy-makers to govern society. Examples might include the state's ability to raise revenue, the strength of the legal system, the success rate in implementing policies, the realization of policy goals and so the extent of poverty, the level of freedom, or the rate of participation. Indicators of the processes of governance measure the extent to which clear goals have been established for the public, and the extent to which problems are resolved through political process.

CONTEXT

The governance indicators developed by the World Bank are the most influential. The World Bank defines governance as the traditions and institutions by which authority in a country is exercised. It then breaks down this broad definition of governance into three components. The first is the processes by which governments are selected, monitored, and replaced. The second is the capacity of the government effectively to form and implement sound policies. The third is the respect of citizens (and state actors) for the various institutions that govern economic and social interactions among them. Finally, the Bank then identifies two sub-components to each of these three components of governance. The result is a total of six aggregate indicators for governance.

To examine the processes by which governments are selected, monitored, and replaced, the Bank measures 'voice and accountability' and 'political stability and absence of violence'. Voice and accountability captures the extent to which citizens may participate in the political process and the level of freedom of association, expression, and the press. Political stability and the absence of violence measures perceptions of the likelihood that the government will be destabilized or overthrown through violence.

To examine whether governments can successfully formulate and implement good policies, the Bank measures 'government effectiveness' and 'regulatory quality'. Government effectiveness captures the quality of public services, the quality of the civil service and the degree of its independence from political pressures, the quality of policy formulation and implementation, and the credibility of the government's commitment to policies. Regulatory quality measures the ability of the government to formulate and implement sound policies and regulations that permit and promote private sector development.

To examine the level of respect the citizens (and state actors) have for their institutions, the Bank measures 'rule of law' and 'control of corruption'. Rule of law captures the extent to which agents have confidence in the rules of society and abide by them, with a particular stress on the quality of contract enforcement by the police and the courts, and the likelihood of crime and violence. Control of corruption measures the extent to which public power is exercised for private gain, including petty and grand forms of corruption, as well as the capture of the state by elites and private interests.

Generally, the Bank relies on two sources of data for aggregating governance indicators. The data comes either from polls answered by experts or from surveys answered by the citizens of a state. These polls and surveys are arranged by international organizations, political and business risk-rating agencies, think tanks, and non-governmental organizations, such as Free House, the Gallop World Poll, and Reporters Without Borders.

The Bank does not claim that its indicators exhaust all the meanings and instances of governance, but the indicators are supposed to capture the most prevalent notions of governance.

DEBATE

There is unsurprisingly a growing debate about the accuracy and fairness of the leading governance indicators. Governance is inherently difficult to measure objectively, especially if the measures have to be quantitative. So, there are numerous methodological concerns about how the measurements are calculated. Relevant issues include the number of samples, the quality of data, the comparability of data across countries, and the role of subjective perceptions and objective measurements and their relationship to one another. Likewise, there are numerous theoretical concerns about the appropriateness of numerical data – especially what often looks like fairly crude data based on simplistic outputs or subjective impressions – for thinking about governance, and more importantly for making crucial political and economic decisions. The World Bank may put too much trust into its own indicators and its ability to impartially and accurately measure governance. The Bank may be trapped by the apparent objectivity and impartiality of numbers at the expense of other forms of knowledge. Finally, governance indicators have been criticized for being non-specific. Even if they give a reasonably good aggregate picture of the state of affairs, they might not provide meaningful guidance to states' actors or other policy actors who want to make specific improvements.

These debates about governance indicators often reflect wider discussions about who wants them and for what purposes. Much of the demand for governance indicators comes from multinational corporations, developed states, and international institutions dominated by them. Yet these policy actors often use governance indicators to recommend policies to developing states or even to impose policies upon them. Critics dislike the power relations involved here, noting the whiff of neo-colonialism. They worry that neoliberal and profit-seeking institutions now develop and deploy governance indicators to discipline poorer, developing states, forcing them to introduce free-market policies and programs.

Such worries clearly refer in particular to the influential role of the World Bank in the development of governance indicators. The Bank describes governance indicators as a diagnostic tool for revealing weaknesses that need to be improved. It can then target these weaknesses in its allocation of aid and loans. But, equally, the Bank clearly uses governance indicators as a guide to the distribution of resources. So, for example, the World Bank may decrease its loans to states that do not demonstrate improvements in governance, and might even go as far as completely to cut off any financial assistance. It is here that governance indicators serve a disciplinary function. Perhaps the moral of such debates is that we should decouple the issue of the advantages and disadvantages of governance indicators from that of the role of the Bank in international affairs.

The distinction between these issues appears in the increasing use of governance indicators by citizens and non-governmental organizations, including those in developing states. Citizens of developing countries are becoming increasingly aware of global governing standards. They are using governance indicators to hold their governments accountable and to demand better performance from them. In developed states too, some citizens are using governance indicators, such as measurements of freedom, to push for progressive reforms.

CROSS REFERENCES

Evidence-based policy, Good governance

FURTHER READING

Arndt, C. and Oman, C. (2006) *Uses and Abuses of Governance Indicators*. Paris: OECD Development Center Studies.

Bovaird, T. and Löffler, E. (eds) (2003) 'Symposium on Evaluating the Quality of Governance', *International Review of Administrative Sciences*, 69: 311–364.

Kaufmann, D., Kraay, A. and Mastruzzi, M. (2006) *Governance Matters*. Washington, DC: The World Bank.

Sudders, M. and Nahem, J. (2004) *Governance Indicators: A User's Guide*. Oslo: United Nations Development Programme.

governance indicators

DEFINITION

The word 'hierarchy' is derived from two Greek words: *hieros*, which means sacred, and *archein*, which means rule or order. Early Christian writers originally used the word to refer to the order of angels. Later the word came to refer to the structure of the Christian Church itself. It described the vertical organization of the early church, which was conceived as both a divine and worldly institution. Hierarchy was the vertical organization of divine authority with local priests at the base and God at the apex.

Hierarchy now refers, similarly, to a form of organization in which people and functions are organized in, and executed through, a well-defined, multi-tiered, vertical structure. Different functional tasks are performed at each level in this structure. In spatial terms, hierarchy might be envisaged as a ladder. Each rung of the ladder represents a tier of the organization, and the tiers form an ascending chain. Power and authority flow up and down this chain. People in the higher tiers have the power to delegate tasks to those below them. Even if the people in the lower tiers have some discretion in performing their tasks, they are ultimately accountable to those above them.

State bureaucracies epitomize hierarchy in most discussions of governance. Departments of state and executive agencies are responsible for executing policy. At their apex are ministers or agency heads who are formally accountable for the institution as a whole. Public officials at lower tiers of the institution are meant to act in accordance with the directives or intentions above them. By the time a directive reaches the lowest level of bureaucracy, it has been shaped and molded in some form by each successive layer higher up in the chain of bureaucracy. The lowest level of the bureaucracy is often the public face of the organization.

CONTEXT

Arguably, the account of hierarchy offered by Max Weber in the early twentieth century remains the most influential. Significantly, Weber actually wrote about modern bureaucracy as a distinct historical product of the process by which societies became increasingly complex and

key concepts in governance

rational. For Weber, bureaucracies embodied a scientific rationality in that they have a central authority that oversees and directs a tightly organized, single chain of command. The central authority acts as the supreme source of power, delegating functions and tasks to subordinates. For Weber, bureaucracies were a response to complexity in that they embodied high degrees of specialization. Functions are differentiated. Each department of state or executive agency, and each subdivision within them, tackles a distinct task or particular domain.

During much of the twentieth century, social science became increasingly formal and ahistorical. Systems theories and classifications became increasingly popular at the expense of the more historical aspects of Weber's story. Historical narratives of the rise of bureaucracy as a distinctive feature of modern society gave way to attempts to describe types of system and even to develop classifications of the possible types of organization. The contemporary concept of hierarchy arose as Weber's narrative of bureaucracy was displaced by accounts of hierarchy as a particular type of system or organization within a broader classification.

Herbert Simon offers a particularly influential account of hierarchy as a type of system. Simon understands hierarchy as a collection of various sub-units organized within chains of command. Unlike Weber, he denies that hierarchy implies top-down systems of authority. Instead, he defines hierarchy in terms of the division of an organization's functions among multiple sub-units where each sub-unit might have its own chain of command. The important point, however, is that Simon evokes hierarchy as an ahistorical category. He uses it to capture an allegedly universal principle of the structure of complex objects. Hence he offers a staggeringly diverse set of examples of hierarchies. He does not limit himself to bureaucracies or even to human organizations. Rather, he argues that books are hierarchies, for they are divided into chapters, sections, paragraphs, phrases, and then words; he argues that the universe is hierarchical, with galaxies being divided into stars; and he even argues that the basic structure of matter is hierarchical, for molecules consist of atoms that are themselves composed of elementary particles. Problems too appear to be a kind of hierarchy, or at least Simon suggests we are better able to solve them if we divide them into sub-problems.

Hierarchy, unlike bureaucracy, is thus widely conceived as one term in an ahistorical classification of different types of organization. Hierarchy is defined here in contrast to both a market and a network. For much of the twentieth century, the Cold War reinforced a simpler dichotomy between hierarchy and market. Hierarchy, planning, and state control stood opposed to markets, capitalism, and individualism. Of course, things were never that simple: almost all social scientists recognized that hierarchies and markets might be better suited to different tasks. It is notable, however, that the end of the Cold War coincided with a crisis of socialism and the dominance of a neoliberalism that hoped to spread markets where once there had been hierarchical bureaucracy. Certainly, the new governance arose as people became increasingly sceptical of the advantages of hierarchy. Reformers have attempted to replace hierarchies with markets and later networks. The provision of some public services has been transferred to the private sector. And hierarchical chains of organization have been broken up by the New Public Management.

DEBATE

Hierarchy has fallen so far out of favor that today there are debates over whether it has or should have a significant role in governance. It is important to emphasize, therefore, that despite the furor over the new governance, hierarchical bureaucracies still dominate within the public sector. Markets and networks generally operate in the shadow of hierarchy.

Many social scientists argue that hierarchy persists because it offers important practical and democratic advantages. In practical terms, hierarchies are often considered especially apt as a way of dealing with tasks that have uncertain outcomes, occur frequently, and require highly specialized knowledge. Even if hierarchies are less flexible than networks, they provide a way of bringing a huge amount of disparate expertise within a singular structure that enables them to operate with fairly high levels of certainty about one another and about their own place and role. A division of labor promotes specialization. A single structure promotes certainty and reliability, and, moreover, allows for certainty and reliability extending over considerable periods of time and repeated interactions.

In democratic terms, hierarchies are often considered to facilitate accountability through the clarity of their chains of command. The division of labor within hierarchies clarifies who is responsible for what. The vertical organization of hierarchies clarifies to whom each individual is responsible. People are answerable to those in the tiers above them all the way up to the minister or agency head, and citizens are thus able to hold the minister or agency head to account for the activities of the relevant organization. This clear accountability is important not only as a form of democracy but also as a means of preventing the spread of political corruption and so protecting our other public values.

While social scientists argue that hierarchy still has much to offer, the new governance has led them to pay less attention to its relationship to rationality and specialization, and more to instances when it ceases to operate effectively. Social scientists often suggest that hierarchies become inefficient when there is excessive layering. When hierarchies contain too many layers, accountability and leadership are stifled. For a start, when decisions have to flow down too many layers of hierarchy, one gets 'buck passing' – the constant shifting of responsibility for tasks on to other individuals – and accountability is thereby weakened. In addition, when people in lower layers feel distant from their superiors, they are less likely to comply with directives, and leadership is thereby weakened. Some social scientists thus conclude that excessive layering leads to a widespread perception that hierarchies are unresponsive and ineffective, thereby providing a kind of popular support for marketization and the New Public Management.

CROSS REFERENCES

Accountability, Bureaucracy, Coordination, Market, New Public Management

FURTHER READING

Du Gay, P. (ed.) (2005) *The Value of Bureaucracy.* Oxford: Oxford University Press.
Gerth, H. and Mills, C.W. (eds) (1973) *From Max Weber: Essays in Sociology.* Oxford: Oxford University Press.
Simon, H. (1969) *The Sciences of the Artificial.* Cambridge, MA: MIT Press.
Williamson, O. (1975) *Markets and Hierarchies: Analysis and Antitrust Implications.* New York: Free Press.

Implementation

DEFINITION

Implementation refers to the set of actions and interactions involved in the execution of public policy. Implementation occurs after a legislature or judiciary creates or modifies policy, and in some cases, it also comes only after appropriate funding has been allocated for the relevant policy. The task of implementing policy falls mainly to the executive branch of government, especially the civil service. Typically, the decisions of the legislature and the judiciary remain ambiguous: they say what is to be done but not how it is to be done. The executive then decides how to implement such decisions and does so. Indeed, the decision on how to implement a policy often determines much of the content of that policy.

CONTEXT

The rise of the new governance in the late 1970s and early 1980s transformed scholars' views on implementation. Before then, implementation was generally conceived as a top-down administrative and hierarchical process. Policy actors operated at different levels and they each had a clearly defined role in the execution of a policy. Lower-level public officials were expected to implement policies in a manner that conformed closely to the policy desires of those above them and so ultimately their political masters. With the rise of the new governance, discussions of implementation began to concentrate on the interactions of various policy actors and how these interactions influence the final form policies assume. We now have a second wave of studies of policy implementation that reject the earlier accounts of the implementation process as an exercise of command and control. The second wave of implementation studies might be described succinctly as studies of bargaining and transformation.

Second-wave studies of policy implementation focus on bargaining and transformation among diverse actors. Policy implementation increasingly requires multiple actors to interact with one another regularly and often over an extended period of time. Constant communication and bargaining between actors are integral to effective implementation. Consider, for example, legislative and judicial oversight. Legislators and courts monitor public officials to ensure that policy is implemented according to the general objectives set forth in legislation or court rulings. If legislators, judges, and civil servants communicate, bargain, and cooperate, implementation is likely to be a relatively smooth and successful process. But if there is conflict between these policy actors, implementation is likely to be delayed and messy, for legislators and judges can often stymie the implementation process.

Some political scientists argue here that the level of consensus required to implement a policy depends on the degree of transformation it entails. Policies that make only minor changes can be implemented with a low level of consensus among the relevant actors, whereas policies that make major changes require a high level of consensus. It certainly seems plausible that various actors have interests in, and commitments to, existing policies and institutions, and that these interests and commitments can hinder reform.

So, policy implementation is increasingly understood in terms of the interactions of multiple actors on multiple levels within a context consisting largely of existing policies and institutions. Implementation requires constant bargaining between the relevant actors, and may also require the transformation of existing policies and institutions.

DEBATE

Debates about policy implementation generally concern either efficiency or fairness. The question of what constitutes effective implementation (and how best to achieve it) is a constant topic of debate. The new governance has arisen in part as policy-makers have looked to find efficiency in markets and networks. Implementation thus increasingly depends on non-state actors. Some critics oppose this trend on the grounds that it is actually inefficient, especially perhaps for the management of public goods and the delivery of public services. Other critics oppose the trend on grounds of fairness. They worry that policies implemented through the market will benefit only those who can afford to pay.

Similar concerns about fairness also appear in debates about the amount of discretion involved in the implementation process. The issue of discretion used to apply mainly to public officials and the extent to which they should be guided by clear rules. Today, it is more likely to apply to different social providers and the extent to which they should be bound by uniform rules or at least minimal standards. Critics of discretion argue that if different agencies implement policies differently, then the public benefits and services citizens receive might vary dramatically with morally arbitrary criteria, such as where they live. Advocates of discretion argue that it allows for negotiations that can have positive sum outcomes. In their view, detailed prescriptions for policy implementation lead to a standardization that denies public officials the ability to execute policies in a way that better serves the goals of the policies. Discretion, in contrast, allows public officials to tailor implementation according to the overall aims of a policy.

CROSS REFERENCES

Bureaucracy, Capacity, Marketization, Policy cycle

FURTHER READING

Barrett, S. (2004) 'Implementation Studies: Time for a Revival? Personal Reflections on 20 Years of Implementation Studies', *Public Administration*, 82: 249–262.

Hill, M. and Hupe, P. (2002) *Implementing Public Policy: Governance in Theory and Practice*. Thousand Oaks, CA: Sage.

Pressman, J. and Wildavsky, A. (1973) *Implementation*. Berkeley, CA: University of California Press.

Van Meter, D. and Van Horn, C. (1975) 'The Policy Implementation Process: A Conceptual Framework', *Administration & Society*, 6: 445–488.

Incrementalism

DEFINITION

The theory of incrementalism draws on pluralism. It purports to explain (and perhaps advocate) a process of gradual policy change that can culminate in large-scale change. Incrementalism assumes that, at any given time, on any given issue, the policy process includes a number of actors who have different knowledge, values, and interests. The various policy actors are competing to enact their respective policies. They also face the constraints of democratic institutions and scarce resources. Hence the policy process is a fragmented one. It is a pluralist system of competition. As a result, policy initiatives are almost always diluted by the compromises needed to generate a broad consensus on any given issue. This dilution of policy initiatives means that policy is generally modest in its scope. Change is small-scale and gradual. Large-scale change occurs not because of a broad, sweeping policy shift, but as a result of the aggregation of small shifts over time.

CONTEXT

Charles Lindblom is generally credited with developing the theory of incrementalism in a 1959 article on the science of 'muddling through'.

key concepts in governance

Incrementalism was a response to approaches to public policy that concentrated on bureaucratic planning. To some extent, indeed, incrementalism was a product of the Cold War: it is part of a broader attempt by American pluralists to construct a theoretical defence of their state and society as democratic and rational when compared with the Soviet Union. As such, we might be wary of simply accepting the caricature of planning that appears in much of the literature on incrementalism.

Bureaucratic planning certainly emphasizes the importance of policy-making based on clear, rational structures. It can appear to assume that public officials are rational decision-makers who understand policy problems and accurately define their scope. Public officials rank order policy problems to keep the most serious ones at the fore, and they determine an appropriate response to each problem. Bureaucratic planning thus appears to make two assumptions. It assumes, first, that all policy actors will be able to agree on a list of priorities. Even if a conflict of values or interests requires a trade-off, all the policy actors will be able to agree on the trade-off. Second, bureaucratic planning assumes that public officials determine the appropriate response to a problem by reviewing all the alternatives and engage in a cost–benefit analysis of each of them. They choose the response that best accords with the aggregate interests of those involved in the policy process, those affected by the policy, or society as a whole.

Proponents of incrementalism argued that the policy process was not structured in the way required by bureaucratic planning. They saw themselves as explaining why the policy process was actually structured as it was. They offered a descriptive theory that stood in stark contrast to the apparently normative content of bureaucratic planning. In particular, incrementalism drew on pluralism to overturn the key assumptions associated with bureaucratic planning. Pluralism undermined the idea that policy actors are able to agree on their respective priorities and goals. It suggested, to the contrary, that different interest groups enter the policy process with different experiences, knowledge, and values, and so with irreconcilable views of the problems. Policy actors represent specific interests, and they define problems relative to those interests. Pluralism also undermined the idea that public officials are fully informed in the way they would have to be to undertake a fully rational cost–benefit analysis of the alternatives available to them. It suggested that public officials were able only to broker the values and interests expressed within the relevant policy networks. Public officials have incomplete information.

Incrementalism thus countered bureaucratic planning with an account of policy-making as a kind of muddling through. Policy actors defend their own corner. Policy arises gradually as they dilute their preferences in order to construct broad coalitions. Once policies arise, they get institutionalized and can be changed only slightly through further processes of negotiation and adjustment. Policy-makers make small changes to tackle new problems or appease new constituencies. Change occurs not through a grand cost–benefit analysis of all possible solutions, but through feedback about the ways existing policies operate. Policies are modified, adjusted, and supplemented as people point to particular difficulties with them. The changes are then slight, due to the need to secure a broad consensus about them.

DEBATE

Many of the most heated debates about incrementalism have concerned its political implications. While incrementalism sometimes masquerades as an entirely descriptive account of the policy process, most formulations suggest that the process of gradual change is in fact a good thing. The questions thus arise: Is incrementalism a superior form of policy-making? Is it more effective and efficient than the alternatives? Is it more in accordance with our democratic values? One problem in answering these questions is that incrementalism has stood in contrast to different political systems at different times.

Advocates of incrementalism argue that it is a superior method of policy-making. First, they argue that because incrementalism enables all the relevant policy actors to participate in the policy process, it allows policy actors to gain a better understanding of one another and of the issues and alternatives that they confront. Second, advocates of incrementalism argue that it grounds policy on constant reflections and modifications based on practical experience. Practical experience is, they add, a better guide to policy-making than the more abstract forms of reasoning found in grand blueprints for sweeping change.

Perhaps the most obvious criticism of incrementalism is that it relies on a caricature of bureaucratic planning that hid important debates about policy-making. Apart from the Cold War rhetoric, the debate has never been between top-down, centralized planning and interest groups muddling through. Rather, the debate has been about the role of science and reason in democratic policy-making. Here critics of incrementalism argue that it goes too far in rejecting the possibility and desirability of a scientific approach to policy-making. In their view, planning is more or less integral to policy-making. Policy actors, like the rest of us, try to assess the likely consequences of their actions. They want to anticipate problems or needs. They hope to coordinate different policies so that they operate well together. Critics of incrementalism have also argued that policy-makers should base their planning on scientific knowledge, not prejudice or negotiated compromises. The current vogue for evidence-based policy-making is just the latest attempt to bring science to bear on policy.

It is worth commenting, finally, on the reversal of the politics of incrementalism after the Cold War. With the collapse of the Soviet Union, the bogeyman of bureaucratic planning has vanished. Contemporary governance exhibits an increasing tendency to rely instead on markets. Arguably, incrementalism now stands most in contrast to a neoliberal rationality that imposes markets against both gradual change and democratic pluralism. Certainly, Lindblom himself argued that the market might be an effective mechanism for creating wealth and innovations, but it is not very good at dealing with all kinds of other collective problems and values, such as distributive justice.

CROSS REFERENCES

Bureaucracy, Evidence-based policy, Pluralism, Policy network

FURTHER READING

Hayes, M. (2001) *The Limits of Policy Change: Incrementalism, Worldview, and the Rule of Law*. Washington, DC: Georgetown University Press.

Hayes, M. (2006) *Incrementalism and Public Policy*. Baltimore, MD: University Press of America.

Lindblom, C. (1959) 'The Science of "Muddling Through"', *Public Administration Review*, 19: 79–88.

Lindblom, C. (2001) *The Market System: What It Is, How It Works, and What to Make of It*. New Haven, CT: Yale University Press.

incrementalism

Institutionalism

DEFINITION

Institutionalism is a general approach to governance and social science. It concentrates on institutions and studies them using inductive, historical, and comparative methods.

Social science, no matter how one defines it, has from its inception put great emphasis on the study of institutions. Institutions have often been understood as formal organizations governed by written laws or rules. Examples of formal institutions include Parliament, the US Presidency, the courts, government departments, and political parties. The concept of an institution can be stretched to include informal organizations. Although informal organizations might lack written rules, they exhibit patterns of behavior that we might unpack in terms of loose norms. Examples of informal institutions might include community groups, voting coalitions, and policy networks. A vague distinction between formal and informal institutions mirrors, albeit roughly and imperfectly, the distinction between hierarchies and networks. The role of written rules in formal institutions seems to make them a good setting for hierarchies in which relationships are based on authority, rules, and subordination. The absence of such rules in informal institutions can suggest that they are more likely to resemble loose networks, with relationships based on trust, negotiation, and reciprocity.

Institutionalism generally uses inductive, legal, historical, and comparative methods to study formal and informal institutions. The inductive and legal methods are mainly concerned with generating adequate accounts of the way an institution operates. Induction relies on observation to provide such descriptions. A preference for induction leads some institutionalists to express skepticism about more general theories of politics. They prefer, in their own terms, to grasp the particular features of each case, and even to let the facts speak for themselves. The legal method is closely associated with the study of formal institutions. It relies on the study of documents and cases to get at constitutional and administrative laws and norms. The historical and comparative methods are arguably more concerned with explaining institutions. The historical method seeks to explain our current institutions by reference to the past. It is widely seen as a way of explaining the unique features of an

key concepts in governance

institution in a way more general laws cannot. The comparative method is used in part to identify those features of an institution, such as a parliament, that are unique to it and those that are found in other legislatures. It also offers a way of trying to explain the common features by reference to other institutions that the relevant states have in common. Of course, these various methods are not incompatible. To the contrary, most studies of institutionalists rely on a combination of them.

CONTEXT

Institutionalism has a rather awkward relationship to the new governance. The New Public Management and contracting-out challenged institutional approaches to the study and practice of public administration. Institutional approaches had concentrated on the importance of rules and laws to define public sector organizations, and especially to ensure that such organizations were properly accountable to the elected representatives of the people. The New Public Management and contracting-out tried to replace formal relationships and laws with ones based on budgets and market mechanisms. No wonder that governments turned not to students of public administration but to economists and business schools for advice on these public sector reforms. To observers, institutionalism seemed increasingly irrelevant.

Before long, however, institutionalists began to redefine their approach. The 1990s witnessed the dramatic rise of the 'new institutionalism'. To some extent, the new institutionalism rests on a caricature of the old institutionalism. The old institutionalism is associated with the study of formal institutions so that the new institutionalism can be identified with a novel concern with informal norms and symbols. In addition, however, the new institutionalism clearly arose in part as an attempt to answer some of the micro-level questions posed by rational choice theory. Rational choice theory deduces models of social life from assumptions about individual behavior. It poses the question: how can we unpack accounts of institutions by reference to individual behavior? Much of the new institutionalism arose in part to answer this question. The new institutionalism pays far more attention than did earlier institutionalisms to the ways in which individuals both affect and are affected by institutional settings, and, in doing so, it grapples with the inner workings of institutions, the sources of differences between institutions, and changes within any given institution.

Just as the institutionalists reworked their approach, some began to study the new governance itself. The greater emphasis on informal institutions helped them to claim as their own the study not only of formal bureaucracies but also of policy networks. They examined the new governance as a further hollowing out of the state through the spread of policy networks. The attempt to bring markets into the public sector weakened the central state. It had further segmented the executive branch of government. And it had thereby made the state more and more dependent on other organizations within a growing number of networks. Many institutionalists concluded that, under the new governance, the state had to rely less on commands or rules and more on indirect management based on negotiation and trust.

DEBATE

There are a number of ways of dividing the new institutionalists into competing factions. The most common is to distinguish between a rational choice institutionalism, a sociological institutionalism, and a historical institutionalism. These different varieties of institutional theory suggest different answers to questions about the nature of institutions, how institutions influence behavior, and how institutions change.

Rational choice institutionalism is best understood as a response to a particular problem within rational choice theory. The problem is that if we assume that people act to maximize their own satisfaction, we are likely to conclude that they will defect from an agreement whenever honoring it will not serve their interests. The continual likelihood of defection appears, in turn, to make it awkward for rational choice theorists to explain stable coalitions and institutions. Some rational choice theorists appeal to institutions to solve this problem. They argue that institutions, such as rules of procedure, structure the information that individuals have and thus the choices that individuals make. In this view, then, institutions are a solution to collective action problems. Institutions try to change and influence behavior by providing the settings within which individuals may seek to maximize the satisfaction of their preferences. Institutions then change because peoples' preferences change.

The sociological institutionalism draws mainly on organizational theory, and it tends to unpack organizations in informal and cultural terms rather than formal and legal ones. Sociological institutionalists thus define institutions primarily by reference to rules, norms, symbols, and beliefs. They argue that institutions influence behavior by giving an individual the beliefs and identities on which he or she then acts. Sociological institutionalists explain changes in an institution by reference to the rise and fall of new symbols and beliefs within the wider cultural environment. New identities arise in society, and as these acquire legitimacy, so they begin to spread across institutions where they open up the possibility of contest and change.

Historical institutionalism is more difficult to explain clearly. The difficulty arises because historical institutionalism is in large part just a flag of convenience adopted by diverse social scientists who want to continue to undertake fairly broad social inquiries without addressing the micro-level issues about individual behavior that are raised by rational choice theory. If we look for the historical institutionalist view of the relation of institutions to behavior, we find vague metaphors, confusion, or oscillation between rational choice institutionalism and sociological institutionalism. Still, historical institutionalists often define institutions as formal or informal procedures, routines, and rules. Some of them adopt a calculus analysis and others a cultural analysis of the way in which institutions influence behavior. The calculus approach echoes rational choice theory: it holds that institutions inform individuals' expectations about how others will behave and so their calculus of how best to attain their ends. The cultural approach, in contrast, echoes sociological institutionalism: it holds that institutions provide familiar patterns that individuals rely on in their attempt to attain satisfactory outcomes. Finally, historical institutionalists explain changes in institutions in terms of 'critical junctures' and 'path dependency'. These metaphorical terms suggest that institutions generally fix their own development, apart from at key moments when crucial decisions are made. The main attempts to give more analytic content to these terms have drawn heavily on rational choice theory.

CROSS REFERENCES

Differentiated polity, Hierarchy, Network, Rational choice theory

FURTHER READING

Adcock, R., Bevir, M. and Stimson, S. (2007) 'Historicizing the New Institutionalism(s)', in R. Adcock, M. Bevir and S. Stimson (eds), *Modern Political Science: Anglo-American Exchanges since 1880*. Princeton, NJ: Princeton University Press.
Hall, P. and Taylor, R. (1996) 'Political Science and the Three Institutionalisms', *Political Studies*, 44: 936–957.
March, J. and Olsen, J. (1989) *Rediscovering Institutions*. New York: Free Press.

institutionalism

Peters, G.B. (1999) *Institutional Theory in Political Science: The New Institutionalism.* New York: Continuum.

Powell, W. and DiMaggio, P. (eds) (1991) *The New Institutionalism in Organizational Analysis.* Chicago: University of Chicago Press.

Interdependence

DEFINITION

Interdependence exists when two or more actors are dependent on one another. Dependence can mean many things, of course, but in social theory, it is most usually defined in terms of resources: an actor is dependent on another actor if it cannot realize its aims without the resources of another actor. The relevant actors might be individuals, organizations, or even states. The goals are whatever these people or groups want to achieve. The resources can include physical and financial ones, but also knowledge and skills, as well as moral resources including legitimacy, and also time and effort. So, interdependence is a relationship in which various actors all need access to each other's resources if they are to attain their goals.

Discussions of interdependence infuse both accounts of the new governance and more abstract theories of governance. Some commentators describe the new governance in terms of growing interdependence. They argue that as policy actors and states have become more interdependent, so they have forged patterns of rule at the local, national, and international levels that are based on networks more than, say, hierarchies. In more abstract terms, social scientists have tried to model the exchange of resources among interdependent actors in a way that clearly owes a debt to rational choice theory. Other social scientists try to explain the extent and nature of social cooperation in terms of the degree of interdependence among actors or the kinds of resources that actors exchange with one another.

CONTEXT

Many social scientists and historians tell narratives of modernity based on the growth of complexity and so of interdependence. In their opinion, modern societies are distinguished from traditional ones by the extent to which they rely on specialization of functions. In modern society, different actors specialize in particular tasks: each actor has an increasingly narrowly defined function within an organization. The more specific the area of specialization of each actor, the more skilled the actors can become in that narrow area; they can do increasingly complex and detailed work in their area of specialization. At the same time, as actors specialize in narrower and narrower fields, so they become more and more dependent on other specialists in other fields. Consider the case of production of a bicycle. If one actor specializes in gears, another in spokes, another in frames, and so on, then each can become increasingly skilled in their area, but each thereby comes to depend more on the others for the production of bicycles. Hence, the argument goes, modern societies are becoming ever more complex with the constant spread of functional differentiation and so interdependence.

Even if the spread of specialization and interdependence are characteristic of modern societies in general, some social scientists believe that these processes sped up considerably in the late twentieth century. These later social scientists often highlight the spread of communication and information technologies, globalization, consumerism, and individualization. It seems that these changes have made individuals, organizations, and states more interdependent. Actors have to interact and collaborate with others if they are to achieve their ends and address the complex problems they now confront; they have to form networks with one another. Some social scientists even describe the result of these trends as 'the network society'.

The narrative of modernity as the rise of interdependence provides one way of making sense of the new governance. It suggests that public sector organizations and even nation states are increasingly dependent on other public and private sector actors: they need to cooperate with other actors if they are to get access to the skills, knowledge, and finance they need to formulate and implement their policies. Hence, the narrative continues, local, national, and international governance have all witnessed a proliferation of networks. Some social scientists bemoan the way in which growing interdependencies appear to have hollowed out the state. Others look to a new world of collaborative networks solving social ills while facilitating new types of participation.

interdependence

DEBATE

Clearly, the concept of interdependence suggests one social theory with which to understand changes in governance. It lurks in many social and historical explanations of the apparent rise of networks within the public sector and even global governance. As such, many of the most prominent debates about interdependence concern concepts such as 'network' and 'managing networks'. Yet, interesting as these debates are, we should not let them obscure the broader debates that have long accompanied historical narratives of the virtues and vices of interdependence. Debates about interdependence have long echoed within discussions of modern life, modern societies, and, most notably, the kind of division of labor that characterizes modern economies. How valuable is self-reliance or self-fulfilment? Does specialization breed alienation or fulfilment in labor? Does commerce lead to concentrations of resources and power, and perhaps thereby to exploitation and injustice?

Most ancient and early modern thinkers placed great store by self-rule, which they defined in contrast to dependency on other people. Some modern political theorists, often inspired by romantic ideals, similarly opposed the rise of specialization or the division of labor on the grounds that it results in dependence on others or in alienation. Radicals and socialists have often argued, in addition, that specialization and modern economies lead to an unequal distribution of resources and power, and so to the exploitation of those who lack resources and power by those who have them. For many radicals, polite talk of interdependence is just an ideological smoke screen obscuring a reality in which some are left considerably more dependent than are others.

Liberal political economists have taken a far more positive view than radicals of the division of labor, specialization, and, of course, modern economies. The classical economists, including, most famously, Adam Smith, argued that actors could specialize in the production of a particular good or service, and then engage in commerce (mutually beneficial exchanges) in order to make themselves and also their communities better off. Typically, the classical economists responded to fears of the degrading effects of dependency on morality by arguing that commerce itself was a way of spreading virtue, morality, and civilization.

CROSS REFERENCES

Global governance, Managing networks, Network

FURTHER READING

Castells, M. (2000) *The Rise of the Network Society*. Oxford: Blackwell.

Keohane, R. and Nye, J. (1977) *Power and Interdependence: World Politics in Transition*. Boston, MA: Little Brown.

Loewy, E. (1993) *Freedom and Community: The Ethics of Interdependence*. Albany, NY: State University of New York Press.

Narula, R. (2003) *Globalization and Technology: Interdependence, Innovation Systems and Industrial Policy*. Cambridge: Polity Press.

Starr, H. (1997) *Anarchy, Order, and Integration: How to Manage Interdependence*. Ann Arbor, MI: University of Michigan Press.

Local Governance

DEFINITION

Local governance refers to all levels of government and administration below the central or national state. The terms here may be confusing since some central states themselves are federations of states. So, in countries such as the USA, local governance refers to individual states (such as California and Florida) as well as county and city governments. In general, we might say that the central state is the level treated as a sovereign power in most international negotiations, and local government consists of the levels of government below the center so conceived. But, of course, even that picture is confused by the rise of regional organizations such as the European Union that then represent their member states in some international negotiations.

The organization and powers of local governance vary considerably across states. The level directly beneath the central state often consists of political and administrative regions. A political region is a territory that contains an elected government. An administrative region is an area that is created to administer a service. Once again, however, generalizations prove difficult to sustain in large part because of disparate terminology. So, in the Netherlands, political regions are not directly below the national government, but rather between the county and the town.

One way to conceive local governance is in terms of the fluctuating fortunes of regionalism and regionalization. Regionalism is the rise of local territorial identities, often in opposition to the center. Regionalization is the attempt by the center, with or without local support, to establish sub-national tiers of government and administration.

Regionalism is an ideology and political movement that promotes the establishment of local government in a region that is associated with a particular identity. Like nationalism, this regionalism flourished in many European states during the nineteenth century. People were increasingly aware of their collective identities as possible bases for political organization. This awareness could lead, as in Germany and Italy, to attempts to forge new nations out of local levels. But it also could lead to attempts to forge new local entities out of states and empires. Belgium provides a good example of this evolution. The Flemings in Belgium opposed the strong powers of the center and sought to promote local control of their community. The result was a new regional pattern of rule. Other regional identities, often dating from the same time, wanted total independence from the center. Some of were successful: the obvious examples being the states forged out of the break-up of the Austro-Hapsburg Empire. Others are still pushing their minority nationalisms, as with the Basques in Spain. Indeed, movements for local autonomy or even independence remain common across the globe.

Regionalization is a more top-down process than regionalism. In addition, it is often more about administrative arrangements than political self-rule. Typically, the central state establishes an authority to run part of its territory. Regionalization can involve the state retaining almost all of its power, or it can see the higher level of government grant significant autonomy to the lower level. It is arguable that financial issues are the most important cause of political fights between the center and such regions. Fiscal relations between different levels of government are often fraught. The center typically wants to keep control since its own economic policies and outcomes often depend heavily on local decisions: for example, the center will have far more difficulty in controlling inflation if local governments are engaging in extensive deficit spending. Equally, however, the local governing bodies typically need some kind of fiscal independence if they are to be more than instruments for the implementation of the center's policies.

The welfare state often pushed processes of regionalization. Between 1945 and 1980, local governance was approached primarily as a way of

key concepts in governance

aiding economically and socially backward regions. The center promoted local arrangements that it thought would be able to secure development. Similarly, regional groups, such as the Northern Ireland Civil Rights Association, often used their identity to demand a greater portion of the wealth of the larger political entity. After the crisis of the welfare state in the late 1970s and early 1980s, however, many central states began to lessen the level of their intervention in local regions. Nowadays regionalization is as likely to be approached as a way of building capacity or legitimacy as a means of redistribution.

DEBATE

There is a debate about whether there has been a shift from government to governance at the local level. Among those who believe there has, there is another debate about whether this shift is a top-down process akin to regionalization or a response to bottom-up demands in a way that more closely resembles regionalism.

Local government used to be conceived in formal institutional and even legal terms. Each level of government was clearly distinguished from those above and below it. The various levels formed a clear hierarchical chain that facilitated government control, clear lines of responsibility, and so accountability. Local networks were typically closed. Policy-making followed routine procedures. The main problems confronting local government, so conceived, arose from blurred responsibilities or excessive centralization. The solutions lay in administrative reorganization or decentralization.

In contrast, local governance is thought to have moved away from such formal and legal patterns. Local governance works through open networks. In particular, it fosters cooperation among diverse governmental actors and even non-governmental actors. While governmental actors may have specific responsibilities or functions, they cannot avoid interdependencies. To the contrary, local actors must cooperate with one another and with non-governmental actors even if the result blurs responsibilities. The shift from local government to local governance has thus brought a larger number of actors into the policy process, a fragmentation of the policy process, more horizontal and vertical networks, and more innovative forms of policy learning and policy formation. From this local governance perspective, the main problems are typically barriers to cooperation, including inflexible rules, inherited mindsets, and actors who have a veto. The solutions lie in deploying strategies of network management so as to promote cooperation.

How might we explain the rise of the new local governance? One possibility would be to see it less as a change in the world and more as a change in the way in which we think about the world. Yet the change is typically presented as one in the nature of local government itself and not our theories. The main explanations of this apparent change appeal to the rise of new challenges for local government. Local actors face new policy issues, such as environmental protection, that require intergovernmental cooperation. Local actors now operate in a more global economy so they have to build transnational alliances and links to secure investment. And local actors often have to respond to the central governments that are promoting the New Public Management and contracting-out. Of course, all these challenges resemble regionalization more than regionalism. They are pressures that promote new administrative systems as more efficient or effective at least in the contemporary world. In addition, however, there are sometimes more bottom-up pressures behind the move from local government to local governance. Regional identities can still demand expression, and sometimes they can seek expression through new administrative and political institutions. Likewise, some citizens are developing and demanding new styles of political participation that alter the character of local politics.

CROSS REFERENCES

Center–local relations, Decentralization, Multilevel governance

FURTHER READING

Agranoff, R. and McGuire, M. (2003) *Collaborative Public Management: New Strategies for Local Governments*. Washington, DC: Georgetown University Press.
Bogason, P. (2000) *Public Policy and Local Governance: Institutions in Postmodern Society*. Cheltenham: Edward Elgar.
John, P. (2001) *Local Governance*. London: Sage.
Rose, L. and Denters, B. (2005) *Comparing Local Governance: Trends and Developments*. Basingstoke: Palgrave Macmillan.

Managing Networks

DEFINITION

If governance is about the presence of networks, then one of the main tasks of the state, as well as of other policy actors, is to manage them. A network is a non-hierarchical, collaborative structure that encompasses various organizations. Typically, these organizations have different expertise, finance, and other resources. They depend on one another to achieve their individual and collective goals. The term 'network' also may refer to the pattern of relationships between such organizations. Networks are often contrasted here with markets and with bureaucracies. A network, unlike a market, does not assume that its members have complete information, and a network, unlike a bureaucracy, can operate without a clearly defined hierarchical leadership. Generally, states manage networks by manipulating the organizations and relationships of which they are composed. States attempt thereby to achieve their policy goals. Of course, other policy actors also might try to manipulate networks for their own ends.

CONTEXT

The rise of the new governance means that the state increasingly depends on other actors to deliver services and coordinate policies. But the new governance also often leaves the state less able to command and control these other organizations. Hence the state must try to manage or steer networks through diplomacy, negotiation, and bargaining.

We might distinguish between the two types of network that most concern the state, namely, policy networks and intergovernmental networks. Policy networks focus on a specific area of public policy, such as agricultural policy or energy policy. They are generally fairly stable. The members of these policy networks have special interests or expertise in the relevant policy area. They may come from government agencies, think tanks, academia, industry, or the community. Policy networks sometimes contain further subdivisions. For example, a policy network that focuses on energy policy may contain within itself smaller networks that focus on wind power, nuclear power, or energy regulation. Political scientists have long recognized the existence of such policy networks. Some argue that they have grown in number or importance with the rise of the new governance.

Whereas policy networks focus on generating policy in a specific area, intergovernmental networks concentrate more on administration and especially policy implementation. The actors in intergovernmental networks are state actors. They may include different levels of governments – local, regional, and national bodies. They may also include state agencies with different policy jurisdictions, such as police, housing, or social security. While the actors in intergovernmental networks can be interdependent, the central state often has notably more resources than more local governments. Like policy networks, intergovernmental networks are generally fairly stable. Repeated interactions over time build trust and reciprocity among the members of the networks. Political scientists have long recognized the existence of intergovernmental networks, but many now argue that they have become far more complex in the new governance. The use of private and voluntary actors to deliver public services means, in particular, that these new types of actor must now be incorporated within intergovernmental networks. Public sectors have become increasingly fragmented. The coordination of policy implementation thus requires new approaches to joining up increasingly diverse actors.

DEBATE

There has been much debate about how the state should try to steer the networks that have become so prominent with the rise of the new governance. We might distinguish between three general approaches to network management in the public sector: the instrumental, the interactive, and the institutional.

An instrumental approach to network management is a top-down form of steering. It concentrates on ways in which a government can exercise its legitimate authority. As such, it typically presumes a governmental department to be the focal organization within a network. The central state is then to devise and impose tools that foster integration in and between policy networks and so enable the state to better attain its objectives. One problem with this instrumental approach is that it relies on the government's ability to exercise effective control when the whole study of networks and governance has exposed the ever-present problem of control deficits.

The interactive approach to network management moves away from hierarchical modes of control. It presumes the mutual dependence of actors in networks: collective action depends on cooperation, with goals and strategies developing out of mutual learning. Management thus requires negotiation and diplomacy; there is a need to understand other actors' objectives and to build relations of trust with them. Chief executive officers in the public sector are urged to develop interpersonal communication and listening skills. This interactive approach is often costly; cooperation is time-consuming, objectives can be blurred, and outcomes can be delayed.

Finally, an institutional approach to network management focuses on the rules and structures that form the background against which interactions take place. Management strategies seek to change relationships between actors, the distribution of resources, the rules of the game, and even values and perceptions. The aim is incremental changes in incentives and cultures. One problem with this approach is that institutions and their cultures are notoriously resistant to change.

Given that all three approaches to network management face problems, perhaps we should conclude, as so often in looking at governance, that there is no simple solution. No one strategy applies in each and every case. No single tool solves all problems. Rather, the state must try to muddle through as best it can, adopting a mixture of strategies depending on the local circumstances, and modifying its strategies as it learns through dialogue with the other policy actors involved.

CROSS REFERENCES

Metagovernance, Network, Policy network

FURTHER READING

Agranoff, R. and McGuire, M. (2003) *Collaborative Public Management: New Strategies for Local Governments*. Washington, DC: Georgetown University Press.

Kickert, W.J.M., Klijn, E.H. and Koppenjan, J.F.M. (eds) (1997) *Managing Complex Networks: Strategies for the Public Sector*. London: Sage.

Mandell, M. (ed.) (2001) *Getting Results through Collaboration: Networks and Network Structures for Public Policy and Management*. Westport, CT: Quorum Books.

McGuire, M. (2002) 'Managing Networks: Propositions on What Managers Do and Why They Do It', *Public Administration Review*, 62: 599–609.

managing networks

Market

DEFINITION

The market refers most generally to an abstract space in which suppliers sell commodities and services to consumers at equilibrium prices. The equilibrium price of an item derives from the amount consumers are willing to pay for it and the cost at which suppliers can produce it. Innumerable factors might alter this relationship of demand to supply and so the price of a commodity. Prices can change as new inventions decrease production costs, as environmental disasters increase production costs, as popular tastes change, and so on. Economic competition implies that suppliers have to price goods not only to maximize their profit but also to attract consumers. Such competition may not exist if, for instance, significant barriers prevent new suppliers from entering the market.

Theoretically, free markets are those in which the state plays no role: the state does not regulate market exchanges either directly or indirectly. In practice, however, the state always seems to play a role. Minimally, the state must provide the legal and institutional infrastructure needed for market exchanges. Markets always require laws and institutions. They depend on a legal system to enforce various rights and responsibilities such as those associated with contracts. Likewise, they depend on financial institutions, such as central banks, to prevent corruption, promote competition, and facilitate market interactions. It is hard to imagine how such legal and financial institutions could be provided apart from by some kind of political authority.

A leading alternative to distribution through markets is distribution through the public sector. When the government provides goods and services, it is often insulated from competition. Hence the prices of the relevant goods and services are often seen as being static. The command economies of the old Soviet Bloc provide an extreme example of services and goods being provided by the public sector. In these command economies, the state is typically the sole producer of all kinds of commodities, and it directs production based on what it deems to be the national need. With the state thus deciding what goods to produce in what quantities, the market relations of supply and demand are conspicuously absent.

CONTEXT

We might think about the relationship between markets and governance in terms of 'market governance' (how the state governs the market) and 'governance by markets' (how markets act as forms of social coordination).

'Market governance' refers to the rules and institutions by which a state governs the operation of the market. The state's main aim here is arguably to ensure that markets are as perfectly competitive as possible. It wants goods and services to be exchanged at price levels that optimize not only the profits of the providers but, more importantly, the utility of the consumers. Hence the state acts to prevent corrupt practices such as price gouging, collusion, and the withholding of information. Examples of state regulation here include anti-trust laws and commerce commissions. Even if the main aim of the state here is the promotion of efficient markets, states often also try to minimize the inequalities and injustices associated with the patterns of distribution that arise out of market exchanges. In so far as markets are intrinsically unequal and arguably unjust, a more activist state might be needed to promote welfare and fairness.

'Governance by markets' refers to the ways in which markets allocate goods and services to the public. States are often called market economies if they rely on the market as the main means of distributing goods and services. Market economies vary immensely according to their varied political, social, and cultural contexts. To simplify matters, we might mention just three main forms of the market economy: the liberal market economy, the developmental market economy, and the coordinated market economy.

Liberal market economies provide the vast bulk of goods and services through a private sector that is only weakly regulated. Liberal market economies have private firms produce for-profit goods and services that in many other states are provided by the state itself. Prominent examples of such economies include the USA and Britain. Advocates of a liberal market economy argue that we get maximum efficiency from a free market that is not weighed down by a heavy state presence.

Developmental market economies involve a heavy state presence, particularly in shaping the infrastructure within which private commerce operates. In developmental states, the state owns large corporations that have a monopoly on the provision of goods and services, such as telecommunications, water, electricity, and air transportation. The state typically runs these services through large institutions that are large employers within the relevant society. A good example would be

market

the French economy, especially in the 1970s and 1980s. Developmental states provide services under market mechanisms of supply, demand, and competition, but, because it has monopolized the provision of certain goods and services, the state can unilaterally set their prices.

Coordinated market economies use corporatist forms of collective bargaining to reach agreements between the state, labor, and business. These agreements then set the parameters of market distribution. Hence the operation of the domestic market depends in large part on political agreements. Within the limits set by these agreements, however, the market acts to determine the prices of goods and services. Prominent examples include Denmark and Sweden.

DEBATE

There are, of course, all kinds of theories of the market. These theories purport to describe how the market works and thereby to show it to be good, bad, or even neutral. They range from neoliberal eulogies to socialist diatribes – although even that is a simplistic claim since most socialists believe the market has an important role to play; some even argue that markets are a perfect system of distribution if only we have a suitably equal society.

Contemporary social scientists are prone to highlighting three main approaches to the study of the market: neoclassical economics, the new institutional economics, and political economy.

Neoclassical economics presents the market as the most efficient mechanism for the distribution of goods and services. The aim of neoclassical economists is to determine market inefficiencies and restructure market governance to eliminate these inefficiencies. One way of understanding the main debates among neoclassical economists is, indeed, in terms of their different analyses of market inefficiencies. On the one hand, neoliberals argue that the most worrying source of market inefficiency is government intervention. State intervention allegedly hinders communication between producers and consumers. Hence neoliberals want to reduce government regulation and to introduce markets and market mechanisms as far as possible. On the other hand, welfare economists argue that markets require government intervention if they are to function efficiently. In this view, the best response to market inefficiencies is often state regulation or intervention. At times such intervention can take the form of public welfare delivered by state agencies.

The new institutional economics provides an alternative approach to the market. Its proponents emphasize that particular rules and regulatory organizations are crucial to market functionality. They highlight the role of institutions in ensuring, say, that property rights are protected and contracts are enforced. All forms of social coordination involve transaction costs. The market is often a peculiarly effective form of coordination since the transaction costs associated with it are generally low. Yet new institutional economists also endorse interventions into the market that decrease market transaction costs and so improve efficiency.

Finally, political economy attempts to understand the ways in which political decisions impact the operation of the market. Economists in this school see the market primarily as a mechanism for distributing resources among groups or classes in society. They emphasize the way in which bargains between dominant social actors and the state typically set the context for market interactions and thereby ensure the dominance of particular groups or classes.

CROSS REFERENCES

Corporatism, Marketization, New Public Management, Regulation

FURTHER READING

Bain, K. and Howells, P. (1989) *Understanding Markets.* Worcester, UK: Billing & Sons.
Bevir, M. and Trentmann, F. (eds) (2004) *Markets in Historical Contexts.* Cambridge: Cambridge University Press.
Pindyck, R.S. and Rubinfeld, D. (2005) *Microeconomics.* Upper Saddle River, NJ: Pearson/Prentice-Hall.
Williamson, O. (1975) *Markets and Hierarchies: Analysis and Antitrust Implications.* New York: Free Press

Marketization

DEFINITION

Marketization refers to the integration of competition and price mechanisms into public services. The most dramatic type of marketization is privatization. Privatization occurs when the state completely abandons the production of a good or the provision of the service by handing it over to the private sector. For example, the state might float a state-owned enterprise on the stock market, or, alternatively, it might sell it to a private firm, a consortium of managers, or a workers' cooperative. Of course, even if the state privatizes an enterprise, it still might introduce regulations in order to limit or control the actions of the new private sector owners of that enterprise.

Another, more common type of marketization is for the state to maintain control of the provision of a public service but to introduce reforms designed to increase market competition in the public sphere. The most common examples of such marketization include contracting-out, purchaser–provider splits, and the creation of government corporations.

Contracting-out refers to the state entering into a contract with a private sector company. The state employs the company to provide a specific service, such as looking after elderly citizens, cleaning a public hospital, or running a prison. Several different private companies compete with one another for the contract, thereby creating a type of market competition. The state gives the contract to the company that offers the best deal, although of course there is considerable room for disagreement over what constitutes the best deal.

Purchaser–provider splits are formed when one state institution buys services or goods from another state institution. For example, in the British National Health Service the general practitioners (primary care physicians) purchase hospital care for their patients from state-run hospitals. Market competition exists here in that several different providers (the hospitals) compete for the custom of the purchasers (the general practitioners).

Government corporations are owned by the state either directly or as a majority shareholder. However, they are legally independent from the state and receive neither privileged monopoly status nor subsidies. Market competition exists here in so far as government corporations compete with private corporations that provide the same service or produce the same goods.

CONTEXT

Marketization arose as an idea in neoliberal economic theory. It became prominent in the 1980s when neoliberal governments in developed states pursued strategies based on this idea. Critics of bureaucratic hierarchies had long claimed that they are inefficient and unresponsive to the demands of citizens. Some economists argued that publicly provided goods are inherently inefficient, given that the government has a monopoly of their provision and so is shielded from the competition of the marketplace. Neoliberals then began to conclude that marketization was necessary to reform sluggish and outdated state enterprises. These neoliberals often found a receptive audience among a public that felt taxation and government expenditure were rising too steeply while standards of public services were declining.

Several developed states elected neoliberal reformers in the late 1970s and early 1980s. The governments of Margaret Thatcher in the UK and Ronald Reagan in the USA attempted to roll back the state through marketization. At the same time neoliberals began to spread the ideas and strategies of marketization to other states. Sometimes neoliberal practices spread under the guise of transnational policy advice. Marketization spread to the formerly communist countries of the Soviet Bloc through neoliberal advisers sent over from the USA and the UK. At other times neoliberal ideas were spread, or even imposed, by international organizations. These ideas became the subject of the 'Washington Consensus' among the International Monetary Fund, the World Bank, and the US Treasury, considering the strategies developing states should pursue. Monetarist policies to control inflation, trade liberalization, the removal of state subsidies and controls, and marketization in the public sector were all imposed on large parts of the developing world by attaching policy conditions – stabilization and structural adjustment programs – to the loans made by the IMF and the World Bank.

Arguably, marketization had peaked by the mid-1990s. All too often, the attempts to spread markets in transitional and developing states had merely exasperated problems of market failure and state performance. Even former neoliberals began to accept that the neoliberal policies that had emerged from developed states were generally inappropriate for other states. The main problem facing many developing states is that the government is too weak and inept to even perform basic functions. We might distinguish here between state scope and state strength. State scope refers to the range of activities pursued by the public sector. State strength refers to how effective the public sector is in pursuing those activities. Neoliberal reforms sought to restrict the scope of state activity. But, it now seems clear that the main obstacle for developing states is a lack of state strength. Hence even institutions such as the World Bank now appear to be paying less attention to marketization and more to building up state capacity.

DEBATE

There are heated debates about the effectiveness and appropriateness of markets within the public sector. Obviously, supporters suggest that the reforms will bring, or even have brought, many of the benefits they were meant to – a more dynamic, efficient, entrepreneurial private sector that provides better services for less money. In contrast, the more negative judgements of the reforms tend to emphasize their role in creating or exacerbating problems such as the fragmentation of service delivery, the state's lack of control over its own policies, and weakening of lines of accountability.

One complaint is that marketization compounds institutional fragmentation. Services are often delivered now by a combination of local government, special-purpose bodies, the voluntary sector, and the private sector. Critics point to an absence of links between organizations. In their view, outsourcing failed to establish proper sustained relationships between state actors and their private sector partners. The worry is that departments of state and their associated agencies are becoming almost unconnected elements. There are no proper mechanisms for ensuring policy coordination.

Another complaint is the decline of the ability of the state to steer other bodies. Marketization undermined the strategic capacity of the center. Critics argue that many agencies work in a policy vacuum. The role of the central state has been restricted to crisis management. When the center does try to exercise some kind of control, it is likely to find that it has rubber levers – pulling the lever does not lead to any action at the other end.

Many commentators are less concerned with issues of capacity or effectiveness than with the way in which marketization relates to civic values. One complaint is that marketization gives aspects of public policy to agencies and private sector organizations that are at best only minimally accountable to politicians and thus the citizens who elect them. Critics argue that public sector managers are now accountable to performance measures but not to their senior administrators and their political masters. At the very least, there has been a shift in the nature of accountability: public sector managers are perhaps more responsible to the citizens who use their services and less to the politicians who represent the public as a whole.

CROSS REFERENCES

Capacity, Market, New Public Management, Public–private partnerships

FURTHER READING

Hodge, G. (2006) *Privatization and Market Development: Global Movements in Public Policy Ideas.* Cheltenham: Edward Elgar.

Nolan, B.C. (2001) *Public Sector Reform.* New York: Palgrave Macmillan.

Pollitt, C. and Talbot, C. (2004) *Unbundled Government: A Critical Analysis of the Global Trend to Agencies, Quangos, and Contractualization.* New York: Routledge.

Salamon, L.M. (ed.) (2002) *The Tools of Government: A Guide to the New Governance.* New York: Oxford University Press.

Metagovernance

DEFINITION

Metagovernance is an umbrella concept that describes the role of the state and its characteristic policy instruments in the new governance. The new governance is such that governing is no longer a state monopoly. Governing is distributed among various private, voluntary, and public actors. Power and authority are more decentralized and fragmented among a plurality of networks. In this context, the role of the state is said to have shifted from the direct governance of society to the 'metagovernance' of the actors that now are involved in governing society. Similarly, in this context, the mode of state action – and so the main policy instruments it uses – are said to have shifted from command and control within a bureaucracy to the indirect steering of the actions and interactions of relatively autonomous stakeholders.

CONTEXT

Generally, then, metagovernance refers to the role and actions of the state in securing coordination in the new governance. It suggests that the state now steers and regulates a range of organizations and networks that perform governance. These other organizations undertake much of the work of governing: they implement policies, they provide public services, and at times they even regulate themselves. The state governs the organizations that thus govern us. It makes sure that they operate efficiently and fairly. Moreover, the other organizations characteristically have a degree of autonomy from the state: they are often voluntary or private sector groups, or they are governmental agencies or tiers of government separate from the core executive. Hence the state cannot govern them solely by the instruments that operate within bureaucracies. It must instead rely on negotiation, diplomacy, and more informal modes of steering.

Metagovernance appears to rise from the leading characteristics of the new governance. States are becoming increasingly fragmented into networks based on a number of different stakeholders. Again, the dividing line between the state and civil society is becoming more blurred since many of the relevant stakeholders are private or voluntary sector organizations. Hence the state appears to face a challenge: it has to recognize the legitimacy of non-state stakeholders in the process of governing while keeping itself apart from these stakeholders sufficiently to ensure that their varied actions are coordinated in a manner that efficiently promotes the public interest. Metagovernance thus entails both recognizing non-state actors (granting them the power to self-regulate) and subtly distinguishing them from the state (letting the state exert macro-control over their self-regulation). The state governs the other actors involved in governance.

The activity of metagovernance is often equated with 'steering' as opposed to the more direct 'rowing' that is involved in governance. There are, however, several ways in which the state can steer the other actors involved in governance. Let us consider some of them. First, the state may adopt a 'framing' approach. It can establish the rules of the game for other actors and then leave them to do what they will in the context of those rules. Second, the state can try to steer other actors through a 'storytelling' approach. It can foster meanings, beliefs, and identities among the relevant actors and thereby influence what they think and do. Third, the state can approach steering other actors through the 'support' it provides them. The state can build and maintain a type of infrastructure or even provide specific financial or logistical resources that make it easier for other actors to do one thing rather than another. Of course, the state need not adopt a single uniform approach to metagovernance. It can use different approaches in different settings or at different times.

DEBATE

One debate about metagovernance concerns the rival merits of the approaches we have just considered. Proponents of a framing approach argue that it allows the state to maintain considerable control over the governing process without having to bear the costs of direct interference. Proponents of a storytelling approach argue that the viewpoints and interests of different actors are so diverse that more intervention is necessary to generate suitable cooperation and coordination among them. It can certainly be difficult to frame the rules of the game in a way that brings the activities of other actors into line with the aims of the state. Storytelling can create coherent social and political meanings and identities that soften the tensions among competing viewpoints and interests. Proponents of the model of support and facilitation argue that both the framing and storytelling approaches neglect the resources that the state has at its disposal for metagovernance. They argue that the state can easily deploy these resources so as to manage other policy actors. Once again, we might want to conclude that the state ideally would deploy different approaches in different contexts.

Another debate about metagovernance concerns its relationship to our democratic values. Some observers point to a number of ways in which metagovernance appears to enhance democracy. They argue that metagovernance opens up all kinds of spaces of self-governance. In this view, metagovernance creates a more pluralistic and active civil society. It adds to the channels by which citizens can exert influence on public policies. It increases the amount of self-governance in the organizations of civil society. It promotes a more vibrant community. All kinds of citizens can develop valuable participatory skills through their involvement in all kinds of organizations. However, other observers point to ways in which metagovernance may undermine democracy. In their view, accountability suffers when elected politicians and the public officials answerable to them have only indirect oversight of governance. Accountability suffers when the fragmentation of the policy process undermines publicity and transparency. Critics also worry that when the state withdraws to metagovernance, governance is likely to become dominated by those private and voluntary actors that possess the greatest resources and who will thus acquire yet more power, thereby widening social inequalities.

Yet another debate about metagovernance concerns whether it decreases the apparatus of government, such as rules and regulations. A few critics argue that it has actually increased the amount of governing since it extends rule more deeply into civil society. Nonetheless, the more widespread view is still that it has in some sense reduced the activity of the state. In this view, even if regulation and self-regulation can appear cumbersome, they are less burdensome and intrusive than the pattern of rule associated with a top-down bureaucracy.

CROSS REFERENCES

Differentiated polity, Enabling state, Managing networks, Regulation

FURTHER READING

Cooper, P. (2003) *Governing by Contract: Challenges and Opportunities for Public Managers*. Washington, DC: CQ Press.

Kooiman, J. (2003) *Governing as Governance*. London: Sage.

Salamon, L.M. (ed.) (2002) *The Tools of Government: A Guide to the New Governance*. New York: Oxford University Press.

Sørensen, E. (2006) 'Metagovernance: The Changing Role of Politicians in Processes of Democratic Governance', *American Review of Public Administration*, 36: 98–114.

Multilevel Governance

DEFINITION

Multilevel governance refers to the set of interactions that occur between policy actors across more than one level of government. These interactions vary greatly in their degrees of complexity. So, multilevel governance may involve well-defined vertical power relationships between the central state and its constituent, subordinate, local entities. But, likewise, it may involve complex interactions that occur among various state and non-state actors on various levels of government. Indeed, multilevel governance often crosses horizontal as well as vertical levels. It is not constrained by traditional jurisdictional boundaries. Uncompartmentalized actors on a particular horizontal level can influence policy on higher or lower political levels.

The United States utilities industry is an example of multilevel governance within a particular state. At a comparatively low level of government, local utility companies compete and cooperate with each other and local public sector actors to provide services to their customers. At a higher level of government, they interact with the state and federal regulatory agencies whose decisions do much to constrain and define the manner in which they compete and provide services.

Political scientists have pointed to the European Union (EU) as an exemplar of multilevel governance reaching above the level of the state. Negotiations over policy occur between the central EU bodies and the member states, among the member states, and between the member states and various sub-state entities within their boundaries. The pattern of interactions thus involves actors from the public and private sectors and from multiple levels of government – sub-state, state, and regional.

CONTEXT

Political scientists have distinguished between two varieties of multilevel governance. One form of multilevel governance provides for relatively restricted interactions among organizations within a particular geographical area. The other form of multilevel governance involves broader interactions among organizations linked by a specific function or policy.

Type 1 multilevel governance resembles federal states. Indeed, a good example is the relationships that exist between the US federal government, the state governments, and the various county and city governments. This Type 1 multilevel governance depicts a distribution of power across a finite number of levels. Power flows from the center, national entity down to sub-state units, each of which is often further subdivided. Cooperation is much more likely to occur between the center and the sub-state entities than between the sub-state entities themselves. Jurisdictional boundaries and the relationship between one level and any other are clearly defined. The jurisdictions of the various levels rarely overlap. Each body serves a general, non-specialized role. Its rule covers a particular territory at the relevant level.

Type 2 multilevel governance involves more complexity and fluidity. It has no set limit of jurisdictional levels. Jurisdictions commonly overlap, and boundaries can expand or shrink as policy needs require. This Type 2 multilevel governance is typically associated with changes in the EU as it incorporated Greece, Spain, and Portugal. The expansion of the EU brought changes that empowered sub-state and non-state actors. Member states built partnerships to acquire and to distribute EU development funds. These partnerships linked actors from the regional (EU) level, the state level (member states), and the sub-state level (local governments). The European Commission also empowered non-state actors at all levels. As a result, all levels of government were in a process of continuous negotiation. Policy actors continuously tried to modify funding flows as conditions changed, so to ensure an effective use of resources. The actors were unconstrained by territorial concerns. They formed partnerships that focused instead on the functional goal of distributing resources appropriately.

DEBATE

The main debates about multilevel governance mirror those about the new governance more generally. Is the state being hollowed out? Are the new patterns of governance more efficient than the old ones? What are the implications for democracy?

Some political scientists argue that Type 2 multilevel governance empowers regional and even global bodies at the expense of states. Other political scientists point out, however, that the state still plays a vital role in multilevel governance. Besides, they add, the distribution of power in multilevel arrangements is not finite or zero-sum. The rising power of supranational entities does not necessarily entail any diminishing of the power of states. To the contrary, supranational entities can yield substantive gains for states and even lower levels. Perhaps, for example, the EU development funds can improve performance and service delivery at lower levels, thereby adding to the legitimacy and power of the member states.

Advocates of multilevel governance, especially of Type 2 multilevel governance, argue that horizontal cooperation between private and public actors and vertical cooperation between different levels of government leads to more effective policies being better implemented. They point to the problems of relying on well-defined, compartmentalized institutions organized by geographical area. They suggest that agencies working together to meet a common functional goal will achieve better results. And they suggest that shifting patterns of cooperation introduce greater flexibility into the policy process. Some sceptics suggest that there is nothing new in all this: policies have always been made and implemented within complex networks of actors drawn from various geographical levels.

What, finally, are the democratic implications of spreading the formation and the implementation of policy across multiple actors at multiple levels of government? The greater complexity of multilevel governance may interfere with public accountability. Clearly defined jurisdictions make it comparatively easy for citizens to identify the level of government at which any failure occurs. Type 2 systems distribute responsibilities across multiple actors at multiple levels in a way that lacks such clarity and transparency. They make it harder for citizens to hold any policy actor to account for any given failure. However, advocates of Type 2 systems argue that they have democratic advantages. Multilevel governance allows for the participation in the policy process of a diverse set of public and private actors. No single actor has a monopoly in the making or implementation of policy. Perhaps, however, differences in the power and resources of policy actors might undermine the pluralism of multilevel governance. Perhaps the reality of multilevel governance is more likely to be an oligopoly.

CROSS REFERENCES

Center–local relations, Metagovernance, Regionalism, Transnationalism

FURTHER READING

Bache, I. and Flinders, M. (eds) (2004) *Multilevel Governance*. Oxford: Oxford University Press.

DeBardeleben, J., Hurrelmann, A. and Leibfried, S. (eds) (2007) *Democratic Dilemmas of Multilevel Governance: Legitimacy, Representation and Accountability in the European Union*. Basingstoke: Palgrave Macmillan.

Doern, G.B. and Johnson, R. (2006) *Rules, Rules, Rules, Rules: Multi-level Regulatory Governance*. Toronto: University of Toronto Press.

Hooghe, L. and Marks, G. (2001) *Multilevel Governance and European Integration*. Lanham, MD: Rowman & Littlefield.

network

Network

DEFINITION

Broadly defined, a network is a group of interdependent actors and the relationships among them. Networks vary widely in their nature and operation depending on the particular actors involved, their relationships, the level and scope at which they operate, and the wider context. The actors within a network might be people, states, transnational corporations, or a mixture thereof. The relationships between actors are always interdependent, but they can vary from close ties, such as those within a family, to occasional impersonal and mediated interactions. Networks can appear at the level of the school playground or high court justices around the world. They appear in unstructured social environments and in highly formalized, rule-bound settings.

The concept of a 'network' is prominent in abstract discussions about governance as social coordination and in specific discussions of the new governance. At the abstract level, social theorists often appeal to a network as a distinct type of social coordination or organization. Networks are contrasted with hierarchies and markets. Their character derives in large part from the interdependence of the actors. This interdependence means that none of the actors can attain their aims unless they cooperate with the others. Hence networks differ from markets in which actors are independent of one another and able to achieve their goals through buying and selling. The interdependence of the actors within a network also means that no one actor can order the others to act in a certain way: no actor is so dependent on another that it has to obey that other's commands. Hence networks differ from hierarchies in which the authority of one actor enables it to ensure the compliance of another.

The distinctive nature of network forms of organization has inspired much of the literature on the new governance. This literature typically suggests that there has been a rise in the quantity and importance of networks. The new governance has emerged, in this view, as networks and perhaps markets have supplanted the hierarchical bureaucracies of an older pattern of government.

CONTEXT

Network theory arose from a number of overlapping trends in social theory. Most of these trends arose as part of a shift to ahistorical forms of social analysis in the first half of the twentieth century. Functionalism, structuralism, systems theory, and other such approaches attempted to explain social facts in terms of synchronic relationships. The nature and behavior of a unit derives from its function or place within a larger whole. The concept of a 'network' appeared here as one way of describing some of the relevant wholes; a network was a whole composed of a set of actors or units and their relations to one another.

Within the social sciences, the concept of a network became popular in all kinds of areas. In ethnography, it provided a way of conceptualizing not only family relationships but also migratory patterns from tribal villages to cities. In social psychology, especially within sociometry, it provided a way to examine the interpersonal relationships within groups so as to identify informal leaders and social rankings. For many people, the most obvious uses of the concept of a network today are within information technology. The World Wide Web is the 'net', a set of interlinked computers form a network, and so forth.

The use of the concept of a 'network' to make sense of social coordination and governance derives mainly from organizational theory. The term 'network' refers here to both the relationships among actors within an organization, and the relationships between various organizations. Today, organization theorists often use typologies that distinguish networks from hierarchies and markets on various dimensions. One dimension is the basis of the relationships between actors: whereas markets are based on property rights and contacts, and hierarchies are based on something like an employment relationship, networks are based on the exchange of resources. Another dimension is the medium of exchange between actors: where markets rely on prices, and hierarchies rely on authority, networks depend on trust. A third dimension is the means of resolving conflicts: market systems use bargaining and the courts, hierarchies use rules and commands, and networks use diplomacy. One final dimension might be culture: it is thought that markets have a competitive culture, hierarchies instantiate a culture of subordination, and networks encourage a culture of reciprocity.

Some social theorists have sought not only to distinguish networks from other types of organization but also to draw up typologies of different types of network. One simple typology is that between formal and informal networks. Formal networks are associated, say, with legalism, planning, the management of decisions, and a structured allocation of resources. Informal networks, in contrast, are linked with trust, discussion, collegiality, and unstructured exchanges. If we ponder the distinction between formal and informal networks, we might notice that formal networks closely resemble hierarchies. It might seem, therefore, that all these typologies should not be taken as offering a discrete set of distinct organizational forms. Rather, they offer us ideal types taken from a larger spectrum of different possibilities.

Just as social scientists have deployed the concept of a network in various settings, so they have developed different ways of analyzing networks. So, for instance, the broad typologies that we have been considering are one way of trying to make sense of the general characteristics of networks. The characteristics of particular networks or types of network have been explored using a range of qualitative and quantitative methods. Mathematical approaches to network analysis began to flourish in the 1950s. Today, there are algebraic theories of relationships, statistical models of the flows through network nodes, and graph theoretical analyses of things such as a network's density.

DEBATE

Most observers today recognize the ubiquity of networks in governance at all levels, from the local to the international. The fragmentation of public services as a result of the rise in special-purpose bodies and contracted-out services is, for example, both obvious and widespread. Debate tends to concern the advantages and disadvantages of the rise of networks within the public sector.

Advocates of networks ascribe a range of advantages to them. Typically, networks are said to offer a kind of dynamism and flexibility that hierarchies cannot, and yet also to foster cooperation and stable relationships in a way markets cannot. Some advocates of networks argue that these advantages are especially relevant to the contemporary world. They argue that the world has become increasingly complex and interconnected, and the pace of change is becoming faster and faster, all of which puts a premium on the kind of dynamism and flexibility associated with networks: many contemporary problems require the state to draw on diverse organizations for specialist funding, resources, and expertise. They also argue that the rise of new knowledge-based industries means that prosperity and efficiency increasingly depend not on competition, but on the kinds of cooperative and open practices that facilitate the exchange of ideas and information: public sector, voluntary sector, and private sector organizations all benefit from stable and creative relationships based on trust and participation.

Not everyone, however, is so enamored of networks. Even advocates of networks often argue that they are not always appropriate, and that the state should rely on a mixture of hierarchies, networks, and markets, adopting whatever organizational form is most apt in any given case. Other critics worry that the explosion of networks has gone too far. They accept that networks have benefits, but they argue that beyond a certain point they lead to a fragmented and unwieldy system of governance. The state loses the ability to effectively implement public policies. Perhaps the main criticism of networks, however, is that they can undermine democratic values, such as accountability. The sheer institutional complexity of networks obscures who is accountable to whom for what. Even if networks are more responsible to citizens, and even if they allow for more participation, they still might threaten some of our democratic values.

CROSS REFERENCES

Hierarchy, Market, Network management, Social capital

FURTHER READING

Mandell, M. (ed.) (2001) *Getting Results through Collaboration: Networks and Network Structures for Public Policy and Management.* Westport, CT: Quorum Books.

O'Toole, L., Jr. (1997) 'Treating Networks Seriously: Practical and Research-based Agendas in Public Administration', *Public Administration Review,* 57: 45–52.

Powell, W. (1990) 'Neither Market nor Hierarchy: Network Forms of Organization', *Research in Organizational Behavior,* 12: 295–336.

Scott, J. (1992) *Social Network Analysis.* London: Sage.

Thompson, G., Frances, J., Levacic, R. and Mitchell, J. (eds) (1991) *Markets, Hierarchies, and Networks: The Coordination of Social Life.* London: Sage.

New Public Management

DEFINITION

New Public Management (NPM) is a loose term, used to categorize a broad set of administrative ideas and reforms. Many observers argue that NPM was a common, or at least overlapping, agenda of the member states of the Organization for Economic Cooperation and Development (OECD) from the late 1970s and through the 1980s. In broad terms, NPM drew on neoliberal and managerial theories to attempt to make the public sector more efficient by rolling back and reorganizing the state through privatization and marketization. NPM tried to reorganize what remained of the state by transferring various tasks to executive agencies and by introducing private sector management techniques to the public sector. The grand aim was thereby to make the state more dynamic and entrepreneurial.

In more concrete terms, the main reforms and ideas associated with NPM include:

- A hands-on professional management in the public sector. Such management was promoted in part on the grounds that efficiency and accountability require a clear assignment of responsibility for particular actions.
- The introduction of explicit, and preferably quantitative, standards and measures of performance. The aim here was to promote efficiency and accountability through a clear statement of goals and objectives.
- The increased use of output controls, including linking the allocation of resources and rewards to measurements of performance. These reforms were intended to shift the focus from procedures to results.
- A disaggregation of administrative units in the public sector. The idea was that disaggregation would create more manageable units, separate provision and production, and so facilitate various types of marketization.
- The spread of markets and competition in the public sector. Contracting-out and public tendering procedures were meant to lead to competition and so drive down costs and promote better standards.
- The introduction of private sector management practices. The underlying idea here appears to be that the greater competition in the private sector had led it to develop better and proven tools of management.
- An emphasis on discipline and frugality in the use of resources. Public sector managers were to cut direct costs, raise labor discipline, and resist union demands, thereby lowering costs and increasing efficiency.

CONTEXT

It is arguable that there is no consistent pattern to NPM. Commentators have disagreed as to which intellectual traditions inspired it, why it spread so widely, and even if it did spread at all. About the only thing that seems clear is that NPM caught many people's imaginations partly because it took off in prominent states, including Britain and the USA, and also partly because it corresponded to a wider sense of crisis in the welfare state. Even here, however, there is disagreement about whether the crisis in the welfare state was more imagined than real. Despite all the disagreement, we might reasonably say that NPM drew on ideas such as neoliberal economics and managerialism to promote a loosely linked set of policies as a suitable response to perceived problems of state overload.

Many observers highlight two, slightly conflicting, schools of thought within NPM: public choice economics and business managerialism. Public choice economics introduced ideas about transactions costs and the principal–agent relationship that cast doubt on the older concept of bureaucratic hierarchies as rational institutions for pursuing public good. Business managerialism suggested that good management consisted of a set of portable techniques that could be transferred from industry to industry, private sector to public sector, as a means of improving the performance of employees and organizations.

To point to the ideas that inspired NPM is not, of course, to explain why these ideas found favor as a basis for public sector reform. NPM appears to have found favor in large part as a response to various social and economic problems that developed states faced in the 1970s and 1980s. Commentators argue, for example, that changes in the level and distribution of income produced an increasingly tax-conscious electorate that favored limiting government expenditure. The growth of service-oriented economies led to an increasingly heterogeneous population. Old solidarities gave way to a new individualism. People became less willing to contribute to social goods through taxation. What is more, this tax-consciousness coincided with international economic developments, such as the oil crisis, that put considerable pressure on the public finances of many developed states. The resulting squeeze on the public sector provided the setting for the cutbacks and reforms that NPM brought.

Social and economic changes provided a setting in which NPM could thrive. NPM appears to have arisen among neoliberals in Britain and the USA. The first countries to introduce related policies were probably Chile and New Zealand – in both of which the policies were adopted as a result of the spread of neoliberal ideas from the USA. However, the main examples of NPM came later, in Reagan's America and Thatcher's Britain. How far NPM spread in other countries is unclear. Some commentators identify a very broad pattern of public sector reform, including marketization and private sector management techniques. Others argue that while all kinds of states have introduced reforms, these often have little in common: the reforms owe more to the administrative traditions of various states than to neoliberalism.

DEBATE

The main debate about NPM is whether or not it is beneficial to the public sector. This debate gets very heated largely because it overlaps with that over the merits of the neoliberal politics associated with Reagan and Thatcher. Some advocates of NPM argue that it is a universal panacea for all the ills of the state. They argue that it is portable and applicable to all states and all levels of government. Rather surprisingly, some of them also argue that it is politically neutral: it consists of technical instruments that make the public sector more efficient and effective irrespective of the political values that are to be pursued.

Critics of NPM disagree. Some see it as an ideological dogma. Others see it as having the ability to improve efficiency but only at the expense of other public values, such as those of fairness and accountability. Yet others see it as possibly beneficial in some contexts – perhaps the strong states of the developed world – but not in others – notably the kind of weak states that are still found in parts of the developing world.

Let us end by briefly looking at some of the very different (arguably even incompatible) criticisms of NPM. The first is that NPM lacks any coherent content and/or has had no real impact. Critics sometimes argue that NPM is a fashionable term that is used to garner support for highly disparate policies. It has changed little. The state has not been rolled back. Public officials might spend more time managing and less on policy advice but the basic structure and problems of the state remain much the same.

A second criticism of NPM is that it has damaged the public service while failing to achieve its central goals of reducing costs and increasing efficiency. It has even been suggested that NPM actually increased bureaucracy with its new systems of accounting and auditing. Perhaps more importantly, NPM stands charged with having weakened accountability and public service ethics. It encouraged an entrepreneurial spirit that verged on illegality.

NPM is criticized, thirdly, for having advanced the interests of a new managerial elite. In practice, the reforms empowered public officials with expertise in economics or accountancy. These officials used their power to advance their own interests at the expense of the public good as well as an older elite rooted in generalist or legal traditions of public service.

CROSS REFERENCES

Marketization, Public–private partnerships, Rational choice theory

key concepts in
governance

144

FURTHER READING

Barzelay, M. (2001) *The New Public Management*. Berkeley, CA: University of California Press.

Bevir, M., Rhodes, R. and Weller, P. (eds) (2003) 'Traditions of Governance: History and Diversity', of *Public Administration* (Special Issue), 81/1.

Christensen, T. and Laegreid, P. (eds) (2001) *New Public Management: The Transformation of Ideas and Practice*. Aldershot: Ashgate.

Pollitt, C. and Bouckaert, G. (2000) *Public Management Reform: A Comparative Analysis*. Oxford: Oxford University Press.

Participatory Democracy

DEFINITION

Participatory democracy is a form of government in which the citizens themselves have the opportunity to make decisions about public policy. Participatory democracy, like its close relative, direct democracy, seeks to promote a form of self-determination or self-rule in which individuals actively make the decisions that determine how they are to be governed. It gives citizens a central role in the making of particular decisions through, for example, public discussion, negotiation, and voting. Indeed, some participatory democrats argue that citizens have an obligation to participate. When participatory democrats assign a role to the state, they often emphasize the importance of educating citizens and providing for a form of communication which promotes political dialogue.

One of the best ways to grasp the nature of participatory democracy is to think of it as an alternative to representative democracy. Most participatory democrats, at least since the late nineteenth century, have been inspired in part by dissatisfaction with the restricted opportunities for participation provided in modern representative democracies. In representative democracies, citizens delegate the tasks of decision-making and policy implementation to elected officials and appointed bureaucrats. Their participation is thus largely restricted to the election of politicians who then 'represent' the interests of their constituents in making decisions and holding the bureaucracy accountable.

Advocates of representative democracy argue that it is more efficient, especially in large states with large populations. Many participatory democrats counter with normative arguments about self-rule and citizenship. People are, perhaps, free only so far as they actively determine the rules under which they live. Yet, some participatory democrats also argue that popular participation leads to more effective policies in that it promotes trust, understanding, and consensus. The arguments for participatory democracy overlap considerably with those for other forms of radical democracy, including associative democracy and deliberative democracy. Associative democrats typically advocate more participation, but only in the context of a pluralist system in which power is divided among a number of groups and associations. Deliberative democrats argue that citizens should decide which laws and policies they ought to pursue through public dialogue and debate.

CONTEXT

Participatory democrats express ideals of self-rule that can be traced back at least as far as early modern forms of civic republicanism. Self-rule is, in this sense, a moral value that predates the rise of liberal democracies. Indeed, after the rise of liberal democracies, civic republican values inspired many radical, and even Marxist and anarchist, critics of liberal government. Current debates about participatory democracy took off, however, in the 1960s, when academics such as Benjamin Barber and Carole Pateman made strong normative arguments for greater citizen involvement. Perhaps more importantly, the 1960s also brought a range of new social movements, including the American Civil Rights movement and the Women's Liberation movement, which championed the causes of groups who were often excluded from representative institutions.

Although participatory democracy can appear to be an alternative to liberal democracy, it is perhaps more helpful to think of participation as a continuum, and participatory democrats as demanding an increase in current levels of participation. Many of the academic voices and social movements of the 1960s wanted to give greater voice to excluded groups, not to do away with all democratic elections, representatives, and assemblies. More generally, democracy, almost by definition, should provide avenues for popular participation. Common forms of participation include electoral participation, group participation, citizen–government participation, and direct participation. The electoral process allows citizens to select their representatives. Group participation allows citizens to combine in associations within civil society to form groups that have a voice in policy-making: common groups include churches, businesses, and trade unions. The concept of 'citizen–government interaction' refers to a diverse set of mechanisms by which citizens may convey their opinions and preferences to politicians; the mechanisms include public meetings, congressional hearings, and citizen surveys. Although participatory democrats value all of these forms of participation, they often place a particular emphasis on more direct forms of participation. Methods of direct participation include the initiative, the referendum, and citizen juries.

Participatory democracy has been implemented within temporary experiments and small groups. There have been televised examples of deliberative opinion polls: political scientists collect a group of diverse citizens and let them make decisions and formulate policies. Various private and voluntary sector organizations have constituted themselves as cooperatives or adopted highly participatory forms of decision-making. Community development corporations arose in response to economic issues within communities and became instruments of participatory democracy, as they promoted the same principles of democracy within the organization, and by means of instigating change in their respective communities. However, critics often argue, despite such experiments, that such extensive participation is simply too costly or too difficult to operate effectively in large, diverse, modern societies.

DEBATE

Discussions about the new governance raise several questions about participation and democracy. One question is whether or not the new governance increases participation. Some commentators suggest that the spread of markets increases choice and so the opportunities for citizens to participate in public decision-making. Neoliberals might argue, for example, that whenever a citizen chooses to use one public hospital or one school rather than another, she participates in determining a public outcome. But most participatory democrats – and, indeed, most commentators – believe that the way in which we participate in markets is not the kind of participation that has democratic value. They argue that we should distinguish the types of choice we make as consumers from the types of participation that are appropriate for citizens.

Yet other commentators suggest that the spread of networks provides enhanced opportunities for participation. In their view, the new governance opens up the possibility of new styles of everyday participation within network partnerships. Citizens and social movements can involve themselves in all kinds of collaborative practices of governance. But some critics of the new governance argue, to the contrary, that the spread of networks undermines the effectiveness of the participation available in representative democracies. They believe that the hollowing out of the state has involved a shift of decision-making power to non-state actors who lack proper legitimacy and who are barely accountable to citizens. In this view, the new governance raises the question of whether or not we need to develop new approaches to participation simply to uphold our standards of legitimacy and accountability.

The challenge for participatory democrats is, it seems, to create opportunities for participation in increasingly complex and differentiated societies. Yet another growing debate about participation and governance concerns e-democracy, that is, the potential of information technology to enhance democratic participation. Advocates of e-democracy argue that recent technical advances can provide solutions to obstacles that otherwise hinder direct participation in large complex societies. Perhaps telecommunications and the internet can facilitate deliberation and referenda among vast populations. There have already been a number of national and local experiments with computer-mediated forms of participation.

CROSS REFERENCES

Dialogic policy-making, Representative democracy

FURTHER READING

Barber, B. (1984) *Strong Democracy: Participatory Politics for a New Age*. Berkeley, CA: University of California Press.

Fung, A. and Wright, E.O. (eds) (2003) *Deepening Democracy: Institutional Innovations in Empowered Participatory Governance*. London: Verso.

Kweit, M. and Kweit, R. (1981) *Implementing Citizen Participation in a Bureaucratic Society*. New York: Praeger.

Pateman, C. (1970) *Participation and Democratic Theory*. Cambridge: Cambridge University Press.

Pauly, L. and Greven, M. (eds) (2000) *Democracy beyond the State?* Lanham, MD: Rowman & Littlefield.

Pluralism

DEFINITION

Pluralism refers to theories or societies in which power is dispersed among a number of different groups. Some pluralists argue that their theory describes the way in which political systems actually operate, at least within advanced western societies. Others see pluralism as a moral theory about how states and societies should order themselves. So, pluralists believe that power either is or ought to be spread out among more or less autonomous groups within the political system or even society at large. Some pluralists argue that as many decisions as possible should be devolved away from the central state to these groups. Others suggest that public policies arise, or should arise, from the interactions between the various groups, where these interactions might be competitive or cooperative. These forms of political pluralism overlap with all kinds of other pluralisms, including value pluralism, legal pluralism, religious pluralism, cultural pluralism, and pluralism in science. In general, pluralism stands for a belief in diversity as a fact, goal, or both. It is opposed to monist theories that promote a single way of doing things.

Contemporary debates about governance owe much to pluralism as both an empirical and a normative theory. Some of the main accounts of the new governance concentrate on networks in a way that recalls pluralist argument about the importance of policy networks. And some accounts of the new governance raise problems of democracy to which pluralism might perhaps offer solutions.

CONTEXT

Contemporary pluralism, as a normative and empirical theory, owes much to intellectual developments in the early twentieth century. Normative pluralism arose in reaction to abstract and idealist theories of the state as an association of unique moral importance embodying the common good. This idealization of the state became problematic during the First World War, partly because it was seen as being rooted in German philosophy, and partly because states were seen as being responsible for that irrational conflict. In the post-war era, political theorists such as G.D.H. Cole and Harold Laski developed pluralist theories. They argued that intermediate associations, including churches or trade unions, were of as much moral significance as the state. They argued that the common good, far from being vested in a unitary state, arose from negotiation and conflict among the various associations or groups in civil society. They also argued that the dispersal of power among such groups provided both a check on abuses of power and greater possibilities for participation and self-rule.

Empirical pluralism arose in reaction to approaches to political science that focused on constitutions and the formal institutions of the state. After the First World War, political scientists began to study what we might call behavioral topics, such as political parties and interest groups. Their studies of behavioral topics prompted a far more fragmented view of the state and the policy process. Many of them suggested that policy arose not from the decisions of a unified and sovereign state but from negotiation among interest groups. This focus on interest groups has inspired many pluralist theories of democracy, from David Truman up to Robert Dahl and, as we should now add, contemporary accounts of governance.

The infamous behavioral revolution in political science in the 1950s fused the behavioral topics we have been discussing with both a range of statistical techniques and a quest for a universal empirical theory of politics. Alas, even today, when political scientists react against behavioralism, they often fail to distinguish topics, techniques, and theory. Hence the trajectories of various approaches to political science can be difficult to trace. In the 1970s and 1980s, some political scientists rejected behavioralism by returning to the state in studies that fused statistical analysis with case studies so as to develop mid-range theories. Equally, some political scientists who gave up on behavioral theory, or simply had never believed in it, continued to study the older behavioral topics such as policy networks. Indeed, one of the most important precursors of studies of governance was just this work on policy networks and the fragmented nature of power and the policy process.

DEBATE

Many pluralists argue that their emphasis on the dispersal of power has a number of democratic advantages. At a very general level, they suggest that pluralism offers a way of accepting, and even affirming, diversity. Historically, pluralists have contrasted their own acknowledgement of the diverse interests and viewpoints to be found in society with totalitarian and particularistic ideologies. More recently, some pluralists have argued that their acceptance of diversity is especially relevant in an age when many societies are increasingly multicultural. In addition, some pluralists argue that a dispersal of power allows for public policies, and so the common good, arising out of a dialogue between all those affected. Several pluralists contrast this account of the common good as a negotiated consensus with oligarchies in which one group imposes its will on society as a whole. Finally, radical pluralists often hope that by devolving decisions to diverse groups within society, they might promote greater citizen participation. In this view, pluralism offers a way of promoting ideals such as democratic self-rule.

Critics of pluralism often focus on practical difficulties. They argue, in particular, that it leads to elitism or, alternatively, that it leads to deadlock. According to some critics of pluralism, groups have widely different resources at their disposal, and pluralist arrangements merely enable the big and powerful groups to dominate the policy process. This criticism suggests that pluralists have been too sanguine about the possibilities of equal participation of various interests. Perhaps pluralism typically leads not to policies that reflect a negotiated consensus among the different groups within society, but to policies that reflect the sectarian interests of immensely powerful groups. Some pluralists, notably empirical theorists, have come to accept the dominance of elite groups within the policy process, and even to suggest that such elitism has various benefits. The most obvious example of elitist pluralism is perhaps corporatism. Other examples arguably include accounts of government as fragmented into various policy networks, access to which is far from open and perhaps even restricted to clientelist groups. Elite pluralism, so conceived, appears in most theories of clientelism, group subgovernments, and iron triangles. In contrast, more participatory pluralists baulk at the idea of elitism. Typically, they have responded to problems raised by a disparity in resources by appealing to the possibility of state or social action to equalize the opportunities for participation across all the groups affected by a policy.

Other critics of pluralism argue that it spreads inefficiencies or irrationalities through the policy process. It has been suggested, for example, that pluralism makes the process of policy formation far too slow: every interest has to have a say, and most will negotiate and bargain until they are satisfied. In this view, pluralism leads to excessive delays, bottlenecks, and even stagnation. It has also been suggested that, especially given the threat of delays, some groups are likely to be able to use procedural niceties and technicalities to extort concessions from others. In this view, some interests are able to use the threat of delay to obtain concessions that have little to do with the common good. Some pluralists have responded to such criticism by trying to identify the conditions under which pluralism operates effectively. Typically, they emphasize the importance of mutual respect and tolerance among groups, and perhaps even a minimal consensus on shared values and norms. Some social scientists argue, in turn, that mutual respect or shared values arise in part from experiences in civil society of family life and community.

CROSS REFERENCES

Corporatism, Differentiated polity, Policy network

FURTHER READING

Dahl, R. (1967) *Pluralist Democracy in the United States: Conflict and Consent.* Chicago: Rand McNally & Company.
Gunnell, J.G. (2004) *Imagining the American Polity: Political Science and the Discourse of Democracy.* University Park, PA: Pennsylvania State University Press.
McLennan, G. (1989) *Pluralism.* Cambridge: Polity Press.
Rhodes, R.A.W. (1997) *Understanding Governance: Policy Networks, Governance, Reflexivity and Accountability.* Buckingham: Open University Press.
Runciman, D. (1997) *Pluralism and the Personality of the State.* Cambridge: Cambridge University Press.

Policy Cycle

DEFINITION

A policy cycle consists of the many constituent phases of a policy's existence. The phases are cyclical because the final phase is not necessarily the end of the matter, but rather an analysis of the policy to provide information that can be used in the first phase of a subsequent cycle. The cyclical or continuous nature of the policy cycle is one of the three main characteristics that theorists ascribe to it. The second characteristic is linearity: the phases of the policy cycle always occur one after another and in the same order: the phases are chronological and mutually exclusive. Third, policy cycles are fractal in that each phase can be divided into sub-phases that are representative of the whole cycle. Many theorists stress that the use and intensity of each division within the cycle varies with the goals of the policy-makers or policy analysts.

CONTEXT

Different schools of thought break down the policy cycle into different phases. There is, however, a general consensus that the policy cycle includes: agenda setting, formulation and decision, implementation, evaluation, and termination or reinstitution.

Agenda setting is the selection process in which policy-makers sift through possible issues and determine which they will tackle. This selection process is generally competitive because of constraints of time, finances, and other resources. The issues that get considered vary from large public ones that seem to require immediate attention to smaller institutional ones promoted by specific organizations. Agenda setting is the most public phase of the policy cycle. In deciding on an agenda, policy-makers typically balance the opinions of their constituency, the wishes of specific interest groups, and their own views.

Once the agenda is set, public actors must develop an effective method to address the selected issues. This is the policy formulation phase. Policy formulations are often written into official statements, papers, and draft bills. However, just as there are many issues from which to choose an agenda, so there are often many different ways in which any given issue might be formulated. The job of policy formulation is to choose the most effective and acceptable way of dealing with an issue. Typically, policy formulation again involves a balance of broad public opinion with specific organized interests. It leads to a decision to adopt a particular policy.

Policy implementation is even less public than policy formulation. In the implementation phase, the state may introduce new programs and new administrative agencies in order to achieve the stated goals. In theory, a well-formulated policy will itself define a specific mode of implementation. In practice, however, policy implementation is often considered the most difficult phase of the policy cycle. The public officials who implement policies often have only vaguely worded policy statements to go on, and they often confront widespread inertia or even hostility to change. Some scholars have even expressed surprise that change ever happens!

If policy implementation is the most difficult phase of the policy cycle, policy evaluation is arguably the most overlooked. A well-written policy will include criteria and modes of evaluation – ideally perhaps, evaluation by non-political actors who are not associated with the formulation or implementation of the policy. Did the policy work? Did it effect the change stated in its goals? Policies that have outlived their usefulness are terminated. Policies that have been useful are reinstated or reassessed. Reassessment of a policy asks whether it could be improved. Did the implementing agencies use their resources wisely? Do they need more or less resources? The answers to these questions help to set a new agenda. The policy cycle then repeats itself.

DEBATE

Discussions of the policy cycle often focus on its scientific credentials as a theory and as an effective aid to policy-making. Both sides in the debate over the importance of developing a more scientific approach to public policy have challenged the policy cycle approach, albeit for very different reasons. Other critics focus on the way in which it seems to privilege administrative processes over democratic contestation.

Social scientists who are anxious to develop a more scientific approach to policy-making believe that the policy cycle approach lacks scientific credentials. They argue that as a theory it lacks explanatory power; it is little more than a loose set of descriptive concepts that cannot be operationalized and tested empirically. Similarly, they argue that as an aid to policy-making it has been supplanted by evidence-based policy-making, which requires a restructuring of the relationship between the phases of the policy cycle.

Other social scientists are sceptical of allegedly scientific approaches to policy-making. These critics often suggest that the policy cycle approach imposes far too rigid a conceptual framework: it offers a formulaic checklist that is all too likely to lead policy-makers to neglect or misunderstand important parts of what is a dynamic, varying process. These critics point, in particular, to the danger of mislabelling. If policy analysts try to squeeze every aspect of a policy process into a predetermined set of categories, they are likely to mislabel some aspects of that process.

Yet other critics suggest that the policy cycle approach mistakenly implies that democratic decisions can be understood in technocratic terms. These critics accept that good processes matter, but they emphasize that the content of policies does not really derive from the processes of the policy cycle. Their underlying claim is that the question of what policy to adopt is less a matter of scientific knowledge than it is a matter of a political decision. Hence they insist that theories of the policy cycle should not be treated as substitutes for democratic decision-making. At times they worry that theories of the policy cycle effectively serve a bureaucratic mechanism for giving an aura of neutrality to political decisions. In other words, the policy cycle shifts attention from the making of difficult decisions to the administrative processes that take place after such decisions have been made.

Advocates of the idea of a policy cycle appear to have retreated in the face of such criticisms. Typically, they now describe the policy cycle not as a theory of the nature of the policy cycle but as a set of flexible, pragmatic concepts that can help policy-makers. In this view, the idea of a policy cycle offers a framework for thinking about policies in terms of phases. It provides a conceptual map by which practitioners can navigate the dizzying world of policy-making. It encourages policy-makers to break down their engagement with a policy into discrete segments so that they will then find it easier to analyze. It provides them with a set of concepts that facilitates more systematic thinking about a policy.

CROSS REFERENCES

Dialogic policy-making, Evidence-based policy, Implementation, Incrementalism

FURTHER READING

Bridgman, P. and Davis, G. (2003) 'What Use is the Policy Cycle? Plenty, if the Aim is Clear', *Australian Journal of Public Administration*, 68: 98–102.

Everett, S. (2003) 'The Policy Cycle: Democratic Process or Rational Paradigm Revisited?', *Australian Journal of Public Administration*, 62: 65–70.

Jones, C.O. (1970) *An Introduction to the Study of Public Policy*. Belmont, CA: Duxbury Press.

May, J. and Wildavsky, A. (1978) *The Policy Cycle*. Beverly Hills, CA: Sage.

Policy Network

DEFINITION

Policy networks consist of governmental and societal actors whose interactions with one another give rise to policies. Typically, these actors are linked through informal practices as well as, or even instead of, formal institutions. The actors are interdependent; they can secure the desired outcomes only by collaborating with each other.

Policy networks can vary widely. At one extreme lie policy communities. Policy communities have a limited number of participant groups, with some groups being excluded. The participants share broad values, beliefs, and preferences. They meet frequently, and they all interact closely on any topic related to the policy area. All of them have significant resources, so their interactions consist of institutionalized forms of negotiation and bargaining. They are usually organized hierarchically so the leaders can secure the acquiescence of the members in whatever policies are agreed upon. At the other extreme lie issue networks. Issue networks generally have far more participants. The participants disagree with one another, so conflict, not consensus, is the norm. They have unequal levels of power and varying degrees of access, so their interactions are often primarily consultative.

CONTEXT

Concepts such as policy network and policy community are part of a broader research program of network analysis, which can be found throughout the social sciences. Network analysis has been used to discuss diverse phenomena, including the information revolution, technological innovation, and urban villages. Policy network analysis is the species of network analysis most relevant to governance. It emphasizes how networks decide which issues will be included and excluded from the policy agenda, shape the behavior of actors, privilege certain interests, and substitute private forms of government for public accountability.

Accounts of governance often concentrate on policy networks. Governance has been described as rule by and through networks. Governance here describes the pattern of rule that arises from the interactions of multiple organizations in networks. Many commentators argue that this pattern of rule has appeared, or at least become far more widespread, in recent times. In this view, the main organization of the state has changed from hierarchy – the bureaucracies of the traditional welfare state – and perhaps markets – the reforms of the New Right – to a contemporary era of networks. The state has become increasingly dependent on other actors; it can get its way only through negotiations with other actors in all sorts of networks.

The concept of governance as networks draws on themes from the earlier literature on policy networks. One such theme is networks as inter-organizational analysis. The literature on inter-organizational analysis emphasizes the structural relationship between political institutions as opposed to the interpersonal relations between individuals within those institutions. These structural relations are taken to be the crucial element in any policy network. The focal organization of the network tries to manage the more dependent organizations using diverse strategies, while the other organizations use similar strategies to attempt to manage each other and the focal one. A network consists, therefore, of numerous over-lapping relationships, each of which depends on the others. This concept of an inter-organizational network has been used to describe and analyze interactions among diverse political actors, including parties, ministries, unions, business associations, and interest groups.

The concept of governance as networks also draws on earlier studies of networks as interest intermediation. The literature on interest intermediation is part of a broader pluralist tradition that paid much attention to sub-governments. Pluralists disaggregated the study of policy-making into subsystems within which bureaucrats, legislators and their staff, and the representatives of interest groups, all interacted with one another. These clusters of individuals were said to make the routine decisions in any given area of policy. Typically, the pluralists concentrated on a few elite groups who had especially close ties to government and who often excluded other groups from access. In this view, the government confronts innumerable interest groups. Some groups are considered to be extreme and unrealistic; they are kept away from the policy process. Others are deemed significant and responsible; they become insiders upon whom government relies to ensure its policies work appropriately. Over time the interactions between government and the insiders become institutionalized. An 'iron triangle' develops between the central agency, the legislative committee, and the elite interest group: they develop an almost symbiotic relationship to one another.

Although concepts of governance draw on the earlier literature on policy networks, they also transform important aspects of this literature. Earlier studies of policy networks typically concentrated on analyzing relations of power around the central state. Concepts of governance, in contrast, often evoke a decline in the power of the central state. Accounts of governance usually focus on the boundary between state and civil society rather than on policy-making in specific areas. They explore the increasing diffusion of state power and authority. Similarly, concepts of governance often invoke international factors that contributed to the decline in the power of the central state. Whereas earlier studies of policy networks concentrated most commonly on policy-making in national policy sectors, concepts of governance are more likely to point outward to transnational networks.

DEBATE

There has been considerable debate about policy network analysis. Some critics complain that the concept of a network is little more than a metaphorical description; it does not do explanatory work. At times, they also complain that the approach fails adequately to specify causal relationships between the characteristics of a network and policy outcomes; it lacks, in particular, a micro-theory capable of accounting for change over time. We might distinguish four approaches to network theory, each of which offers a different response to such criticisms: power dependence, rational choice, dialectical, and decenterd.

The power dependence approach unpacks policy networks as made up of resource-dependent organizations. Their relationships are such that any organization depends on others for resources that they thus have to exchange to achieve their goals. Each organization within the network deploys its resources, whether these be financial, political, or informational, in order to maximize its influence on outcomes. Although one might suggest that the relationships between organizations thus resemble a game rooted in trust and regulated by rules, advocates of the power dependence approach rarely explain outcomes by reference to rational behavior within a game. Instead, they explain differences in outcomes in a network and variations between networks by reference to, say, the distribution of resources and the bargaining skills of participants.

Rational choice approaches to policy networks have flourished, particularly in the work of Renate Mayntz, Fritz Scharpf, and their colleagues. Scharpf explains how policy networks operate in terms of an actor-centerd institutionalism that combines rational choice with the new institutionalism. Networks are institutional settings in which public and private actors interact. They consist of rules that structure the opportunities for actors to realize their preferences. Actors adopt strategies in order to maximize their satisfaction and their resources within the context of such rules. It is arguable that this rational choice approach differs from the power dependence approach mainly in the extent to which it uses formal game theory to analyze and explain rule-governed networks.

Advocates of a dialectical approach to policy networks oppose the methodological individualism associated with the rational choice one. They argue that network structures and the agents within them have a mutually determining effect upon one another. At the micro-level, networks comprise strategically calculating subjects whose actions shape network characteristics and policy outcomes. However, the beliefs and interests of these actors are products of the macro-level nature of the relevant networks and their contexts. These macro-level factors are understood, in turn, to be ones of power and structure – terms that often carry a Marxist echo – rather than rules of a neutral game.

Decenterd theory shifts the attention to the social construction of policy networks. It eschews the search for generality, correlations, and models found among the other approaches. Policy networks are seen as the contingent products of the actions of diverse individuals, where these individuals might act on very different beliefs and understandings informed by conflicting traditions. At the micro-level, we can explore networks in terms of the behavior of a host of everyday makers – citizens and junior public servants as well as politicians, senior bureaucrats, and members of interest groups. At an aggregate level, we can explain the behavior of clusters of everyday makers by reference to the traditions and dilemmas that inform their webs of belief. Change within networks arises because people change their patterns of action in response to various dilemmas.

Ironically, the study of policy networks has contributed to the transformation of contemporary governance. Some policy actors, convinced by those who sing the praises of networks, actively promote networks and partnerships within the public sector. A faith in the virtues of networks has inspired programs of holistic, joined-up, and whole-of-government approaches, for example, in Australia, Canada, and the UK. Public sector bodies are expected to collaborate within quality networks so as to better deliver services and tackle problems that cut across traditional functional divisions. They are also supposed to form partnerships with private and voluntary bodies to gain access to resources and to encourage greater diversity and flexibility in the delivery of policies.

CROSS REFERENCES

Differentiated polity, Managing networks, Network

FURTHER READING

Marin, B. and Mayntz, R. (eds) (1991) *Policy Networks: Empirical Evidence and Theoretical Considerations*. Frankfurt am Main: Campus Verlag.

Marsh, D. (ed.) (1998) *Comparing Policy Networks*. Buckingham: Open University Press.

Rhodes, R.A.W. (1997) *Understanding Governance: Policy Networks, Governance, Reflexivity and Accountability*. Buckingham: Open University Press.

Scharpf, F. (1997) *Games Real Actors Play: Actor-centered Institutionalism in Policy Research*. Boulder, CO: Westview Press.

Public–Private Partnerships

DEFINITION

Public–private partnerships (PPPs) are relationships between governing institutions and private or voluntary entities. They allocate the burdens of providing resources and taking risks in the provision of public goods and services. They also allocate the rewards to be gained from the provision of these goods and services. PPPs have proved most popular as ways of providing the public with highly complex services or with services that require substantial capital investment. Yet, far from being limited to business ventures, they are found in education, health, transport, technology, and other policy sectors.

Theoretical discussions of PPPs suggest that each actor will provide a particular resource or ability. Advocates suggest, in particular, that they combine the strengths of the private and public sectors. In this view, PPPs bring together the political access and long-term stability found in the public sector with the entrepreneurial creativity and ability to raise capital found in the private sector.

CONTEXT

One problem in exploring PPPs is the vagueness of the concept of 'partnership'. At a very general level, almost any kind of relationship might be described as a partnership. Typically, however, PPPs are understood more narrowly as a contractual relationship. Yet even this narrow definition would mean that the forms of contracting-out that arose along with marketization and the New Public Management would count as PPPs. So, more narrowly still, we might thus say that a PPP is a contractual relationship in which the relevant public and private agencies agree to fairly stable long-term links so as to fulfil a social purpose in a way that also profits the private agency. Alternatively, we might simply distinguish between collaborative and substantive partnerships. Substantive partnerships occur when the private agency more or less replaces the public one: they include many of the arrangements established through marketization. Collaborative partnerships, in contrast, occur when both the public and private agencies perform active functions. Finally, we might point out here that the archetypal PPP is one in which the private agency agrees to provide capital or to run a service in return for some sort of share in the profits thereby generated.

While PPPs have spread recently as part of the new governance, with its shift from hierarchy to markets and networks, various forms of partnerships between the public and private sectors are anything but new. Such partnerships have existed since at least the middle of the seventeenth century. At that time they were used to finance and maintain infrastructure projects. An early example was the creation of the Canal de Briare in 1638. By the eighteenth century, the French state was using such partnerships extensively to build infrastructure for water, sanitation, and other public needs.

Contemporary PPPs flourished in the late 1980s in both developed and developing states. There are, of course, a range of reasons for their rise, varying across states and sectors. Many observers agree, however, that PPPs possess a flexibility that makes them particularly suited to the new governance. In this view, public problems are increasingly complex, involving qualitative differentiation on particular occasions and also requiring the joining-up of various agencies. Hence public administration needs to make more use than it did before of horizontal agreements between diverse actors. So, if joined-up governance promotes horizontal agreements between different state agencies, PPPs represent similar agreements between public agencies and other actors.

A prominent subset of PPPs is Private Finance Initiatives (PFIs). PFIs try to deliver the policy goals of governments while transferring the capital costs to the private sector. Private companies provide the capital finance for a public project. In return, the government grants the private company at least some sort of temporary share in the ownership or rents associated with the project upon its completion. The government thus gets access to capital without having to raise taxes. The private company gets to make a profit, usually with government protection, by charging citizens or public sector groups for access to goods or services. PFIs have spread rapidly recently: in the UK, they accounted for over £12 billion of the capital works contracts signed in the first two years of the New Labor governments.

DEBATE

Public–private partnerships are, not surprisingly, extremely contentious. To some they are a panacea. To others they are a necessary evil. To yet others they are a threat to public virtues. And, of course, there are plenty of social scientists who want to examine their effectiveness in particular contexts or within particular sectors of the economy.

Most advocates of PPPs argue that they bring gains of efficiency. Others argue that they are simply necessary to provide the capital for public projects in an age when taxpayers appear increasingly reluctant to do so. Some advocates of PPPs also claim that involving more private actors in the policy creation realm creates a more transparent form of governance.

A more pragmatic approach to PPPs attempts to assess their success within specific sectors of the economy or social life. This approach typically leads to an emphasis on the widespread acceptance of PPPs as ways of developing roads, railways, and other transport infrastructure. The apparent success of PPPs in this area stands in contrast with the uncertainty and hostility that often surrounds them in areas such as national and international health partnerships. Yet, this pragmatic approach misses the point in so far as it tries to turn what should be a debate about public values and goods into a more technocratic one. Critics point out, for example, that there are immense difficulties in defining, let alone measuring, what we mean by success when we talk about PPPs. Should a viable concept of success try to accommodate values such as social justice as well as measures of public approval, capitalization, and profitability?

Certainly, much of the most heated opposition to PPPs derives from suspicions that the increasing role of the private sector in governance is a threat to public values such as accountability and fairness. Some critics fear that the PPPs are likely to evolve into longer-term partnerships or even act as a pathway to privatization of the relevant public enterprises. PPPs might be the beginnings of private sector expansion in all kinds of public activities.

CROSS REFERENCES

Enabling state, Marketization, New Public Management, Network

FURTHER READING

Bouvaird, T. (2004) 'Public–Private Partnerships: From Contested Concepts to Prevalent Practice', *International Review of Administrative Science*, 70: 199–215.

Brinkerhoff, D.W. and Brinkerhoff, J.M. (2004) 'Partnerships Between International Donors and Non-governmental Development Organisations: Opportunities and Constraints', *International Review of Administrative Science*, 70: 253–270.

Bull, B. and McNeill, D. (2007) *Development Issues in Global Governance: Public–Private Partnerships and Market Multilateralism*. New York: Routledge.

Grimsey, D. and Lewis, M.K. (2005) *The Economics of Private Public Partnerships*. Cheltenham: Edward Elgar.

Rational Choice Theory

DEFINITION

Rational choice theory deduces models of social life from the assumption that individuals act to maximize the satisfaction of their personal preferences. Although it is sometimes called the economic approach to politics, and also draws heavily on the neoclassical approach to micro-economics, it also makes extensive use of decision theory and game theory.

The exact nature of the assumptions made by rational choice theory remains a matter of discussion. The most important discussion is perhaps over whether or not rational choice theory assumes that people are selfish. Critics sometimes suggest it does. Technically, however, rational choice theory is agnostic over the content of people's preferences: it assumes that people act rationally in accordance with whatever preferences they have, and it deduces the content of their preferences as being revealed by their actions. Nonetheless, although rational choice does not technically assume that people are self-interested, its exponents are generally unable to apply their models to real-world situations without assuming that the people have certain preferences, and at this point they do tend rather blithely to assume that people are selfishly concerned with their own wealth, status, and power.

CONTEXT

Rational choice theory offers one of the leading ways of thinking about social coordination in general and about the new governance in particular. At a very general level, rational choice theorists often try to explain the stability of social and political coordination and cooperation, given that their theory seems to imply that individuals will break up such stability as soon as it is in their interests so to do. One explanation is that the state or another authority creates incentives and disincentives such that individuals have an interest in sustaining a stable order. But this explanation leaves unanswered the question of how orders remain stable in the absence of any higher authority, and so the question of how a higher authority could arise in the first place. Hence rational choice theorists often discuss issues of governance in abstract terms. They hope to reconcile self-interest, the existence of coordination, and the absence of any enforcement mechanism.

In more concrete terms, rational choice theory has been applied to the changing nature of contemporary governance. There are, for example, rational choice models of the ways in which bureaucrats influence the process of public sector reform. Some rational choice theorists adopt a budget maximization model. They assume that bureaucrats increase their status and salary by maximizing the budget and size of their departments. They conclude that bureaucrats try to expand their departments even if there is no good reason for them to do so. Other rational choice theorists adopt a bureau-shaping model. They assume that bureaucrats are less interested in increasing the size of their budget than in their own career paths: bureaucrats seek an appropriate rank within a suitable department, and they try to shape their department to increase their role within it, and, more especially, to secure interesting work. In this view, bureaucrats will be willing to accept budget cuts and downsizing of their department if they thereby can shape that department to advance their individual career goals. Rational choice theorists argue about the rival merits of these models in part in terms of their explanatory power when applied to changes in governance. The bureau-shaping model seems better able to explain why some bureaucrats might support the shift from government to governance: bureaucrats might accept the contracting-out of their functions and cuts in their budgets if they were consequently able to focus on activities of more interest and higher status.

DEBATE

As we have seen, there are debates about the nature of the assumptions made by rational choice theory. The ideal case for rational choice theory would perhaps be one that exhibited the following three characteristics. First, the individual agent would know the outcome of each action that she might perform; the outcome of an action would not depend on how others act. Second, the agent would have a clear rank order of preferences among the various outcomes: she would know that she preferred one to another or that she was indifferent between them. Third, the agent's preferences would be transitive: if she prefers outcome A to an alternative outcome B, and if she prefers B to another alternative, C, she necessarily prefers A to C. If these three characteristics are present, then the agent acts rationally if she seeks the outcome she prefers (or if there is a tie, one of the outcomes she prefers).

Many of the debates or developments within rational choice theory have been about relaxing the characteristics exhibited by the ideal case. The most important of these developments is the rise of game theory. Game theory applies where there is strategic interdependence among agents, that is, where an agent's behavior affects what is the best choice for another agent and vice versa. A more contentious development is the rise of concepts such as bounded rationality and procedural rationality. These concepts arise from recognition that agents have limited information, time, and cognitive capacity. As a result, the argument continues, agents typically rely on relatively simple heuristic devices to make decisions on how to act. Perhaps agents are not maximizers so much as satisficers: perhaps individuals do not select the actions that best accord with their preferences so much as the first action they think of that leads to a satisfactory outcome. Although game theory and concepts of procedural rationality relax the first two characteristics of the ideal case for rational choice theorists, it is sometimes difficult to imagine how rational choice theory might proceed in the absence of some sort of an assumption about the transitive nature of preferences.

Criticisms of rational choice theory generally challenge its assumptions of individualism, rationality, and selfishness. Sociological critics reject individualism on the grounds that individuals are largely the product of social structures. Some of them even argue that actions can only be rational relative to particular systems of meaning or sets of values. In their view, people do not act in accordance with their selfish self-interests but in ways that reflect their socialization and so their adherence to social norms and ideologies. Psychological critics of rational choice theory might reject individualism on the grounds of group memory or instinct. More often, however, they concentrate their critique on the idea that we are rational: they point to the role that the unconscious plays in determining human action. Many of them argue that people are motivated not only, or even mainly, by self-interest, but by a range of emotions, including envy, altruism, revenge, and love.

CROSS REFERENCES

Collective action problem, Market, New Public Management

FURTHER READING

Amadae, S. (2003) *Rationalizing Capitalist Democracy: The Cold War Origins of Rational Choice Liberalism*. Chicago: Chicago University Press.

Friedman, J. (ed.) (1996) *The Rational Choice Controversy*. New Haven, CT: Yale University Press.

Fudenberg, D. and Tirole, J. (1991) *Game Theory*. Cambridge, MA: MIT Press.

MacLean, I. (1987) *Public Choice*. Oxford: Blackwell.

Monroe, K. (ed.) (1991) *The Economic Approach to Politics: A Critical Reassessment of the Theory of Rational Action*. New York: Harper Collins.

Regionalism

DEFINITION

Regionalism means somewhat different things in the contexts of domestic and international politics. Within a state, regionalism refers to a process in which sub-state actors become increasingly powerful and independent of the state: power devolves from the central state to regional governments within it. Sub-state regionalism thus overlaps somewhat with the processes discussed under the entry in this book on decentralization. This entry, in contrast, will consider regionalism in international politics. At the international level, regionalism refers to transnational cooperation to achieve a common goal or resolve a shared problem.

Sometimes regionalism is defined more narrowly as transnational cooperation among states rather than other actors. This narrower definition implies a distinction between regionalism and the related process of regionalization. Regionalism is a top-down process in which states cooperate. Regionalization is, in contrast, a bottom-up process in which private and voluntary sector actors pursue transnational cooperation. Relevant sub-state actors include multinational corporations, non-governmental organizations, and civil society groups. In practice, of course, regionalism and regionalization often follow similar paths and even overlap. Nonetheless, we can identify key examples of each. Examples of regionalism are state-based groups such as the Association of Southeast Asian Nations (ASEAN), the European Union, or the North American Free Trade Association (NAFTA). Examples of regionalization include non-governmental organizations and civil society groups, such as the Caribbean Conservation Association or the Asian Human Rights Commission.

CONTEXT

The development of regionalism is often divided into two waves. The first wave arose in the 1950s during the Cold War. It gave rise to the 'old regionalism'. The second wave arose in the late 1980s and early 1990s at the end of the Cold War. It gave rise to a 'new regionalism'.

The old regionalism reflected the global balance of power during the Cold War. This bipolar power arrangement limited the number of regional organizations, their scope, and the number of members they contained. The USA and USSR, as the dominant superpowers, shaped the goals of regional organizations, especially regional security alliances such as the Warsaw Pact and the North Atlantic Treaty Organization. Hence discussions of regional governance tended to concern the role of the superpowers as leaders.

Old regional organizations were characteristically closed. They were formed specifically for the interests of their members. Hence these regional organizations generally opposed moves towards globalization. In this closed regionalism, the members of regional organizations often granted one another trade concessions that were not extended to other states. Examples included free trade areas, which lower trade barriers among members, and customs unions, which lower trade barriers and also coordinate external tariffs among members. Developing states combined this closed regionalism with a developmental strategy called import substitution industrialization. Regional governance was intended to keep exports out of the region so as to encourage the rise of domestic companies manufacturing the relevant commodities. Import substitution suggested that states should thus replace the goods it imported with domestically-produced alternatives.

Regionalism declined in the 1970s only to re-emerge in the 1980s and 1990s. This second wave, or new regionalism, overlapped with several other changes in world politics. The changes included:

- The end of the Cold War and a shift from a bipolar balance of power.
- A decline in the Westphalian state system (see the entry on sovereignty).
- The apparent instability of the General Agreement on Tariffs and Trade (GATT) trading regime and the consequent formation of regional economic organizations like NAFTA.
- The rise of neoliberalism and, with it, the turn to export-oriented development strategies.

These changes, notably the decline of the bipolar balance of power, gave regional organizations greater scope. A new regionalism arose in which regional organizations tackled more diverse issues than had their predecessors. The new regionalism moved from a focus on economics and security to encompass environmental and social issues. Similarly, the absence of dominant superpowers gave more power to the members of regional organizations. The new regionalism involves more extensive negotiations and bargaining among a wider number of states. Finally, the new region-alism is usually described as open rather than closed. The interests of regional organizations extend beyond their members. Moves towards trade liberalization have replaced the protectionism evident in first-wave regionalism. Examples include the Asia Pacific Economic Cooperation Forum (APEC) and the Mercado Común del Sur (Mercosur).

The open nature of the new regionalism is less antagonistic to global-ization. Whereas the old regionalism can be seen as directly opposing the aims of globalization and global integration, the new regionalism has been framed as a dual response to the pressures of globalization. Regional organizations now both promote globalization and mitigate some of its undesirable effects. On the one hand, the new regionalism can advance globalization in that it promotes greater trade and the formation of cross-national production networks. On the other hand, regional organizations can still sometimes insulate member states from aspects of globalization – currency blocs help to stop fluctuations in the values of particular cur-rencies, trading agreements can protect particular industries, and so on. Hence the new regionalism has been seen as both a building block of the new global economy and a possible source of protectionism.

DEBATE

The main debates about the new regionalism concern its overall shape and how it is to be explained. Accounts of the shape of the new region-alism often emphasize meso-regionalism or a north–south regionalism. Meso-regions are 'regions within regions'. They are sub-regions of a larger regional, geographic entity. Examples of meso-regions include ASEAN as a sub-region of Asia and Mercosur as a sub-region of the Americas. Meso-regions may be transitory steps in the formation of a larger regional orga-nization, perhaps incorporating all of Asia or all the Americas. Equally, however, they can be identity markers that are established by the con-stituent states in order to distinguish them from the larger region.

North–south regionalism revolves around the creation of regional agreements between developed and developing states. These agreements spread rapidly in the late 1980s, notably as multinational corporations extended their production networks across state borders. Developing nations see the agreements as an export-oriented strategy of develop-ment, for the agreements typically give them preferential access to the markets of a developed state. Equally, developed states generally hope thereby to bind the economic elite of the developing state to them. The agreements also typically allow the developed states to press their preferred regulatory and legal structures onto their developing partners.

Let us turn now to some of the main ways of explaining regionalism: neo-functionalism, institutionalism, and neo-realism. Neo-functionalism spreads mainly as an account of the old regionalism. For neo-functionalists, regional organizations arise to satisfy the functional needs of the states involved in them. Yet neo-functionalists also suggest that the functional needs of an organization can become the functional needs of its constituents. In other words, national values and interests are redefined as the values and interests of the entire region. The concept of spillover plays a significant role here. For neo-functionalists, regionalism develops through the spillover effects from the economic sector to other sectors. As the economies of countries became more closely linked, so there is a spillover from the economic sector to other sectors, such as the governmental and military.

Some new institutionalists explain regionalism as a means of lowering the transaction costs of cooperative action. Regional institutions help constituent members to develop the trust in each other that they need to solve various collective action problems. When states work together in a transparent fashion, they lessen the chances of individual states 'cheating' or not fulfilling their mutual obligations. Hence states form regional institutions to reduce the possibility of such cheating and thereby enable them to work together for mutual gains.

Neo-realists typically analyze regionalism in terms of states' attempts to make relative gains over issues of security. In this view, the success of regional institutions depends on their ability to mitigate the uneven distribution of relative gains. If a state stands to gain less from joining a regional organization than do others, then it is unlikely to join. Hence regionalism has prospered as the potential gains it offers have been evened out among states.

CROSS REFERENCES

Global governance, Globalization, Multilevel governance, Transnationalism

FURTHER READING

Gamble, A. and Paine, A. (eds) (1996) *Regionalism and World Order*. Basingstoke: Macmillan.

Hettne, B., Inotai, A. and Sunkel, O. (eds) (1999) *Globalism and the New Regionalism*. Basingstoke: Macmillan.

Mansfield, E. and Milner, H.V. (eds) (1997) *The Political Economy of Regionalism*. New York: Columbia University Press.

Mattli, W. (1999) *The Logic of Regional Integration: Europe and Beyond*. Cambridge: Cambridge University Press.

Regulation

DEFINITION

Regulation refers to the state's attempts to monitor (and thus direct) conduct. It gives rise to rules that structure the behavior of individuals and groups in a state's domain. As we will see, some observers believe that the new governance has brought the rise of a new regulatory state and perhaps also a new emphasis on self-regulation.

The term 'regulation' appears in various contexts. Nonetheless, most uses of the term share a common structure: a subject (e.g. the state or a specialized agency) regulates an object (e.g. the economy, firms, or citizens) by means of certain instruments (e.g. laws or norms). In political economy, the state can impose specific rules to govern the micro-level conduct of firms and individuals, or, alternatively, the state can make broad adjustments to macro-level policy instruments such as taxation and interest rates. In public policy, the state can promulgate targets or rules in an attempt to ensure policy actors conduct themselves in certain ways or move towards certain goals. In the social sciences, regulation may refer to any kind of social control, including the effects of public policies and also social norms.

CONTEXT

The crisis of the state in the late twentieth century encompassed the then-leading styles of regulation. Worries about state overload and inefficient bureaucracies eroded faith in state control.

Neoliberals tried to roll back the state, restricting its regulatory presence in the economy. They promoted not only privatization but also liberalization. To some extent the result was a deregulation of large parts of the market economy, most notably including financial services. Yet, even neoliberals often wanted the state to be able to steer these deregulated bits of the economy or at least to oversee them so as to prevent market failures and abuses. Hence the state set up a range of new regulatory authorities to govern sectors such as finance, transport, and telecommunications.

Neoliberals also promoted public sector reforms such as marketization. They wanted the state to concentrate on steering not rowing. Other organizations should take on some of the functions of the state. The state should then set general policy goals and oversee these other organizations. Public services that had been provided by the state itself were contracted-out to non-governmental organizations. Hence the state set up all kinds of regulatory mechanisms to oversee these non-governmental organizations.

The result of neoliberal reforms was thus the rise of a complex network of regulatory authorities and mechanisms as an alternative to older, more hierarchical forms of state control. Some commentators evoke the concept of a regulatory state to refer to this shift towards indirect modes of state steering. Many developed states have set up all kinds of new regulatory agencies and mechanisms. The states only have direct control over the regulatory agencies, leaving them to oversee individuals and corporate groups.

Regulatory agencies have also become more common in international politics. In this case, however, the motivation appears to have been less to roll back the state than to try to gain some control over exploding transnational interactions. States often respond to the dilemmas of globalization by setting up new suprastate regulatory agencies. These regional and international regulatory bodies characteristically operate without a single unitary subject of regulation, such as the state is often thought to be. The European Union (EU) provides many examples. The EU relies on agreements among its member states to steer in all kinds of sectors, including e-commerce and telecommunications.

Even as the new regimes of regulation appeared within and across states, so their limitations became clear. Some social scientists argue that regulatory agencies compete for governmental resources to augment their size and power beyond the socially optimal point. In their view, regulatory agencies thus use more resources than necessary, which makes a mockery of the idea that they promote efficiency. These kinds of views help to explain the trend of self-regulation.

Self-regulation occurs when those to whom regulations apply are also responsible for devising, maintaining, and enforcing the regulations. It generally refers, therefore, to non-governmental regulations established by voluntary and private sector actors, often as an alternative to governmental regulations. Chemical firms across the world have set up, for example, a Responsible Care Initiative, under which they agree voluntarily to abide by certain standards for emissions and operations. Similar cases of self-regulation appear to have become increasingly prevalent – perhaps because of rising public discontent with the perceived limitations of state regulation.

DEBATE

Does regulation serve the public interest or private interests? Economists used to envisage regulation as a governmental attempt to promote the public interest in cases of market failures or market abuses. They argued that state regulation might be necessary to address problems such as monopolies, externalities, transaction costs, and asymmetric information. However, other economists now warn that regulation itself can exacerbate these market failures and so become self-defeating. The Chicago School particularly challenged the older view of regulation. It explained regulation not in terms of the public interest but in terms of the self-interest of the relevant policy actors. In this view, regulatory policies emerge from competition among interest groups seeking their own advantage. The winners of this competition are the groups which can align their interests with those of the politicians and public officials involved in the process. Hence, far from protecting the public interest, regulation is an expression of the rent-seeking activities of various groups and individuals.

Is the regulatory state a new form of state? Those who argue that it is typically claim that the extent, responsibilities, and power of regulatory agencies have increased dramatically, and, as a consequence, the state now has considerably less power than it once did. Those who argue that the regulatory state is not a new form of state typically respond by arguing that the areas of policy in which the state has given up direct control are less important than those over which they retain direct control, so the rise of new regulatory agencies has not altered the fundamental relationship between the state and its citizens.

What are the implications of the regulatory state for democracy? Critics of the rise of regulatory agencies worry that the public officials who head them are often unelected. These officials do not represent the people. In many cases, they are not even answerable to the people. Some critics even suggest that the rise of the regulatory state, and the rise of transnational links among regulatory officials, means that policies are being made by all kinds of networks of unelected technocrats. Other commentators are more sanguine. They point out that most regulators are themselves appointed by democratically elected governments, to whom they are then accountable.

How can regulation be made effective? Regulatory enforcement can rely on either deterrence or persuasion. Deterrence is rule-bound. It relies on formal punitive measures, such as fines and criminal prosecutions, to deal with disobedience and deter others from disobeying. Persuasion focuses on education and negotiation. Its advocates believe that the regulators should hold meetings and discussions with the groups or individuals whom the regulations affect. These meetings facilitate exchanges of information. They improve the content and implementation of regulations, and they make disobedience less likely. Yet, critics still worry that such meetings will favor insider groups rather than reflecting all the interests involved. There is even a danger of regulatory agencies being captured by the very actors they are meant to be overseeing. Some social scientists have suggested that the most effective regulation should balance deterrence and persuasion, perhaps in accordance with the level of resistance in the regulated domain. Perhaps it really is the mix that matters.

CROSS REFERENCES

Enabling state, Managing networks, Metagovernance

FURTHER READING

Baldwin, R., Scott, C. and Hood, C. (eds) (1998) *A Reader on Regulation*. Oxford: Oxford University Press.

Jordana, J. and Levi-Faur, D. (eds) (2004) *The Politics of Regulation: Institutions and Regulatory Reforms for the Age of Governance*. Cheltenham: Edward Elgar.

Majone, G. (1996) *Regulating Europe*. London: Routledge.

Moran, M. (2003) *The British Regulatory State: High Modernism and Hyper-innovation*. Oxford: Oxford University Press.

key concepts in governance

Regulation Theory

DEFINITION

Regulation theory is a Marxist approach to political economy. It examines how particular forms of capitalism achieve a temporary stability. Karl Marx famously argued that capitalism was inherently unstable: first, because it led to over-accumulation of capital and so periodic crises, and, second, because it generated an unstable set of social relations that resulted in class struggle. These instabilities would result, Marx added, in a working-class revolution to establish a communist society. Regulation theory focuses on the ways in which material, institutional, policy-driven, and discursive supports allow capitalism to 'regulate' its instabilities in order to ward off revolution.

The concern with the temporary stability of capitalism leads regulation theorists to explore its varieties across time and space. Several regulation theorists identified a Fordist variety of capitalism, associated with Keynesian economic policies and a welfare state, which had achieved a temporary stability for much of the twentieth century. Yet, from the late 1970s, Fordism and the Keynesian welfare state came under attack from the neoliberals of the New Right. The rise of neoliberalism coincided with the introduction of the New Public Management, and, more broadly, with the rise of the new governance. Regulation theorists were among the most prominent Marxists to explore these changes in society and the state. Typically, they explained the rise of the new governance as part of a shift from a Fordist to a post-Fordist form of capitalism.

CONTEXT

Marx himself had different views of the prospects for revolution at different times in his life. Up until the end of the First World War, however, Marxists commonly believed that the workers' revolution would come soon. The prospects for revolution looked far bleaker by the 1920s. The call to war had found the workers not uniting to overthrow capitalism but rallying to nationalist causes. Even the Russian revolution had failed to spark similar uprisings in the more advanced economies of Western Europe.

Much twentieth-century Marxism can be read as an attempt to explain the absence of revolution and the persistence of capitalism. One well-known explanation came from Antonio Gramsci, an Italian Marxist imprisoned under Mussolini. Gramsci argued that the bourgeoisie had established an ideological hegemony; the bourgeoisie had propagated an ideology that dominated throughout society and that lent a spurious legitimacy to the capitalist social order. Although the concept of hegemony certainly offered one way of explaining the persistence of capitalism, it did so by emphasizing the role of culture and ideas – an emphasis that inspires the critical and Marxist strains in interpretive theories of governance – in a way that broke somewhat with the more orthodox, economic strands of Marxist thought. Regulation theory tried to explain the persistence of capitalism in terms closer to Marx's economic writings.

The earliest exponents of regulation theory are called the New French School, or more commonly the Parisian School. They explained the temporary stability of various types of capitalism primarily in terms of economic institutions. Their emphasis on such institutions explains why their work is often described in relation to other institutionalist challenges to neoclassical economics. Yet, their institutionalism remained firmly located within a Marxist theory, according to which capitalism inherently suffered from unstable development (crises of over-accumulation) and social relations (class struggle). Hence they concentrated on the ways in which institutional arrangements managed to persist in spite of such instabilities.

The main institutional arrangements studied by the Parisian School were regimes of accumulation and regimes of regulation. As a rough but oversimplifying rule, we might say that regimes of accumulation do most to mask the instabilities associated with the over-accumulation of capital, while regimes of regulation do most to mask the instabilities associated with the class struggle. A regime of accumulation refers to the institutions or regularities that facilitate a stable and proportional distribution of capital across departments of production. It includes norms for the organization of work and production, the relationship between branches of the economy, modes of industrial and commercial management, and the norms that govern the division of income between wages, profits, and taxation. The regime of regulation refers to the legal and political institutions that enable capitalist societies, and so regimes of accumulation, to persist over time. It includes laws, industrial codes, styles of negotiation, state policies, political practices, and patterns of consumption.

DEBATE

Regulation theory seeks to analyze the different ways in which the tendencies to crisis inherent in capitalism are managed by the historically specific types of capitalism. It does so by describing the different regimes of accumulation and modes of regulation, and by examining the social embedding of economic institutions through extra-economic factors. In general terms, regulation theory explores governance and patterns of rule within capitalist society by exploring their role within a general system for dealing with over-accumulation and the class struggle. In addition, because regulation pays attention to different types of capitalism, it offers a framework within which to discuss the rise of the new governance. Regulation theorists typically view the rise of the new governance as part of a broad shift from a Fordist form of capitalism to a post-Fordist (and arguably neoliberal) one.

Fordism gets its name from the methods of mass production and the rules of management that were pioneered by Henry Ford in his car factories during the 1920s and 1930s. Regulation theorists use Fordism to refer to a combination of an intensive regime of accumulation with a monopolistic mode of regulation. This combination lay behind the temporary stability of western capitalism, with its Keynesian welfare state, up until the mid to late 1970s. The intensive regime of accumulation comprised mass production, the intensificaton of work, semi-skilled labor, a detailed division of tasks, and increasing mechanization. The monopolistic regulation embraced the separation of ownership and control, monopoly pricing, the recognition of trade unions, wages being indexed to growth in productivity, the use of Keynesian policies to secure aggregate demand, and standardized consumption of mass-produced commodities. Regulation theorists argue that intensive accumulation and monopolistic regulation created something akin to a virtuous circle. Mass production brought economies of scale and so rising productivity and increased wages. Rising wages led to increased demand and so a fuller utilization of capacity and greater profits. Rising profits then led to the new investment in technologies of mass production needed to start the cycle again.

According to regulation theorists, neoliberalism and new patterns of governance arose when the inherent instabilities of capitalism finally disrupted the temporary stability created by Fordism. We might distinguish here between several different but compatible explanations for the end of Fordism. Some regulation theorists argue that productivity gains declined because of both social limits (e.g. worker resistance) and technical limits (e.g. the difficulties of balancing ever longer lines of production). Others argue that the expansion of production led to increased global economic flows and thereby undermined the ability of the state to regulate its national economy. Yet others argue that Fordism relied on ever-greater state expenditure, which led to inflation and overload. The demise of Fordism, whatever its cause, entailed a whole social formation; it was the end of mass production, large industrial complexes, blue-collar work, full employment, mass markets for standardized goods, mass political parties, the nation state, and, crucially for our purposes, centralized and bureaucratic management systems.

Regulation theorists have often been reluctant to engage in prediction. They did not claim to be able to predict what regimes of accumulation and regulation would arise in the post-Fordist era. In recent years, however, several regulation theorists have begun to suggest that neoliberalism itself has developed a kind of temporary stability. In this view, the new governance of markets and networks presumably acts as a way for the state and other actors to collectively manage capital overaccumulation and the class struggle.

CROSS REFERENCES

Institutionalism, Regulation, State

FURTHER READING

Boyer, R. (1990) *The Regulation School*. Chicago: University Chicago Press.
Boyer, R. and Saillard, Y. (eds) (2002) *Regulation Theory: State of the Art*. London: Routledge.
Jessop, B. and Sum, N. (2006) *The Regulation Approach and Beyond: Putting Capitalist Economies in their Place*. Cheltenham: Edward Elgar.
Lipietz, A. (1993) 'The Local and the Global: Regional Individuality or Interregionalism?', *Transactions of the Institute of British Geographers*, 18(1): 8–18.

Representative Democracy

DEFINITION

Representative democracy is a type of democracy in which the citizens of the state exercise their popular sovereignty through legitimately elected representatives. In a representative democracy, the citizens choose their representatives by voting in elections. Typically, the chosen representatives then congregate in a legislative assembly where they debate policy and determine legislation. Such representative democracy is often contrasted with more direct or participatory forms of democracy in which citizens play an active role in the decision-making process.

The classical theory of representative democracy suggests that the representatives should act in accordance with the will or interests of the citizens. Yet, the representatives do not simply act as a proxy for the relevant citizens; rather, they have considerable discretion, and so can adopt the positions that they believe will most benefit their constituents or even the nation state as a whole. Besides, representative democracies often include political parties, with citizens voting for particular representatives in large part because of the party to which they belong, in a way that arguably requires the representative to adopt the positions to which his or her party was committed at the time of the election.

Since the role of the representatives is, at least in part, to act on behalf of their constituents, it is important that the voters have a way of holding the representatives to account. Accountability has generally been linked here to transparency and to periodic elections. Transparency enables the citizens to keep track of the actions of their representatives. Periodic elections enable the citizens to replace their representatives should they be unhappy with their actions.

CONTEXT

As we have seen, the classical theory of representative democracy broadly supposed that elected politicians would act in accordance with the will or interests of their constituents. This supposition has been challenged by several themes that have become prominent in the literature on governance, including the dominance of some policy networks by vested interests, the complexity of modern governance, and declining levels of trust and political participation.

From the early twentieth century onwards, social scientists have shown how business groups become involved with the political process and even come to dominate areas of it. Corporate interests have used their extensive resources to become powerful lobbyists, financiers, and advisers for politicians and at times public officials. The worry is that their involvement can lead to political representatives, perhaps intentionally or perhaps unintentionally, acting as voice for these kinds of elite interests rather than their constituents.

Classical accounts of representative democracy are also threatened by the sheer complexity of modern governance, and especially the rise of non-governmental modes of collective decision-making. The classic account of representative democracy suggested that laws (and perhaps public policy) were made by elected representatives in a transparent manner and within a national context. Not much of that account remains. For a start, many non-elected officials clearly make policy and law within administrative agencies, judicial settings, and other such domains. Although the legislature creates statutes, these statutes are generally vague, so typically their interpretation, application, and enforcement all fall to administrative and judicial bodies that have the relevant technical expertise. Hence much of our collective decision-making now occurs in contexts where neither citizens nor their elected representatives have much of a presence. In addition, the complexity of the technical issues that are involved in defining, applying, and enforcing laws and policies inevitably entails a certain loss of transparency. Few citizens can grasp the legal language, let alone the scientific knowledge, on which many policies are based. Finally, the growing complexity of intergovernmental and transnational ties means that the lives of people within a specific nation state are increasingly being governed by laws and policies decided upon not by their own government but by transnational decision-making bodies. For example, while rules on environmental regulation, trade treaties, and migration all affect people living inside national borders, they are often made by international organizations that are certainly not directly accountable to the affected constituents in specific countries.

The declining rates of trust and political participation also challenge classical accounts of representative democracy. A representative democracy depends on regular political participation from citizens to function. Voting is, after all, the way in which citizens select their representatives.

Falling rates of voter turnout undermines the claim that elected politicians adequately represent the voice of their constituents. Much of the public voice remains silent and unheard.

DEBATE

The challenges to representative democracy have led many of its advocates to worry that their ideal is increasingly out of touch with political realities. Some of them still hope to transform society and politics in accordance with the ideal. Others appear to be more interested in redefining the ideal so as to make it less demanding. Perhaps, they suggest, the number of citizens who vote does not matter as long as we have elections. Perhaps, they continue, the complexity of collective governance and decision-making does not matter as long as elected representatives are involved at some point. And perhaps, they conclude, policy networks can be seen less as dangerous clusters of vested interests and more as beneficial ways of bringing voices into the decision-making process.

The debate among advocates of representative democracy over how to respond to the new governance is, however, increasingly influenced by debates about the desirability of representative democracy. Radical, participatory, and deliberative democrats all believe that we should renounce, or at least supplement, the representative ideal with other forms of citizen involvement. For some, representative democracy isn't very democratic at all. Democracy literally means the rule of the *demos*, or people, and radical democrats want the people, not the people's representatives, to rule. Some radical democrats point mainly to the worries about self-interest and corruption within representative bodies: the representatives might not act in good faith. Other radical democrats argue that political freedom consists in active participation within the process of ruling: much of the value of democracy lies in the experience it affords citizens of collective deliberation and wielding power.

Advocates of representative democracy often counter more radical schemes by arguing that they could not work in the modern world. Radical schemes will not work, they tell us, because of the size of modern states and the complexity of problems they confront. In this view, direct democracy might have worked in ancient Athens, but Athens was just a single city: if every eligible voter participated directly in a modern democracy, the political process would more or less grind to a halt. Likewise, in this view, modern politics deals with complex issues, including macro-economics, the environment, and health and safety – issues on which the ordinary voter lacks the technical expertise necessary to make informed decisions. Some advocates of representative democracy have also defended it on the grounds that it might check some illiberal tendencies found in more radical proposals. They argue that radical democratic schemes encourage a tyranny of the majority: the power given to majority choices is liable to lead to the repression of minorities. In their view, representative democracy provides a bulwark against such tyranny in so far as representatives are more moderate than the average citizen.

CROSS REFERENCES

Accountability, Participatory democracy

FURTHER READING

Benz, A. and Papadopoulos, I. (eds) (2006) *Governance and Democracy: Comparing National, European, and International Experiences*. London: Routledge.
Manin, B. (1997) *The Principles of Representative Government*. Cambridge: Cambridge University Press.
Przeworski, A. Stokes, S.C. and Manin, B. (eds) (1999) *Democracy, Accountability, and Representation*. Cambridge: Cambridge University Press.
Sisk, T. (2001) *Democracy at the Local Level: The International IDEA Handbook on Participation, Representation, Conflict, Management, and Governance*. Stockholm: International IDEA.

Rule of Law

DEFINITION

The rule of law requires that the state be based on a set of laws that apply equally to everyone, including agents of the state. The rule of law is in part a normative concept that distinguishes just rule from despotism. The state should not be based on the arbitrary will of the sovereign, whether the sovereign be a king, president, or parliament. Rather, the sovereign should fall within the law. The agents of the state should be bound by the law just like other citizens. They should not have any more legal privileges than regular citizens. More generally still, the rule of law requires that the law be applied equally to every citizen. The application of the law does not depend on arbitrary characteristics such as, say, socio-economic status, race, gender, or religion.

Clearly, the concept of the rule of law has implications for the content and character of law itself. The general idea is that rule becomes rather arbitrary if citizens are unable to know or obey the laws by which they are governed. Hence laws must be understandable so citizens may comprehend and comply with them. More particularly, laws should be transparent and stable in order that citizens may easily grasp what is required of them. Laws should be consistent so that citizens are able to comply with them, and if contradictions do arise in the law, then the law itself should provide the means to resolve them. Laws should not place an undue burden on citizens. Finally, laws, at least under most circumstances, should not apply retrospectively since citizens would then not have known what was required of them.

No doubt the rule of law may exist within widely different forms of government. Nonetheless, some general institutions are thought to be especially important for the rule of law. One such institution is an independent judiciary. Judges and courts should be shielded from political intervention from other agents of the state sufficiently to enable them to interpret and apply the law in a fair way. Another relevant institution is arguably an inclusive legal system: all citizens should have reasonable access to legal advice, institutions, and remedies. Another institution that has sometimes been tied to the rule of law is a written constitution. The idea here seems to be that the constitution can act as a fundamental law that constrains agents of the state and provides citizens with a basis on which to appeal against actions of the state. Despite the association of the rule of law with these kinds of institution, it is important to remember that the rule of law is a moral concept rather than an institutional blueprint.

CONTEXT

The concept of the rule of law arose as early modern and Enlightenment thinkers challenged the doctrine of the divine right of kings. This latter doctrine suggested that monarchs acquired their legitimacy directly from God. Philosophers such as Locke and Rousseau challenged this doctrine by appealing to reason, natural law, and consent as the basis of political obligation. They thereby suggested that political authority ceased to be legitimate if it became capricious and arbitrary. By the time of the Enlightenment, the rule of law had thus come to be seen by many as a prerequisite of political legitimacy. The rule of law thus arose as a clearly normative concept, demarcating legitimate rule from despotism. However, when later modernist social scientists began to press a distinction between empirical and normative claims, the concept of the rule of law sometimes acquired a more descriptive content. Max Weber distinguished, for example, legal-rational authority from other forms as a basis for a largely empirical theory of modern societies. He argued that modern authority typically had a legal-rational basis as opposed to a charismatic or traditional one.

In contemporary discussions of governance, the concept of the rule of law again seems to have a largely empirical content, even if normative themes continue to appear from time to time. The rule of law plays a particularly prominent role, for instance, in analyses of good governance, but good governance itself is often defined here primarily in terms of economic development rather than political legitimacy. We might worry that the concept of the rule of law is in danger of being valued only as a technical means to economic growth, and, more tendentiously, as a means to a competitive market economy. Alternatively, we might welcome attempts to promote the rule of law even if the reasons for doing so now appear to differ somewhat from older ones about political legitimacy.

Proponents of good governance offer several overlapping economic arguments in favor of the rule of law. They argue that foreign investors are reluctant to pour capital into political regimes that are not based on the rule of law since these regimes are unstable. They argue that businesses thrive in stable environments characterized by the consistent and predictable application of laws. They argue that the absence of the rule of law often encourages corruption. And they argue that the rule of law is necessary to secure private property rights and enforce contractual obligations in the ways required by a free market economy. Today these kinds of argument have led global economic institutions and developed states to treat the rule of law as something like a prerequisite of any developing state in which they are to invest. The same arguments, and the need for such investment, have led several developing states to try to promote the rule of law.

DEBATE

There is a long-standing debate about whether the rule of law is a negative or a positive concept. Analyses of the rule of law as a negative concept emphasize its links to non-arbitrariness. They concentrate on the problems of basing legitimate authority on irrational bases such as personal caprice. In this view, the rule of law serves primarily to protect citizens from arbitrary and tyrannical intrusions by the state and its agents, and secondarily to provide citizens with equal protection under the law. Clearly, this negative analysis of the rule of law has little to say about the substantive ethical content of the law; it has little to say about cases in which the consistent and rational application of the law results in unexpected or even undesirable consequences.

More positive analyses of the rule of law focus on the content of law or at least the moral ends it should serve. They place less emphasis on the value of the rule of law in itself, and more on its role in promoting substantive ethical values such as human rights, justice, and equality. In this view, the law is not just a series of procedural guidelines, but rather substantive values that promote a greater good. Critics argue that this more positive analysis of the rule of law gives excessive power to the state as the creator of law. They complain that the state should not promote a particular ethic, but merely leave individuals free to do so in their own ways.

Finally, we should remember that although the rule of law is surely a good thing, there is also something profoundly undemocratic about it. If we allow law to override the decisions of the sovereign, we allow it to override the decisions of democratically elected institutions. There is, it seems, a trade-off between, on the one hand, a rule of law that protects citizens from the state, and, on the other, the danger that judges and courts will act as an unaccountable barrier to democratic authorities instituting the will of the people.

CROSS REFERENCES

Accountability, Good governance

FURTHER READING

Hart, H.L.A. (1961) *The Concept of Law*. Oxford: Oxford University Press.
Selznick, P. (1999) 'Legal Cultures and the Rule of Law', in M. Krygier and A. Czarnota (eds), *The Rule of Law after Communism*. Aldershot: Dartmouth.
Shapiro, I. (ed.) (1994) *The Rule of Law: NOMOS XXXVI*. New York: New York University Press.
Shklar, J. (1998) 'Political Theory and the Rule of Law', in J. Shklar (ed.), *Political Thought and Political Thinkers*. Chicago: University of Chicago Press.
Tamanaha, B. (2004) *On the Rule of Law: History, Politics, Theory*. Cambridge: Cambridge University Press.

rule of law

Social Capital

DEFINITION

Social capital is defined by the conjunction of its two terms. 'Social' refers to institutions, organizations, and networks through which individuals interact to achieve common goals. 'Capital' refers to the aspects of these interactions that can be used to achieve common goals and political gains. Hence social capital includes all interactions that develop bonds and trust between community members and that thereby increase the capacity of citizens to influence the political process.

Social capital can grow out of almost any everyday human interaction. Yet, while all kinds of interaction are important, some feed more directly into governance than do others. Again, while all kinds of governing institution might foster trust, social scientists often suggest that local governing groups, such as city councils and school boards, are of particular value to the creation of a cohesive society.

CONTEXT

To simplify matters, we might think of the institutions that foster social capital as being either private or state ones. Private groups, such as non-profits and local networks, can help to develop social capital outside the state. Even when social capital develops outside the state, it often helps to give people access to particular state resources, such as funding for schools or the repair of local roads. Here, social capital fosters trust and communication within local communities, thereby enabling people to cooperate and thus interact more effectively with government. Equally, of course, such social capital can enable people to act collectively to pursue interests and concerns in ways that simply by-pass the state. One example would be a local voluntary group that takes it upon itself to protect and clean a park or other zone.

Social capital can also arise from government institutions. State agencies can stimulate communication, trust, and understanding between community members. A dramatic example of governmental interest in stimulating social capital is the White Paper on European Governance published by the Commission of the European Communities in 2001. The White Paper explicitly aimed to develop means to connect the

European Union more closely to its citizens and to increase participation in governmental affairs. These aims are unpacked in terms of five principles: openness, participation, accountability, effectiveness, and coherence. These principles then inspire proposals for change under four headings: better involvement in shaping and implementing policy, better policies and better delivery of policies, contributions to global governance, and refocused institutions and policies. The main idea is to expand democratic participation by opening up the policy-making process through a shift in the role of governing institutions from command and control in hierarchies to facilitation and negotiation in networks. Governance in and through networks is thus invoked as a means of building social capital.

DEBATE

The European Union and other governments might be increasingly convinced of the importance of building social capital, but by no means does everyone agree with them. Some social scientists think that the concept of social capital is sheer nonsense. Others debate about how to define it, or its role in society, governance, and democracies. Consider its definition. Some people define social capital as an omnipresent resource arising out of each and every interaction. Others associate it more narrowly with only those social interactions that produce norms of trust and reciprocity. While these definitions overlap, they often lead to different analyses of the relationship between social capital to society and to governance.

Consider the role of social capital in civil society. Do high levels of social capital sustain communities in a way that leads to a strong and inclusive civil society? Alternatively, we might suggest that some forms of social capital actually hinder wider trust and cooperation. Close-knit social groups often exclude other members of society with different identities or concerns: wealthy gated neighbourhoods might express the common concerns of their residents for privacy and security, but they also physically remove their residents from the greater community. What is more, close-knit groups can restrict the effective freedom of their members by imposing draconian rules or norms. Yet, on the other hand, some social scientists argue strongly that even exclusive or repressive groups entail interactions that generate social capital. In this view, even if such groups make it harder to develop broader forms of trust and cooperation, they nonetheless increase the capacity of their members to engage in governance and influence the state.

However, the effect of social capital on the state is also a matter of debate. The dominant view is that social capital stimulates the state to respond to its citizens. When citizens develop trust and cooperation, they are better able to get the state to respond to their demands. Yet, we might suggest that social capital sometimes encourages the state to divest from communities. For example, if local community groups and non-profits tackle problems, state actors might come to believe that they need not do so. In the absence of successful community cooperation, the state itself might address the relevant issues.

Another debate concerns the relationship between social capital and democracy. Social capital is, it seems, weak in authoritarian states. Some political scientists thus argue that democracy depends on the presence of certain levels of social capital within civil society and independent of the state. Social capital in civil society serves to check abuses of power and prevents government corruption. However, other political scientists argue that democracy does not presuppose social capital so much as create it. Democracy encourages the state to pay more attention to public opinion, thereby giving social actors more reason to interact and organize themselves. Authoritarian states, in contrast, often restrict free speech and free organization, thereby undermining the growth of social capital.

CROSS REFERENCES

Communitarianism, Policy network, Social inclusion

FURTHER READING

Bourdieu, P. (1986) 'The Forms of Capital', in J. Richardson (ed.), *Handbook of Theory and Research for the Sociology of Education*. New York: Greenwood Press.

Coleman, J. (1988) 'Social Capital in the Creation of Human Capital', *American Journal of Sociology*, 94: s95–s120.

Fine, B. (2001) *Social Capital versus Social Theory: Political Economy and Social Science at the Turn of the Millennium*. London: Routledge.

Portes, A. (1998) 'Social Capital: Its Origins and Applications in Modern Sociology', *American Review of Sociology*, 24: 1–24.

Putnam, R. (1993) *Making Democracy Work: Civic Traditions in Modern Italy*. Princeton, NJ: Princeton University Press.

Social Constructivism

DEFINITION

Constructivists argue that social reality is constructed out of human knowledge, beliefs, or meanings. Typically, they add that human knowledge too is constructed. Constructivism stands in stark contrast to accounts of our knowledge as resting directly on facts. It denies that our knowledge can derive from pure experiences of an independent reality. On the contrary, it emphasizes the positive role played by social traditions and cultural conventions in determining the content of our experiences. Hence constructivism often acts as a form of critique. It suggests that ideas that might appear to be inherently rational or natural are in fact the artifacts of particular traditions or cultures. Likewise, it implies that our social and political practices are not the result of natural or social laws, but are the product of choices informed by contingent meanings and beliefs.

Social constructivism has been applied to a range of concepts. Perhaps the most controversial in philosophical terms are concepts such as truth and reality. The most controversial in social terms have perhaps been race, sexuality, and gender, all of which might be thought to have a basis in given facts about human bodies. Constructivism has also been applied to social and political institutions, including nations, corporations, agencies, and governments. A constructivist view of institutions challenges many of the leading approaches to social science and also related approaches to public policy. Constructivist theories of governance stress the role of tradition, discourse, and culture in constructing contemporary patterns of rule. They thereby highlight the contingency and contestability of governance in contrast to those who see it as inevitable, rational, or explicable by reference to natural or social processes. They suggest that contemporary governance arose out of particular discourses or traditions.

CONTEXT

All forms of social constructivism emphasize the constructed nature of the social world. However, there are different ways of unpacking constructivism, such as linguistic constructivism and critical constructivism, and we should distinguish between them. Although it is tempting to think of each type of constructivism as an account of society as a whole, each type might apply to some (but not all) of our concepts.

Constructivism asserts only that we make the social world by acting on our beliefs. Linguistic constructivists would add that we make the very beliefs and meanings on which we act. Our concepts are contingent products of particular traditions rather than natural or inevitable ways of conceiving and classifying objects: various traditions or cultures categorize objects very differently. For example, the Inuit have words for different types of 'snow', while the people of the Kalahari Desert have words that discern various shades of red. Constructivism thus entails anti-essentialism. Linguistic constructivism implies that our concepts do not have essences: our concepts do not pick out intrinsic properties that are common to all the things to which we might apply them and thus explain the other facets and behavior of those things.

Linguistic constructivism can lead to pragmatic or critical accounts of particular concepts. Pragmatic concepts are vague; they are ways of dividing up continuums, rather than names for discrete chunks of experience. However, although pragmatic concepts do not refer to essences, they do refer to groups of objects, properties, or events. Social factors determine pragmatic concepts because there are innumerable ways in which we may classify things, and because our purposes and our histories lead us to adopt one classification and not another. Yet the role of social factors in determining a concept does not mean that the concept has no basis in the world. Rather, we can justify adopting a particular pragmatic concept by arguing that it best serves our purpose. We might justify a pragmatic concept of the 'New Public Management' by saying that it picks out family resemblances among public sector reforms. We might defend ascribing particular content to concepts such as 'neoliberalism' on the grounds that doing so best explains the family resemblances between public sector reforms. And we might adopt a particular concept of 'democratic accountability' on the grounds that it best captures those patterns of rule that we regard as legitimate.

Critical constructivism arises when we want to suggest a concept is invalid. In such cases, we might argue that the concept is determined by social factors and that it fails to capture even a group. For example, we might reject the concept 'New Public Management' as unfounded, especially if it is meant to refer to a global trend. We might argue that different states have introduced very different reforms with widely varying results. And we might add that the reforms drew upon and resembled each state's own individual traditions of administration far more than they did a common neoliberal blueprint. In such cases, we dismiss concepts as unfounded by arguing that there is no fact of the matter – neither an essence nor a group – that they accurately pick out.

Some anti-realists have adopted a kind of global critical constructivism, applying it to all of our concepts. Typically, these anti-realists argue that the role of prior theories and traditions in constructing our experiences precludes our taking these experiences to be accurate of a world independent of us. They argue that we only have access to our world (things as we experience them) rather than some world as it exists independent of us (things in themselves). They then conclude that this means that we have no basis from which to assert that our concepts are true to the world. In their view, there is nothing outside the text and therefore no world outside our linguistic constructions.

DEBATE

Different types of social constructivism might inspire different approaches to governance. Whatever the merits of anti-realism as a global theory, it is important to say that there is nothing incoherent about anti-realist or critical accounts of governance. The new governance is often defined in terms of the hollowing out of the state: the state is said to have lost the ability to impose its will, and comes to rely instead on negotiations with other organizations with which it forms networks. In contrast, we might suggest that the state never had the ability to impose its will; the state always had to operate with and through organizations in civil society; it always has been plural and dispersed. Hence we might conclude that there is no fact of the matter that can be accurately picked out by the concept 'the new governance'.

Even if we took an anti-realist stance towards 'the new governance', we still might be interested in abstract questions about governance conceived as an account of features of all patterns of rule. The general and pragmatic versions of social constructivism are most relevant to these abstract questions. Because constructivists argue that we make the social world by acting on contingent sets of meanings, they generally analyze changing patterns of governance in terms of competing discourses and traditions. They favor the interpretive approaches to governance that concentrate on elucidating the meanings that make possible any particular pattern of rule. Similarly, because constructivists emphasize the contingency of traditions, they sometimes highlight the diversity of traditions at play within a pattern of rule and the contests between these traditions. They favor bottom-up approaches to governance that explore how meanings are created, sustained, contested, and transformed by human activity within practices saturated with relations of power. Finally, when constructivists emphasize the contingent and diverse nature of traditions, they offer critical genealogies of alternative accounts of governance. They reject any suggestion that a natural or social logic determines the content or the development of any given pattern of rule. They argue that political scientists efface the contingency of social life when they attempt to ground their theories in apparently given facts about human rationality, the path-dependence of institutions, or the inexorability of social developments.

Although constructivists favor interpretive, bottom-up, and critical approaches to governance, there are differences between, say, governmentality and decenterd theory. Governmentality theorists often imply that concepts exist as quasi-structures since their content derives from their relationship to one another within discourses: individuals are just the passive supports or constructs of such discourses. In contrast, decenterd theorists take meanings to arise from the ways individuals use language to express their beliefs; discourses are just clusters of intersubjective beliefs adopted against the background of similar traditions.

Constructivists adopt different views of meaning largely because they hold different views of the individual. Governmentality and decenterd theory alike reject the idea of an autonomous individual: they insist that individuals are inherently located in the social contexts that influence them. Yet governmentality theorists sometimes appear to reject the idea of human agency. They generally concentrate exclusively on the ways in which social discourses give individuals their intentions and beliefs. Decenterd theorists, in contrast, want to defend the idea of situated agency. They argue that individuals can reason and act in novel ways, although they can do so only against the background of the inherited traditions that influence them.

CROSS REFERENCES

Dialogic policy-making, Differentiated polity

FURTHER READING

Barry, A., Osborne, T. and Rose, N. (1996) *Foucault and Political Reason: Liberalism, Neo-liberalism and Rationalities of Government*. London: UCL Press.

Berger, P. and Luckmann, T. (1966) *The Social Construction of Reality: A Treatise in the Sociology of Knowlege*. New York: Anchor Books.

Bevir, M. and Rhodes, R. (2003) *Interpreting British Governance*. London: Routledge.
Bevir, M. and Rhodes, R. (2006) *Governance Stories*. London: Routledge.
Bevir, M., Rhodes, R. and Weller, P. (eds) (2003) 'Traditions of Governance: History and Diversity', of *Public Administration* (Special Issue), 81/1.

Social Inclusion

DEFINITION

Social inclusion is a concept and policy agenda for social justice. It refers to processes of involving citizens in civil society and in collective decision-making. Such involvement may take many forms, including employment, church attendance, and voting. As a positive vision, the concept of social inclusion implies that the involvement of citizens in such activities helps to create a fair and cohesive community.

When social inclusion is defined in more negative terms, it appears as the opposite to or overcoming of social exclusion. Social inclusion seeks to overcome barriers that prevent particular groups or segments of the population from full and equal participation in civil society. Many of these barriers reflect historical patterns of prejudice. Excluded groups have often been defined by criteria: if people met the criteria, they were included; if they did not, they were excluded. Historically, these criteria included gender, age, ethnicity, property ownership, and religious affiliation. Certainly adult white male property-owners have often dominated western states. Minorities – such as people of colour, women, and youth – have had far fewer opportunities for participation in both state and society.

It is important to recognize, however, that social inclusion differs from affirmative action and restorative justice. Social inclusion is not an attempt to right past wrongs. It does not seek to include groups as a way of making amends for past disadvantages. On the contrary, social inclusion is a vision of a good society based on a notion of what everyone is entitled to by virtue of membership of that particular society. It seeks to include groups because of the intrinsic value of a cohesive and inclusive society. Hence social inclusion extends not only to groups who have suffered from historical patterns of prejudice, but also to divisions of far more recent origin. For example, there is much discussion of social inclusion as a way of overcoming the 'digital divide' between those with and without adequate access to computer technology and the internet.

CONTEXT

Both the concept and the policy agenda of social inclusion appear to have risen to prominence as part of the more social democratic second wave of public sector reforms.

The shift to a concept of social inclusion reflected widespread concerns about the plausibility and desirability of historic socialist policies. Social inclusion has often found its most ardent supporters among political parties and governments associated with social democracy, such as the New Labor governments in the UK and the European Commission. To some extent, social inclusion thus appears to be a modified version of the older socialist commitment to equality. Most socialists see equality in terms of income disparity: equality involves closing the gap between rich and poor. Socialists supported redistributive policies based on high, progressive rates of taxation. In contrast, social inclusion appears to conceive equality in terms of opportunities to participate: it requires all citizens to have the opportunity to get a job, to interact with agencies, to access information, and to vote. But the outcome of their participation may lead to great disparities of wealth. Hence social inclusion appears to mirror a shift in the concept of poverty away from material deprivation and towards an inability to exercise social and political rights. In this view, poverty reflects various types of social exclusion, such as inadequate education, homelessness, loss of family support, and unemployment. Perhaps the main question to ask is: does social inclusion represent an alternative or a supplement to wealth equalization?

Governments have generally tried to promote social inclusion through local partnerships. There are, of course, attempts to promote inclusion by means of the further extension of political and social rights. Typically, however, social inclusion is seen as requiring stronger links between political institutions and civil society, and also a transformation of parts of civil society itself. In this view, the state can promote social inclusion only through working with voluntary and private sector bodies in processes of collective problem-solving. Some of the new partnerships aim to involve citizens in the policy process: they might provide opportunities for consultation, deliberation, or even involvement in the delivery of public services. Other new partnerships aim to transform society by stimulating social action: they are intended, for instance, to bring about economic regeneration, tackle poverty, provide community services, or spread access to the internet.

DEBATE

We might distinguish debates on social inclusion according to whether they concern the concept itself or the policies that it has inspired.

Conceptual debates often focus on the question: what constitutes inclusion? Some people argue that social inclusion depends primarily on paid employment. Employment brings self-respect, interaction with others, and also the resources one needs to engage in other social activities. Others put more emphasis on the ability to participate in a range of political processes. Still others argue that irrespective of people's involvement in politics, poverty often precludes any kind of meaningful participation in civil society, while also resisting the argument that employment is the way to think about poverty. This last view tends to push the content of social inclusion towards the historic socialist commitment to reducing disparities of wealth. Finally, some critics argue that the very concept of social inclusion is profoundly flawed. Perhaps it places too much emphasis on who is excluded as opposed to who is doing the excluding. Perhaps the simple dichotomy between inclusion and exclusion hides more important questions about kinds and degrees of exclusion. Perhaps the concept of social inclusion focuses on outcomes in a way that fails to recognize exclusion as a process.

Other debates arise over the policies by which governments typically seek to promote social inclusion. Do local and other partnerships live up to the rhetoric of cohesion, trust, and integration? There have been several empirical studies of the capacity of local partnerships, their inclusiveness, their accountability, and their outcomes. These studies typically suggest that the new partnerships have managed to involve more non-governmental actors in the processes of governance. Equally, however, they suggest that it is not necessarily the case that all (or even most) of the key actors in shaping the future of a locality are among those involved in the partnerships. The new partnerships are often weakened by problems of complexity and coordination, and by the limits of institutional capacities and capabilities. In some cases, the new partnerships actually strengthen a kind of vertical integration leading up to the central state rather than horizontal networks at the local level.

CROSS REFERENCES

Collaborative governance, Communitarianism, Enabling state, Good governance

FURTHER READING

Askonas, P. and Stewart, A. (eds) (2000) *Social Inclusion: Possibilities and Tensions*. Basingstoke: Palgrave Macmillan.

Levitas, R. (1998) *The Inclusive Society? Social Exclusion and New Labour*. Basingstoke: Palgrave Macmillan.

Percy-Smith, J. (ed.) (2000) *Policy Responses to Social Exclusion*. Buckingham: Open University Press.

Van Berkel, R. and Moller, I. (eds) (2003) *Active Social Policies in the EU: Inclusion through Participation?* Cambridge: Polity Press.

Sovereignty

DEFINITION

Sovereignty is the exclusive authority that a state has within its territorial boundaries. Generally, sovereignty acts as a legitimizing concept: we ascribe authority and legitimacy to whoever is deemed to hold it. Effective sovereignty thus comes in large part from the recognition of legitimacy by at least some actors within and outside the given territory.

As well as being a legitimizing concept, sovereignty has both domestic and international dimensions. Domestically, sovereignty regulates all of the relationships between the 'rulers' and 'ruled' within a given territory. Internationally, sovereignty dictates the relationships of states to one another and the norms that govern their treatment of one another. Both of these aspects of sovereignty are thus closely tied to the concept of the state.

A sovereign state is one that holds a monopoly on the legitimate use of force in a given geographical area. It is also often conceived to have an exclusive right to make and enforce laws within its boundaries. Sovereignty thus implies that there is a final authority within a distinct political community. Decisions made by that authority on behalf of the community cannot be overruled by another authority elsewhere.

It has been argued that state sovereignty implies indivisible power. This idea of indivisibility might appear to be contradicted by the presence of local governments and the division of the central state into different departments and agencies. Yet, it is argued that the practical division of administration and policy-making does not contradict the idea of an indivisible sovereignty since the central state itself retains some ability to revoke the powers delegated to local governments and agencies.

CONTEXT

The concept of sovereignty emerged along with the modern state. At the end of the Thirty Years' War, the Treaty of Westphalia (1648) divided Europe into separate sovereign states. The Treaty established that states and monarchs were not allowed to invade other territories for the purpose of saving souls. It thereby established territorial sovereignty as a corollary of a principle of non-interference in the affairs of other territories. Each state or territory was an independent sovereign entity.

Between the Treaty of Westphalia and the French Revolution of 1789, the concept of sovereignty changed along with ideas about who rightly governs. At first the concept of sovereignty was generally tied to the rule of independent kings and princes. The king had supreme authority over a territory and the guilds and feudal lords within it. Indeed, the legitimacy of the rule of a king was sometimes ascribed to the will of God: kings had a divine right to rule. Yet, over time, political theorists began increasingly to challenge the idea of divine right. Political theorists began to argue that the king ruled by the will of the people. The people were the sole 'holders' of sovereignty, and the king ruled only by virtue of their tacit consent. It was thus an agreement between the king and the people, not divine right, which made the king sovereign. Later still, the French Revolution saw citizens take power and proclaim new rights. Thereafter, the idea of popular sovereignty as implying rule by the people came to inform much modern democratic theory.

While the domestic location of sovereignty thus became associated with the people rather than a king, state sovereignty continued to define the theory and practice of international relations. International affairs were conducted by sovereign states, each of which had exclusive jurisdiction over its own territory and each of which thus respected the rights of the others to decide their own internal policies. Indeed, state sovereignty implies a kind of anarchical view of world politics. No world

sovereignty

government can dictate what states must do without infringing on their sovereignty; international agreements are binding only because states agree that they are so. Equally, however, state sovereignty entails a set of rules that are constitutive rules of a world order – rules about the equality of states, self-determination, reciprocity, non-intervention, and even membership and participation in a kind of society of states.

DEBATE

Globalization and the new governance raise questions about the adequacy of sovereignty as a realistic account of the world and perhaps even as a legitimizing concept. Many political scientists argue that the state is increasingly lacking in the power to impose its will within its territory: it has instead to rely on forming networks with other public, voluntary, and private actors. Likewise, political scientists often argue that the rise of transnational actors and linkages has undermined the very idea of a distinct territory that might have a unique source of authority. Finally, international relations scholars often point to the rise of a new regionalism within which numerous states appear to have given up much of their autonomy to bodies such as the European Union. All these kinds of changes have led to what is sometimes described as a hollowing out of the state. There is, of course, considerable debate as to whether or not the state has been hollowed out. Some of these debates are considered in the entry on the state. What matters here is that the idea of a hollow state has some tension with our historical concept of sovereignty.

Another debate concerns the desirability of our historical concept of sovereignty. The practice of state sovereignty has become increasingly contentious when it serves to shield states from intervention when, say, they violate human rights, foster terrorists, or develop weapons of mass destruction. Hence there are debates over whether and to what extent a principle of sovereignty should be sacrificed to international agreements and treaties, and even to cosmopolitan ethical norms. What rights should states have over their territories? What rights should the international community have to intervene in a state for humanitarian purposes? What rights should other states have to overthrow authoritarian governments?

CROSS REFERENCES

Global governance, State, Transnationalism

FURTHER READING

Bartelson, J. (1995) *A Genealogy of Sovereignty*. Cambridge: Cambridge University Press.
Hinsley, F.H. (1986) *Sovereignty*. Cambridge: Cambridge University Press.
Spruyt, H. (1994) *The Sovereign State and Its Competitors*. Princeton, NJ: Princeton University Press.

State

DEFINITION

The word 'state' arose from the Latin *status*, which referred to the different legal standings that people might have. A revival of Roman law in fourteenth-century Europe saw the word 'status' being used to pick out the different estates of the realm – king, lords, and commons – and to discuss the unique standing of the king within the realm. This use of 'status' chimed well with Roman discussions of the *status rei publicae* (the standing of the republic). By the end of the fourteenth century, terms like 'status' and 'state' could thus be used to refer to the condition and legal order of a given territory under an individual monarch.

Today the state is still used to designate both a geographical territory and the set of institutions that hold sovereign and independent control over that territory. A state consists of a single political unit that is usually represented by a head of state, such as a monarch or president. Nonetheless, a state – as opposed to a nation or nation state – is not associated with a particular ethnic group.

The state can also be defined by its formal properties and role in domestic and international politics. A state is often said to have a monopoly on the legitimate use of force within its territory. Similarly, states typically act as single units in negotiations with other states, where governments require the explicit acceptance of other states around the world if they are to be declared states.

States can have very different characteristics from one another. Generally they contain several layers of local and regional government. Generally they contain clear executive, legislative, and judicial branches even if these are not always strictly separate from one another. Generally they have a standing army and a police force by which they exercise their monopoly of the legitimate use of force.

CONTEXT

Most scholars agree that the modern state emerged around the fifteenth century in Europe. Monarchs then began to centralize power, raise taxes, and command larger armies. Later still, the Treaty of Westphalia (1648) established the principle of state sovereignty in international relations. States became recognized as the principal actors in world politics.

The state changed considerably between the seventeenth and the late twentieth centuries. Many of the changes foreshadowed ones now associated with the rise of the new governance. Consider, first, internal changes in the state. When the state first emerged, most governments could be identified with a single king or prince. No doubt even kings must balance the interests of various domestic actors if they are to consolidate their rule. Nonetheless, over time the state became more pluralistic and more entwined with civil society. The rise of democracy and interest group politics led to states being seen more obviously as composites of (or sites of contest between) diverse voices ranging from corporations to non-profit groups. The broad story here is of the state's transition from a unified actor to an arena of conflict among competing groups. Certainly, many social scientists believe that democratization increases the dependency of the state on civil society and even on the approval of its citizens.

Consider, next, changes in the place of the state in international affairs. As the principle of state sovereignty developed, states were conceived as autonomous entities with control over their own territories. Of course there have always been weak states that found it more or less impossible to maintain such control. Nonetheless, over time, states have become increasingly entwined through transnational flows across borders that are beyond their powers to control. The growth of international trade made state autonomy increasingly problematic, for corporate actors could negotiate internationally without the presence of the state.

Thus, the concept and perhaps nature of the state had already changed dramatically by the late twentieth century. Some political scientists argue, however, that the last half-century has seen a hollowing out of the state. Indeed, one of the main debates in the literature of governance is whether or not the state has become increasingly powerless.

DEBATE

The concept of a hollow state evokes a decline in the power of the state. The state was often conceived as the sovereign authority over a territory with the power to get most of what it wanted done. The thesis of the hollowing out of the state asserts that in the new governance the authority and power of the state have waned: the state is increasingly fragmented and less able to impose its will upon its territory.

Several processes have contributed to the hollowing out of the state. Some of the state's functions have moved upwards to international and regional organizations such as the European Union. Although states remain important institutions, the growth of regional blocs, international law, and economic globalization have combined to limit their autonomy. Some of the state's functions have moved downwards to local levels of government and to special-purpose bodies. Devolution takes control of activities away from the center. Finally, some of the state's functions have moved outwards as a result of the increased use of markets and networks as means of service delivery. Even when the state retains a dominant role within networks, it still has to enter negotiated relationships with organizations in civil society if it is to effectively implement policies.

Claims about the hollowing out of the state raise further debates about accountability, fragmentation, and steering. First, representative democracies typically hold civil servants and agencies accountable to citizens by way of elected politicians. If these politicians are no longer able to control agencies, how is such accountability to operate? Second, the hollow state is fragmented in that decisions and services are made by numerous organizations, which often have different cultures. This fragmentation makes communication and coordination especially difficult. Third, when functions are transferred to other organizations, the state arguably needs to find ways of influencing and coordinating the various actions of these organizations. These problems often require politicians and civil servants to adopt new roles and new techniques if they are to govern effectively.

The concept of the hollow state has met with several criticisms. It has been argued that because the state voluntarily gave up functions, these functions were no loss. But one might reply that the concept seeks to describe the effects of actions irrespective of the motives behind them. It has also been suggested that the state remains powerful since it retains regulatory control over many of the functions it appears to have lost. This criticism raises further questions about contemporary governance. How many of the lost functions are covered by regulatory bodies? Is the state able to steer regulatory bodies effectively? Have regulatory bodies been 'captured' by those they are supposed to oversee?

CROSS REFERENCES

Corporatism, Differentiated polity, Enabling state, Sovereignty

FURTHER READING

Fukuyama, F. (2004) *State Building: Governance and World Order in the Twenty-first Century.* London: Profile Books.

Skinner, Q. (1989) 'The State', in T. Ball, J. Farr and R. Hanson (eds), *Political Innovation and Conceptual Change.* Cambridge: Cambridge University Press.

Weiss, L. (1998) *The Myth of the Powerless State: Governing the Economy in a Global Era.* Cambridge NY: Polity Press.

Weller, P., Bakvis, H. and Rhodes, R. (eds) (1997) *The Hollow Crown.* London: Macmillan.

Systems Theory

DEFINITION

The concept of a 'system' is very abstract. It can be little more than a metaphor used to describe any complex set of parts forming a larger whole. At its most abstract, the concept of a system is thus just a way of thinking about macro-structures in terms of the relations of their units. It breaks down objects into their parts and the relations between these parts, often in an attempt to facilitate problem-solving. This concept of a system can be found in diverse academic subjects, including biology, chemistry, and engineering, as well as economics and political science. For example, some biologists think of humans as a system composed of subsystems (such as the vital organs), each of which performs a process essential to the maintenance of the system as a whole.

Systems theorists typically see governance as a system composed of a series of subsystems operating within specific environments. A system consists of a set of subsystems or processes that are coordinated to accomplish defined goals. Each system or subsystem operates within an environment that is defined by fixed factors that constrain that system. Governance is the product of a complex network of interdependent systems. Many systems theorists also argue that systems are capable of regulating themselves so as to ensure that they evolve in a way that keeps their subsystems in harmonious relations with one another.

CONTEXT

Many systems theorists emphasize the self-organizing properties of systems. The self-organizing nature of systems can seem to make systems theory peculiarly appropriate to the new governance, conceived as the rise of markets and especially networks in place of bureaucratic hierarchy. In the absence of a dominant center or sovereign entity capable of guiding the whole, governance appears to resemble a self-organizing set of networks or subsystems. Historically, social scientists often concentrated on hierarchical exchanges in idealized bureaucratic structures. Advocates of systems theory suggest that it provides a way of exploring horizontal and exogenous interactions within networks as they respond to complex environments.

How are we to analyze governance networks conceived as systems and subsystems? Social scientists distinguish five different dimensions to systems analysis. These dimensions are: the objective of the system, the environment that contains the system, the system's resources, the system's subsystems and their respective goals, and the management of the system.

The objective of a system is not always readily apparent: it can be concealed by the complexities of the system. Social scientists often identify the objective of a system by asking for what ends the system actually sacrifices external goals.

The system's environment consists of fixed external factors that define its operating parameters. So conceived, the environment does not include everything that surrounds the system but only static factors.

A resource is anything that enables a system to fulfil its functions. A system may vary its resources depending on the circumstances. Systems often contain internal mechanisms that periodically increase resource levels. An example of such a mechanism would be a production improvement within a firm. The firm's technological improvement may increase the amount of labor that can be utilized in the production process and thus increase the resources within the system.

The actions of a system are often performed by coordinated subsystems. An analysis of the subsystems allows social scientists to consider their respective value to the system as a whole. In addition, they can consider which processes are critical and which might safely be removed.

System management ensures that the system's infrastructure is maintained and that the system is meeting its objectives. As long as these two conditions are met, the system will continue to exist.

The application of systems theory to governance generates several different approaches to system management. How can policy actors manage new self-organizing governance systems? The autopoetic approach suggests that any system that persists over time will be self-regulating. In this view, the system steers itself, and it does so through closed, self-referential processes. The autopoetic approach thus leads to pessimism over the possibility of the state (as a subsystem) steering society. The interactionist approach, in contrast, identifies governance as a product of interactions within the system. It highlights the impact of relationships between governors and those being governed, between public and private actors, and between institutions and the social forces they regulate. All these interactions offer sites at which the state, and also societal actors, might intervene so as to steer self-governing systems. In this view, recognition of the importance of interactions helps us to understand how steering becomes possible.

DEBATE

Systems theorists debate the implications of the theory for governance and the possibility of consciously steering networks. Yet these debates already assume that the theory has a defined and valid content. In fact, systems theory is, as we have seen, often little more than a metaphor. Hence there are arguably more important debates about the content and compatibility of different types of systems thinking.

More general debates about systems theory often concern the rival merits and compatibility of distinct variants. Schematically, we might distinguish at least four types of systems thinking: hard systems, organismic systems, soft systems, and critical systems. Hard systems thinking arose in operations research methods and engineering design where it is used to solve physical problems within clearly defined limits. Engineers break processes down into systems and subsystems in order to work on individual components in an efficient, organized manner. Second, organismic systems thinking arose in the biosciences. Organisms or their environments appear here as whole units or systems that in turn are composed of subsystems that possess varied characteristics. Organismic systems thinking leads to a more holistic approach than does hard systems thinking with its focus on breaking down a problem into small parts. Third, social scientists devised soft systems thinking by drawing on organismic systems thinking in order to examine social problems. Many other social scientists had adopted atomistic approaches that broke society or social phenomena down into smaller and smaller institutions, groups, and the like. In contrast, soft systems thinking tried to grasp the nature of the whole before looking at the place of each component part within that whole. Finally, critical systems theory improves system design by bringing a greater awareness of human needs and actions to other types of systems thinking.

To conclude, we might note that these different types of systems thinking often use the concept 'system' to describe different objects and to champion different ways of studying these 'objects'. If systems theory is to be seen as more than a metaphor flowing uncritically from one type of object to another, it is necessary to examine more critically the differences between these objects or macro-structures and so the different forms of analysis and explanation appropriate to them.

CROSS REFERENCES

Collaborative governance, Interdependence, Network

FURTHER READING

Banathy, B. (1996) *Designing Social Systems in a Changing World*. New York: Plenum Press.
Kooiman, J. (2003) *Governing as Governance*. London: Sage.
Luhmann, N. (1995) *Social Systems*. Stanford, CA: Stanford University Press.
Parsons, T. (1971) *The System of Modern Societies*. Englewood Cliffs, NJ: Prentice-Hall.

systems theory

Transnationalism

DEFINITION

Transnationalism refers to economic, political, and cultural links that transcend borders. Many transnational links exist between organizations. Some organizations operate across various states. Examples include multinational corporations as well as non-governmental organizations such as Médecins sans Frontières and Oxfam. Other transnational links arise from the flow of ideas. Policy transfer occurs, for example, whenever the policies, institutions, or administrative practices in one setting serve as inspiration for the development of similar arrangements in some other setting. Yet other transnational links and flows involve individual people. Migrants and refugees are obvious examples. Even after people settle in a new state, they often maintain social, cultural, and political ties with their countries of origin. Indeed, some social scientists argue that people's conceptions of themselves are inexorably tied to where they come from even if they have resided elsewhere for an extended period of time.

CONTEXT

Many observers argue that transnationalism has increased dramatically as a result of a range of globalizing processes. Transnational links within and between organizations have increased along with the growth in international trade and improved means of transportation and communication. The liberalization of trade and finance enables corporations to make agreements and exchanges in increasingly disparate settings. Innovations in transportation and information technology enable them to 'modularize' their production over multiple states and to manage operations across a wide expanse. Many production chains now consist of several organizations performing different functions in separate states. Non-governmental organizations, too, have taken advantage of changes in laws, transportation, and information technology to establish operations in areas previously deemed inaccessible.

Globalization may also be increasing the extent of policy transfer. There has been a huge increase in the extent of international education. Rising numbers of people travel abroad for at least part of their graduate and professional education before returning home. Public policy schools, such as the Kennedy School at Harvard, spread particular approaches and styles of social science and policy analysis to a global elite. Sometimes policy transfer is even more direct. States can arrange, formally or informally, for experts to be sent to other states to advance, promote, advise, or implement policies.

The processes of globalization may also increase transnational flows of people. Indeed, some economists argue that the growth of transnational organizations has increased the need for labor in developed states, and migrants have moved to fill such labor needs. During the 1950s and 1960s, Britain encouraged such immigration from Commonwealth countries. Then, during the 1970s and 1980s, France and Germany encouraged immigration to fill its labor shortages. More recently, there has been a huge migration of workers from Eastern Europe to states such as Britain, Germany, and Italy. Information technology and improved transportation then enable these migrant laborers to maintain close ties with their places of origin. Emails, phone calls, money remittances, and international air travel are all common.

Greater transnational links on the individual level undermine older ideas of citizenship and especially nationalism. Citizens of a state typically have particular legal privileges and rights that are not granted to other people, even if they reside with that state's borders. These privileges and rights are often associated with acceptance of a national identity. For immigrants to become citizens of a state, in this view, they should accept the values and perhaps the culture of the relevant nation. Indeed, many states require applicants for citizenship to past tests that examine their values and/or knowledge of the politics and history of the state. Nationalism often implies here that individuals living within the borders of a state have (or should have) a common language, culture, or values.

Transnationalism represents a marked departure from these ideas of nationalism and citizenship. Some observers argue that we are witnessing the rise of a new breed of transnational citizens who are less vested in upholding any shared culture, language, or values associated with the states in which they reside, and more interested in maintaining cultural and political markers of their places of origin. Arguably, migrants eventually used to integrate into their host countries. Today they seek to maintain their pre-migration identities.

transnationalism

DEBATE

How might we respond to the erosion of the nation state and national citizenship? Should we welcome it or bewail it?

States have generally responded to transnationalism by seeking to develop less formal forms of citizenship, control, and accountability. In the case of citizenship, the new policies often aim at a multicultural society that embraces difference rather than assimilation. They try to enable distinct cultures to coexist under the umbrella of a common set of political institutions. Many states have even become more accommodating of dual citizenship. They are increasingly comfortable allowing transnational migrants to have a formal political loyalty to their country of origin as well as their new home. In the case of control and accountability, states have generally tried to establish a range of transnational institutions or networks to enable them to coordinate their activities and thereby gain a measure of control over transnational flows. Examples of such institutions and networks include bilateral ones, such as the 1961 agreement between Turkey and West Germany facilitating the temporary migration of workers, regional ones, such as the European Union, international agreements, such as the Kyoto Protocol, and the kind of informal networks that have arisen among high court judges or central bankers.

The debate on the merits of transnationalism might seem to involve two straightforward positions. On one side, nationalists and those who have strong national loyalties will bewail transnationalism. On the other, multiculturalists and those who hold cosmopolitan ideals will welcome it. There is much truth in this stark dichotomy. Equally, however, some social scientists have offered more complex reasons for worrying about the rise of transnationalism. They focus less on the nation as an ideal and more on the instrumental benefits of cultural nations for the welfare state and even liberal democracy. Social democrats worry that the decline of national solidarities leaves people increasingly reluctant to support welfare programs. In this view, people have supported welfare for others, whom they think are like them, but they are now far less likely to vote for taxation to support others for whom they feel no cultural sympathy. Similarly, liberal democrats sometimes argue that shared norms and beliefs, social integration and trust, and even democratic dialogue and deliberation, all presuppose something like a single national culture. To some extent, therefore, the debate over the merits of transnationalism is about the requirements of democratic politics.

CROSS REFERENCES

Differentiated polity, Global governance, Globalization

FURTHER READING

Anderson, J. (ed.) (2002) *Transnational Democracy*. London: Routledge.

Dingwerth, K. (2007) *The New Transnationalism: Private Transnational Governance and its Democratic Legitimacy*. Basingstoke: Palgrave Macmillan.

Hedetoft, U. and Hjort, M. (eds) (2002) *The Postnational Self: Belonging and Identity*. Minneapolis, MN: University of Minnesota Press.

Kramsch, O., and Hooper, B. (ed.) (2004) *Cross-border Governance in the European Union*. Abingdon: Routledge.

transnationalism

Bibliography

Adcock, R., Bevir, M. and Stimson, S. (2007) 'Historicizing the New Institutionalism(s)', in R. Adcock, M. Bevir and S. Stimson (eds), *Modern Political Science: Anglo-American Exchanges since 1880*. Princeton, NJ: Princeton University Press.

Agranoff, R.J. (1986) *Intergovernmental Management*. Albany, NY: State University of New York Press.

Agranoff, R. and McGuire, M. (2003) *Collaborative Public Management: New Strategies for Local Governments*. Washington, DC: Georgetown University Press.

Amadae, S. (2003) *Rationalizing Capitalist Democracy: The Cold War Origins of Rational Choice Liberalism*. Chicago: Chicago University Press.

Anderson, J. (ed.) (2002) *Transnational Democracy*. London: Routledge.

Ansell, C. (2000) 'The Networked Polity: Regional Development in Western Europe', *Governance*, 13: 303–333.

Arndt, C. and Oman, C. (2006) *Uses and Abuses of Governance Indicators*. Paris: OECD Development Centre Studies.

Askonas, P. and Stewart, A. (eds) (2000) *Social Inclusion: Possibilities and Tensions*. Basingstoke: Palgrave Macmillan.

Bache, I. and Flinders, M. (eds) (2004) *Multilevel Governance*. Oxford: Oxford University Press.

Bain, K. and Howells, P. (1989) *Understanding Markets*. Worcester, UK: Billing & Sons.

Baldwin, R., Scott, C. and Hood, C. (eds) (1998) *A Reader on Regulation*. Oxford: Oxford University Press.

Banathy, B. (1996) *Designing Social Systems in a Changing World*. New York: Plenum Press.

Barber, B. (1984) *Strong Democracy: Participatory Politics for a New Age*. Berkeley, CA: University of California Press.

Bardhan, P. and Mookherjee, D. (2006) *Decentralization and Local Governance in Developing Countries: A Comparative Perspective*. Cambridge, MA: MIT Press.

Barnett, Michael N. and Finnemore, M. (2004) *Rules for the World: International Organizations in Global Politics*. Ithaca, NY: Cornell University Press.

Barrett, S. (2004) 'Implementation Studies: Time for a Revival? Personal Reflections on 20 Years of Implementation Studies', *Public Administration*, 82: 249–262.

Barry, A., Osborne, T. and Rose, N. (1996) *Foucault and Political Reason: Liberalism, Neo-liberalism and Rationalities of Government*. London: UCL Press.

Bartelson, J. (1995) *A Genealogy of Sovereignty*. Cambridge: Cambridge University Press.

Barzelay, M. (2001) *The New Public Management*. Berkeley, CA: University of California Press.

Beetham, D. (1996) *Bureaucracy*. Buckingham: Open University Press.

Behn, R.D. (2001) *Rethinking Democratic Accountability*. Washington, DC: Brookings Institution Press.

Benz, A. and Papadopoulos, I. (eds) (2006) *Governance and Democracy: Comparing National, European, and International Experiences*. London: Routledge.

Berger, P. and Luckmann, T. (1966) *The Social Construction of Reality: A Treatise in the Sociology of Knowlege*. New York: Anchor Books.

Bevir, M. (2005) *New Labour: A Critique*. London: Routledge.

Bevir, M. and Rhodes, R. (2003) *Interpreting British Governance*. London: Routledge.

Bevir, M. and Rhodes, R. (2006) *Governance Stories*. London: Routledge.

Bevir, M., Rhodes, R. and Weller, P. (eds) (2003) 'Traditions of Governance: History and Diversity', of *Public Administration* (Special Issue), 81/1.

Bevir, M. and Trentmann, F. (eds) (2004) *Markets in Historical Contexts*. Cambridge: Cambridge University Press.

Bogason, P. (2000) *Public Policy and Local Governance: Institutions in Postmodern Society*. Cheltenham: Edward Elgar.

Bohman, J. (1996) *Public Deliberation: Pluralism, Complexity, and Democracy*. Cambridge, MA: MIT Press.

Bourdieu, P. (1986) 'The Forms of Capital', in J. Richardson (ed.), *Handbook of Theory and Research for the Sociology of Education*. New York: Greenwood Press.

Bouvaird, T. (2004) 'Public–Private Partnerships: From Contested Concepts to Prevalent Practice', *International Review of Administrative Science*, 70: 199–215.

Bovaird, T. and Löffler, E. (eds) (2003) 'Symposium on Evaluating the Quality of Governance', *International Review of Administrative Sciences*, 69: 311–364.

Boyer, R. (1990) *The Regulation School*. Chicago: University Chicago Press.

Boyer, R. and Saillard, Y. (eds) (2002) *Regulation Theory: State of the Art*. London: Routledge.

Bridgman, P. and Davis, G. (2003) 'What Use is the Policy Cycle? Plenty, if the Aim is Clear', *Australian Journal of Public Administration*, 68: 98–102.

Brinkerhoff, D.W. and Brinkerhoff, J.M. (2004) 'Partnerships Between International Donors and Non-governmental Development Organisations: Opportunities and Constraints', *International Review of Administrative Science*, 70: 253–270.

Bull, B. and McNeill, D. (2007) *Development Issues in Global Governance: Public–Private Partnerships and Market Multilateralism*. New York: Routledge.

Cameron, A. and Palan, R. (2004) *The Imagined Economies of Globalization*. London: Sage.

Castells, M. (2000) *The Rise of the Network Society*. Oxford: Blackwell.

Cawson, A. (1986) *Corporatism and Political Theory*. New York: Basil Blackwell.

Cheema, G. and Rondinelli, D. (eds) (2007) *Decentralizing Governance: Emerging Concepts and Practices*. Washington, DC: Brookings Institution Press.

Cheema, S. and Rondinelli, D. (eds) (2003) *Reinventing Government for the Twenty-first Century*. Bloomfield, CT: Kumarian Press.

Chisholm, D. (1989) *Coordination without Hierarchy: Informal Structures in Multiorganizational Systems*. Berkeley, CA: University of California Press.

Christensen, T. and Laegreid, P. (eds) (2001) *New Public Management: The Transformation of Ideas and Practice*. Aldershot: Ashgate.

Coleman, J. (1988) 'Social Capital in the Creation of Human Capital', *American Journal of Sociology*, 94: s95–s120.

Cooper, P. (2003) *Governing by Contract: Challenges and Opportunities for Public Managers*. Washington, DC: CQ Press.

Cox, A. and O'Sullivan, N. (1988) *The Corporatist State*. Cheltenham: Edward Elgar.

Dahl, R. (1967) *Pluralist Democracy in the United States: Conflict and Consent*. Chicago: Rand McNally & Company.

DeBardeleben, J., Hurrelmann, A. and Leibfried, S. (eds) (2007) *Democratic Dilemmas of Multilevel Governance: Legitimacy, Representation and Accountability in the European Union*. Basingstoke: Palgrave Macmillan.

Demmers, J., Fernández Jilberto, A.E. and Hogenboom, B. (eds) (2004) *Good Governance in the Era of Global Neoliberalism: Conflict and Depolitisation in Latin America, Eastern Europe, Asia and Africa*. New York: Routledge.

Dingwerth, K. (2007) *The New Transnationalism: Private Transnational Governance and its Democratic Legitimacy*. Basingstoke: Palgrave Macmillan.

Dodson, A. (2000) *Green Political Thought*. London: Routledge.

Doern, G.B. and Johnson, R. (2006) *Rules, Rules, Rules, Rules: Multi-level Regulatory Governance*. Toronto: University of Toronto Press.

Doornbos, M. (2001) '"Good Governance": The Rise and Decline of a Policy Metaphor?', *Journal of Development Studies*, 93: 93–108.

Du Gay, P. (ed.) (2005) *The Value of Bureaucracy*. Oxford: Oxford University Press.

Dunsire, A. (1978) *Control in a Bureaucracy*. New York: St Martin's Press.

Etzioni, A. (1993) *The Spirit of Community: Rights, Responsibilities, and the Communitarian Agenda*. New York: Crown.

Etzioni, A. (ed.) (1998) *The Essential Communitarian Reader*. Lanham, MD: Rowman & Littlefield.

Everett, S. (2003) 'The Policy Cycle: Democratic Process or Rational Paradigm Revisited?', *Australian Journal of Public Administration*, 62: 65–70.

Fine, B. (2001) *Social Capital versus Social Theory: Political Economy and Social Science at the Turn of the Millennium*. London: Routledge.

Fischer, F. and Forester, J. (eds) (1993) *The Argumentative Turn in Policy Analysis and Planning*. Durham, NC: Duke University Press.

Friedman, J. (ed.) (1996) *The Rational Choice Controversy*. New Haven, CT: Yale University Press.

Fudenberg, D. and Tirole, J. (1991) *Game Theory*. Cambridge, MA: MIT Press.

Fukuyama, F. (2004) *State Building: Governance and World Order in the Twenty-first Century*. London: Profile Books.

Fung, A. and Wright, E.O. (eds) (2003) *Deepening Democracy: Institutional Innovations in Empowered Participatory Governance*. London: Verso.

Gamble, A. and Paine, A. (eds) (1996) *Regionalism and World Order*. Basingstoke: Macmillan.

Gerth, H. and Mills, C.W. (eds) (1973) *From Max Weber: Essays in Sociology*. Oxford: Oxford University Press.

Gilbert, N. and Gilbert, B. (1989) *The Enabling State: Modern Welfare Capitalism in America*. New York: Oxford University Press.

Grant, W. (1985) *The Political Economy of Corporatism*. London: Macmillan.

Grimsey, D. and Lewis, M.K. (2005) *The Economics of Private Public Partnerships*. Cheltenham: Edward Elgar.

Gunnell, J.G. (2004) *Imagining the American Polity: Political Science and the Discourse of Democracy*. University Park, PA: Pennsylvania State University Press.

Habermans, J. (1985) *The Theory of Communicative Action*, 2 vols, trans. T. McCarthy. Boston: Beacon Press.

Hajer, M. and Wagenaar, H. (eds) (2003) *Deliberative Policy Analysis: Understanding Governance in the Network Society*. Cambridge: Cambridge University Press.

Hall, P. and Taylor, R. (1996) 'Political Science and the Three Institutionalisms', *Political Studies*, 44: 936–957.

Hardin, G. (1968) 'The Tragedy of the Commons', *Science*, 162: 1243–1248.

Hardin, R. (1982) *Collective Action*. Baltimore, MD: Johns Hopkins University Press.

Hart, H.L.A. (1961) *The Concept of Law*. Oxford: Oxford University Press.

Hay, C. and Marsh, D. (eds) (2001) *Demystifying Globalization*. Basingstoke: Palgrave Macmillan.

Hayes, M. (2001) *The Limits of Policy Change: Incrementalism, Worldview, and the Rule of Law*. Washington, DC: Georgetown University Press.

Hayes, M. (2006) *Incrementalism and Public Policy*. Baltimore, MD: University Press of America.

Healey, P. (1997) *Collaborative Planning: Shaping Places in Fragmented Societies*. London: Macmillan.

Hedetoft, U. and Hjort, M. (eds) (2002) *The Postnational Self: Belonging and Identity*. Minneapolis, MN: University of Minnesota Press.

Henderson, P. and Salmon, H. (1998) *Signposts to Local Democracy: Local Governance, Communitarianism, and Community*. London: Community Development Fund.

Hettne, B., Inotai, A. and Sunkel, O. (eds) (1999) *Globalism and the New Regionalism*. Basingstoke: Macmillan.

Hewson, M. and Sinclair, T. (eds) (1999) *Approaches to Global Governance Theory*. Albany, NY: State University of New York Press.

Hill, M. and Hupe, P. (2002) *Implementing Public Policy: Governance in Theory and Practice*. Thousand Oaks, CA: Sage.

Hinsley, F.H. (1986) *Sovereignty*. Cambridge: Cambridge University Press.

Hodge, G. (2006) *Privatization and Market Development: Global Movements in Public Policy Ideas*. Cheltenham: Edward Elgar.

Hooghe, L. and Marks, G. (2001) *Multilevel Governance and European Integration*. Lanham, MD: Rowman & Littlefield.

Im, S. (2001) *Bureaucratic Power, Democracy and Administrative Democracy*. Burlington, VI: Ashgate.

Jessop, B. and Sum, N. (2006) *The Regulation Approach and Beyond: Putting Capitalist Economies in their Place*. Cheltenham: Edward Elgar.

John, P. (2001) *Local Governance*. London: Sage.

Jones, C.O. (1970) *An Introduction to the Study of Public Policy*. Belmont, CA: Duxbury Press.

Jordan, A. and Schout, A. (2007) *The Coordination of the European Union: Exploring the Capacities of Networked Governance*. New York: Oxford University Press.

Jordana, J. and Levi-Faur, D. (eds) (2004) *The Politics of Regulation: Institutions and Regulatory Reforms for the Age of Governance*. Cheltenham: Edward Elgar.

Kaufmann, D., Kraay, A. and Mastruzzi, M. (2006) *Governance Matters*. Washington, DC: The World Bank.

Keating, M. (ed.) (2004) *The New Regionalism in Western Europe: Territorial Restructuring and Political Change.* Cheltenham: Edward Elgar.

Keohane, R. and Nye, J. (1977) *Power and Interdependence: World Politics in Transition.* Boston, MA: Little Brown.

Kickert, W.J.M., Klijn, E.H. and Koppenjan, J.F.M. (eds) (1997) *Managing Complex Networks: Strategies for the Public Sector.* London: Sage.

Kooiman, J. (2003) *Governing as Governance.* London: Sage.

Kramsch, O. and Hooper, B. (eds) (2004) *Cross-border Governance in the European Union.* Abingdon: Routledge.

Kweit, M. and Kweit, R. (1981) *Implementing Citizen Participation in a Bureaucratic Society.* New York: Praeger.

Latham, M. and Botsman, P. (eds) (2001) *The Enabling State: People before Bureaucracy.* Sydney: Pluto Press.

Levitas, R. (1998) *The Inclusive Society? Social Exclusion and New Labour.* Basingstoke: Palgrave Macmillan.

Levy, D. and Newell, P. (eds) (2004) *The Business of Global Environmental Governance.* Cambridge, MA: MIT Press.

Lindblom, C. (1959) 'The Science of "Muddling Through"', *Public Administration Review*, 19: 79–88.

Lindblom, C. (2001) *The Market System: What It Is, How It Works, and What to Make of It.* New Haven, CT: Yale University Press.

Lipietz, A. (1993) 'The Local and the Global: Regional Individuality or Interregionalism?', *Transactions of the Institute of British Geographers*, 18(1): 8–18.

Loewy, E. (1993) *Freedom and Community: The Ethics of Interdependence.* Albany, NY: State University of New York Press.

Luhmann, N. (1995) *Social Systems.* Stanford, CA: Stanford University Press.

MacLean, I. (1987) *Public Choice.* Oxford: Blackwell.

Majone, G. (1996) *Regulating Europe.* London: Routledge.

Mandell, M. (ed.) (2001) *Getting Results through Collaboration: Networks and Network Structures for Public Policy and Management.* Westport, CT: Quorum Books.

Manin, B. (1997) *The Principles of Representative Government.* Cambridge: Cambridge University Press.

Mansfield, E. and Milner, H.V. (eds) (1997) *The Political Economy of Regionalism.* New York: Columbia University Press.

March, J. and Olsen, J. (1989) *Rediscovering Institutions.* New York: Free Press.

Marin, B. and Mayntz, R. (eds) (1991) *Policy Networks: Empirical Evidence and Theoretical Considerations.* Frankfurt am Main: Campus Verlag.

Marinetto, M. (2003) 'Governing Beyond the Centre: A Critique of the Anglo-governance School', *Political Studies*, 51: 592–608.

Marsh, D. (ed.) (1998) *Comparing Policy Networks.* Buckingham: Open University Press.

Mattli, W. (1999) *The Logic of Regional Integration: Europe and Beyond.* Cambridge: Cambridge University Press.

May, J. and Wildavsky, A. (1978) *The Policy Cycle.* Beverly Hills, CA: Sage.

McGuire, M. (2002) 'Managing Networks: Propositions on What Managers Do and Why They Do It', *Public Administration Review*, 62: 599–609.

McLennan, G. (1989) *Pluralism*. Cambridge: Polity Press.

Meadowcroft, J. (1999) 'Cooperative Management Regimes: Collaborative Problem Solving to Implement Sustainable Development', *International Negotiation*, 4: 225–254.

Monroe, K. (ed.) (1991) *The Economic Approach to Politics: A Critical Reassessment of the Theory of Rational Action*. New York: Harper Collins.

Moran, M. (2003) *The British Regulatory State: High Modernism and Hyper-innovation*. Oxford: Oxford University Press.

Mulhall, S. and Swift, A. (1996) *Liberals and Communitarians*. Oxford: Blackwell.

Munishi, S. and Abraham, B. (eds) (2004) *Good Governance, Democratic Societies and Globalization*. New Delhi: Sage.

Narula, R. (2003) *Globalization and Technology: Interdependence, Innovation Systems and Industrial Policy*. Cambridge: Polity Press.

Nolan, B.C. (2001) *Public Sector Reform*. New York: Palgrave Macmillan.

Nutley, S.M., Smith, P.C. and Davies, H.T.O. (2000) *What Works?: Evidence-based Policy and Practice in Public Services*. Bristol: The Policy Press.

Nye, J. (2001) 'Globalization's Democratic Deficit: How to Make International Institutions More Accountable', *Foreign Affairs*, 80: 2–6.

Olson, M. (1965) *The Logic of Collective Action: Public Goods and the Theory of Groups*. Cambridge, MA: Harvard University Press.

Osborne, D. and Gaebler, T. (1992) *Reinventing Government*. Reading, MA: Addison-Wesley.

O'Toole, L., Jr. (1997) 'Treating Networks Seriously: Practical and Research-based Agendas in Public Administration', *Public Administration Review*, 57: 45–52.

Oxhorn, P., Tulchin, J. and Selee, A. (2004) *Decentralization, Democratic Governance, and Civil Society in Comparative Perspective: Africa, Asia, and Latin America*. Washington, DC: Woodrow Wilson Center Press.

Page, E. (1985) *Political Authority and Bureaucratic Power*. Brighton: Wheatsheaf Books.

Page, E. (1991) *Localism and Centralism in Europe: The Political and Legal Basis of Local Self-government*. Oxford: Oxford University Press.

Page, E. (ed.) (2007) *From the Active to the Enabling State: The Changing Role of Top Officials in European Nations*. Basingstoke: Palgrave Macmillan.

Painter, M. and Pierre, J. (eds) (2005) *Challenges to State Policy Capacity*. Basingstoke: Palgrave Macmillan.

Parsons, T. (1971) *The System of Modern Societies*. Englewood Cliffs, NJ: Prentice-Hall.

Pateman, C. (1970) *Participation and Democratic Theory*. Cambridge: Cambridge University Press.

Pauly, L. and Greven, M. (eds) (2000) *Democracy beyond the State?* Lanham, MD: Rowman & Littlefield.

Pawson, R. (2006) *Evidence-based Policy: A Realist Perspective*. London: Sage.

Percy-Smith, J. (ed.) (2000) *Policy Responses to Social Exclusion*. Buckingham: Open University Press.

Peters, G.B. (1999) *Institutional Theory in Political Science: The New Institutionalism*. New York: Continuum.

Pindyck, R.S. and Rubinfeld, D. (2005) *Microeconomics*. Upper Saddle River, NJ: Pearson/Prentice-Hall.

Pollitt, C. and Bouckaert, G. (2000) *Public Management Reform: A Comparative Analysis*. Oxford: Oxford University Press.

Pollitt, C. and Talbot, C. (2004) *Unbundled Government: A Critical Analysis of the Global Trend to Agencies, Quangos, and Contractualization*. New York: Routledge.

Portes, A. (1998) 'Social Capital: Its Origins and Applications in Modern Sociology', *American Review of Sociology*, 24: 1–24.

Powell, W. (1990) 'Neither Market nor Hierarchy: Network Forms of Organization', *Research in Organizational Behaviour*, 12: 295–336.

Powell, W. and DiMaggio, P. (eds) (1991) *The New Institutionalism in Organizational Analysis*. Chicago: University of Chicago Press.

Pressman, J. and Wildavsky, A. (1973) *Implementation*. Berkeley, CA: University of California Press.

Przeworski, A., Stokes, S.C. and Manin, B. (eds) (1999) *Democracy, Accountability, and Representation*. Cambridge: Cambridge University Press.

Putnam, R. (1993) *Making Democracy Work: Civic Traditions in Modern Italy*. Princeton, NJ: Princeton University Press.

Radin, B. (2006) *Challenging the Performance Movement: Accountability, Complexity, and Democratic Values*. Washington, DC: Georgetown University Press.

Rhodes, R.A.W. (1988) *Beyond Westminster and Whitehall: The Sub-central Governments of Britain*. London: Routledge.

Rhodes, R.A.W. (1997) *Understanding Governance: Policy Networks, Governance, Reflexivity and Accountability*. Buckingham: Open University Press.

Rhodes, R., Carmichael, P., McMillan, J. and Massey, A. (2003) *Decentralizing the Civil Service: From Unitary State to Differentiated Polity in the United Kingdom*. Buckingham: Open University Press.

Roberts, N. (ed.) (2002) *The Transformative Power of Dialogue*. Oxford: Elsevier.

Rose, L. and Denters, B. (2005) *Comparing Local Governance: Trends and Developments*. Basingstoke: Palgrave Macmillan.

Runciman, D. (1997) *Pluralism and the Personality of the State*. Cambridge: Cambridge University Press.

Salamon, L.M. (ed.) (2002) *The Tools of Government: A Guide to the New Governance*. New York: Oxford University Press.

Sanderson, I. (2002) 'Evaluation, Policy Learning and Evidence-based Policy Making', *Public Administration*, 80: 1–22.

Sandler, T. (1992) *Collective Action: Theory and Applications*. Ann Arbor, MI: University of Michigan Press.

Scharpf, F. (1997) *Games Real Actors Play: Actor-centered Institutionalism in Policy Research*. Boulder, CO: Westview Press.

Schmitter, P. and Lehmbruch, G. (1982) *Patterns of Corporatist Policy Making*. London: Sage.

Scholte, J. (2005) *Globalization: A Critical Introduction*. Basingstoke: Palgrave Macmillan.

Scott, J. (1992) *Social Network Analysis*. London: Sage.

Selznick, P. (1999) 'Legal Cultures and the Rule of Law', in M. Krygier and A. Czarnota (eds), *The Rule of Law after Communism*. Aldershot: Dartmouth.

Shapiro, I. (ed.) (1994) *The Rule of Law: NOMOS XXXVI*. New York: New York University Press.

Shklar, J. (1998) 'Political Theory and the Rule of Law', in J. Shklar (ed.), *Political Thought and Political Thinkers*. Chicago: University of Chicago Press.

Siddiqui, T. (2001) *Towards Good Governance*. New Delhi: Oxford University Press.

Simon, H. (1969) *The Sciences of the Artificial*. Cambridge, MA: MIT Press.

Sisk, T. (2001) *Democracy at the Local Level: The International IDEA Handbook on Participation, Representation, Conflict, Management, and Governance*. Stockholm: International IDEA.

Skinner, Q. (1989) 'The State', in T. Ball, J. Farr and R. Hanson (eds), *Political Innovation and Conceptual Change*. Cambridge: Cambridge University Press.

Slaughter, A. (2004) *A New World Order*. Princeton, NJ: Princeton University Press.

Smith, B.C. (1988) *Bureaucracy and Political Power*. New York: St Martin's Press.

Sørensen, E. (2006) 'Metagovernance: The Changing Role of Politicians in Processes of Democratic Governance', *American Review of Public Administration*, 36: 98–114.

Spruyt, H. (1994) *The Sovereign State and Its Competitors*. Princeton, NJ: Princeton University Press.

Starr, H. (1997) *Anarchy, Order, and Integration: How to Manage Interdependence*. Ann Arbor, MI: University of Michigan Press.

Strange, S. (1996) *The Retreat of the State: The Diffusion of Power in the World Economy*. Cambridge: Cambridge University Press.

Sudders, M. and Nahem, J. (2004) *Governance Indicators: A User's Guide*. Oslo: United Nations Development Programme.

Tamanaha, B. (2004) *On the Rule of Law: History, Politics, Theory*. Cambridge: Cambridge University Press.

Thompson, G., Frances, J., Levacic, R. and Mitchell, J. (eds) (1991) *Markets, Hierarchies, and Networks: The Coordination of Social Life*. London: Sage.

Van Berkel, R. and Moller, I. (eds) (2003) *Active Social Policies in the EU: Inclusion through Participation?* Cambridge: Polity Press.

Van Meter, D. and Van Horn, C. (1975) 'The Policy Implementation Process: A Conceptual Framework', *Administration & Society*, 6: 445–488.

Weiss, L. (1998) *The Myth of the Powerless State: Governing the Economy in a Global Era*. Cambridge, NY: Polity Press.

Weller, P., Bakvis, H. and Rhodes, R. (eds) (1997) *The Hollow Crown*. London: Macmillan.

Wholey, J.S., Hatry, H.P. and Newcomer, K.E. (eds) (1994) *Handbook of Practical Programme Evaluation*. San Fransisco: Jossey-Bass.

Wilkinson, R. (ed.) (2005) *The Global Governance Reader*. London: Routledge.

Williams, D. and Young, T. (1994) 'Governance, the World Bank, and Liberal Theory', *Political Studies*, 42: 84–100.

Williamson, O. (1975) *Markets and Hierarchies: Analysis and Antitrust Implications.* New York: Free Press.

Wondolleck, J. and Yaffee, S. (2000) *Making Collaboration Work: Lessons from Innovation in Natural Resource Management.* Washington, DC: Island Press.

World Commission on Environment and Development (1987) *Our Common Future.* Oxford: Oxford University Press.

Young, O. (1998) *Global Governance: Learning Lessons from the Environmental Experience.* Cambridge, MA: MIT Press.